A PROFESSOR'S DUTIES

ISSUES IN ACADEMIC ETHICS

General Editor: Steven M. Cahn

Campus Rules and Moral Community: In Place of *In Loco Parentis*
by David A. Hoekema

University-Business Partnerships: An Assessment
by Norman E. Bowie

A Professor's Duties: Ethical Issues in College Teaching
by Peter J. Markie

A PROFESSOR'S DUTIES

Ethical Issues in College Teaching

Peter J. Markie

ROWMAN & LITTLEFIELD PUBLISHERS, INC.

ROWMAN & LITTLEFIELD PUBLISHERS, INC.

Published in the United States of America
by Rowman & Littlefield Publishers, Inc.
4720 Boston Way, Lanham, Maryland 20706

3 Henrietta Street, London WC2E 8LU, England

British Cataloging in Publication Information Available

Library of Congress Cataloging-in-Publication Data

Markie, Peter J., 1950–
A professor's duties : ethical issues in college teaching / Peter J.
Markie.
p.   cm. — (Issues in academic ethics)
Includes bibliographical references and index.
1. College teachers—Professional ethics.   2. College teaching—
Moral and ethical aspects.   I. Title.   II. Series.
LB1779.M37   1994   378.1'25—dc20   94–1953 CIP

ISBN 0–8476–7951–9 (cloth : alk. paper)
ISBN 0–8476–7952–7 (pbk. : alk. paper)

Printed in the United States of America

 ™ The paper used in this publication meets the minimum requirements of
American National Standard for Information Sciences—Permanence of
Paper for Printed Library Materials, ANSI Z39.48–1984.

For Elizabeth and Bob
with thoughts of
Laurie DeCourcy and Bob Gurland

May the first two be taught as the second two taught me:
going far beyond what's obligatory

Issues in Academic Ethics

Academic life generates a variety of moral issues. These may be faced by students, staff, administrators, or trustees but most often revolve around the rights and responsibilities of the faculty. In my book *Saints and Scamps: Ethics in Academia* (Rowman & Littlefield), published in 1986 and revised in 1994, I set out to enumerate, explain, and emphasize the most fundamental of these professional obligations. To do justice to the complexities of academic ethics, however, requires the work of many scholars focused on numerous areas of investigation. The results of such an effort are embodied in this series.

Each volume concentrates on one set of connected issues and combines a single-authored monograph with sources chosen by the author to exemplify or amplify materials in the text. This format is intended to guide readers while encouraging them to develop and defend their own beliefs.

In recent years philosophers have examined the appropriate standards of conduct for physicians, nurses, lawyers, journalists, business managers, and government policymakers but have not given equal attention to formulating guidelines for their own profession. The time has come to observe the Delphic motto "Know thyself." Granted, the issues in need of critical examination are not exotic, but as the history of philosophy demonstrates, self-knowledge is often the most important to seek and the most difficult to attain.

Stephen M. Cahn

Contents

Preface

Professors, administrators, and trustees talk a lot about education but give little attention to teaching, especially at major research universities. We inscribe the names of high ideals on campus buildings but seldom examine the ethical dimension of what goes on inside. These familiar complaints about contemporary higher education come together in concerns about the ethics of college teaching. We cannot adequately respond to them, whether the response be rebuttal or reform, without a full study of this part of our professional lives.

This work takes a narrow focus on the topic. Part One concentrates on the obligations of individual professors, primarily with regard to issues about what and how to teach. I do not examine any ethical dimension other than the obligatory—for example, the ethical virtues that characterize a good teacher. I do not discuss the ethical obligations that groups such as department and college faculties have in the area of teaching. I do not consider the ethical obligations of administrators and trustees. The essays in Part Two cover some of what I ignore, but there still remains much more to study. This work is, then, an entry point into what should be a much more expansive and continuing discussion. By no means a last word, it is intended to be a start.

Acknowledgments

Several people helped in the development of this work. Thomas Huffman tracked down and provided initial evaluations of several secondary sources. Michael Hosokawa provided extremely useful comments on an early draft and was a constant source of encouragement. Larry Clark, the dean of my college, generously provided funding for a research assistant at the start of the project.

Steven Cahn deserves special thanks. He invited me to do this work, provided encouragement and critical comments along the way, and, perhaps most of all, has been a fine example of a professional life informed by a thoughtful dedication to principle.

As always, Kate Murphy Markie has been a constant source of encouragement and advice; but for her, little would be done and less would be worth doing.

Finally, the work would not exist if those holding the copyright on the essays in Part Two had not generously allowed them to be republished here.

PART ONE

CHAPTER ONE

To Be a Professor

Hundreds of times on hundreds of campuses, a familiar event occurs at the start of each academic session. Faculty walk into their classes, look out over the assembled students, and announce that they are the professor for the course. It is part self-introduction and part assumption of a particular role within a cooperative venture. What is that role? We must have some idea of what it is to be a professor, if we are to appreciate the ethical dimensions—the ethical duties, rights, and dilemmas—that go with being one.

Basic Roles

Let's begin with characteristics obvious enough to need no argument.

Professors teach, and the verb is transitive; what we teach is the subject matter and those to whom we teach it are the students. To teach isn't just to present the subject to the students. The bookstore clerk does that by handing them their books. To teach isn't just to get students to believe the subject matter. A mathematics professor who gets students to believe a theorem without understanding why it is true has not taught them the theorem. Teaching produces knowledge, and knowledge is true belief based upon good reasons. To teach is to guide students through the course material in such a way that they come to form a series of rationally based true beliefs with regard to it. Guiding students to this goal entails mapping out the best way to proceed, directing their attention to the most important details, helping them develop the skills necessary to progress, and assisting those who need help.

Professors represent the subject matter. Plato, Cervantes, Maxwell,

Faulkner, Boyle, Einstein, and the rest cannot be present in the classroom to explain their ideas. The Hopi Indians cannot be there to explain their culture. No theorem in calculus ever explained itself. This responsibility is ours as professors. We take it upon ourselves to speak for the course material, and speaking for the material includes presenting it accurately and explaining it so it can be both understood and appreciated. Students introduced to new ideas should come away, not only with an understanding of what the ideas are, but also with a clear sense of why whoever had them had them in the first place. Attorneys don't truly represent a client to the judge and jury unless they get them, at least momentarily, to see the case as the client does. So too, we don't truly represent the subject to our students unless we get them, at least momentarily, to see the world in terms of it.

Professors also represent certain values. We are supposed to inspire our students by communicating a vision of intellectual excellence and to help them acquire the qualities needed to make that vision a reality in their lives. Some of the qualities—analytic skills, verbal skills—are intellectual abilities, some—self-discipline and perseverance—are traits of character, and others—a commitment to the truth and objectivity, a belief in the value of free inquiry—are moral values.[1] Like all values, these last are best taught by word, example, and expectation. Our role includes acknowledging them in word, displaying them in action, and holding students to them in their course work.

To be the professor for a course is to be the certifier of students' knowledge and ability. We judge how well each student masters the course material and certify that level of achievement to the student and to the academic community. Education certainly does not require any particular structure of grades, degrees, and the like. Nonetheless, we cannot guide students successfully without giving them a regular assessment of where they are relative to where they are attempting to go, and so long as education is expected to yield an academic degree, success must be certified to the community expected to grant it.

Professors are academic advisors. Students enroll in each course to complete a general program of study, and their educational goals are often linked to a career objective. Part of being a professor is to be a source of advice to students on the relation between their career objectives and different programs of study and how to best pursue whatever program they select. Note that professors are *academic* advisors. We are not charged as professors to be psychotherapists or personal confidants to our students. We are sometimes drawn into such roles—and some seek them out—but they are not part of what it is to be a professor, and those who take them on do so as an addition to their professional responsibilities.[2]

Finally, to be a professor is to be engaged actively in one's intellectual discipline in a way that supports one's teaching. To be a professor of philosophy is to be a philosopher, to be a professor of mathematics is to be a mathematician, and so on.[3] Some find this idea hard to accept. They interpret it as the expectation that every professor engage in original, creative research, and they object that it is unrealistic, since many fine teachers are incapable of such activity, and that it actually encourages faculty to engage in trivial, valueless research at the expense of their teaching. Faculty come to think of "their work" as their research and of their teaching as an unwelcome distraction, as in "I had to advise so many students today that I couldn't get any of my own work done."[4]

I shall examine these concerns in detail later, but a few points must be made now. First, the expectation is not simply that professors actively engage in their disciplines; it is that we engage in our disciplines in a way that supports our teaching. Professors bring the practice of their discipline into the classroom. Thus, properly understood, the expectation does not encourage us to engage in trivial research at the expense of our teaching. Second, the expectation is part of what separates university teachers from teachers at lower educational levels; and it is unimaginable that any excellent university teacher will be unable, or even fail, to meet it. To guide students through advanced subject matter and to serve as that material's representative to students, we must be able to think through it critically, and that requires regularly practicing the discipline.

In short, we take on a complex role when we walk into class and declare that we are the professor: the students' guide to the subject and the subject's representative to the students, representative of intellectual excellence and related virtues, certifier of student progress, academic advisor, and practitioner of an intellectual discipline. To be a professor is to function effectively and successfully in all these ways, though in any particular course with any particular group of students, all of us play some parts better than others. Being a professor is an ideal we pursue rather than an activity we simply perform.

Agents, Cooperation, Power, and Autonomy

Professors are members of a university rather than independent contractors. Students are admitted by the university and pay their tuition to it. We teach students on behalf of the university. As a member of the university, each professor inherits the institution's educational commitments to students.

Each professor also acts within a cooperative venture aimed at the good of higher education. The cooperative relations sometimes break down, but they are intended to be there, and they take a variety of forms. Our relationship to our students is intended to be such that they are active learners and we are their guide. Our relationship with our colleagues is intended to be such that each of our courses is part of the general educational effort by our department, college, and university. Even those outside the university are part of the cooperative venture. Parents, taxpayers, educational foundations—all provide financial support.

What is especially distinctive about this cooperative relationship is the significant amount of power and autonomy that the other participants grant to each professor. Our individual power is most obvious in the classroom. We are in charge. We determine what tasks are to be done and by whom. We evaluate performance. We determine the overall environment in which students learn or fail to do so. We can make it supportive or destructive. The professor-student relationship is a power relationship, and just about all the power is the professor's. Short of withdrawing from the course or venting anger in a nasty teaching evaluation at the semester's end, the student is at our mercy.

Our individual autonomy is almost without limit. The material taught in a particular course, the texts used, the number and nature of exams, the policy on make-up exams and delayed grades, the grading scale, the number and times of office hours, all these matters are generally determined by the individual professor with little or no restriction or supervision. Seldom are we bound by any institutional rules, and the few rules that occasionally apply are regularly limited to such mechanical aspects of teaching as the length of time before a delayed grade becomes a failing grade. Beyond the level of introductory courses, our individual teaching assignments are generally determined by our areas of specialization, which are in turn determined by our own interests and abilities. When it comes to whether to direct a student in an independent readings course or research project, the decision is typically ours alone.

All the points just made about individual professors apply with equal force to department, college, and university faculties. The faculty of each department has the role of guiding students to knowledge in their discipline, representing that subject and academic values to students, certifying student progress, providing students with advice, and practicing their intellectual discipline. The college and university faculty have a similar role at a more general level. As in the case of the individual professor, the faculty of each department, college, or university acts as part of the university within a cooperative venture and generally performs its role with a great deal of power and autonomy. The faculty creates and maintains the curriculum, decides what courses must be completed and special exams taken for each degree, certifies the progress of each candidate, and determines the overall environment in which learning takes place. All colleges and universities—and more than a few departments—have experienced attempts by other groups (e.g., administrators, students, or state legislators) to interfere with the faculty's control, say by forcing the addition or discontinuation of a certain program or degree requirement. These occurrences are relatively few, however, and they have done little to decrease the faculty's day-to-day power in curricular matters. In a few cases, a department or college faculty finds its autonomy limited by the demands of a professional accrediting agency, but this too is more the exception than the rule.

An Ethical Dimension

As a result of accepting a certain role within the cooperative venture of higher education, professors gain significant power over others and a great deal of discretion in its use. If we use the power appropriately, we educate students; if we use it inappropriately, we deprive them of an education and may harm them in other ways as well. Even more surely than winning the lottery brings new friends, becoming a professor should bring new ethical duties. We have ethical obligations to our students, our colleagues, our university, and in general to all those who join us in the activity of higher education.

Many people, indeed many professors, seem to think otherwise. We write a great deal on ethical issues in other fields—law, medicine, business, engineering—but very little on ethical issues in our own. Indeed, we generally speak as though the issues we face in exercising our power and autonomy are matters of taste rather than ethics. We say things like: "I like to discuss current political issues in my class, but my older colleagues don't." "She likes to be friends with her students." "He likes to just give one exam in his course." What one professor likes another dislikes; it is just a matter of taste. Could it be that there really are no important ethical issues for us to consider here? It is worth considering three lines of argument that lead to this conclusion; I suspect that in some form or another they are present in our thinking about what we do as professors and are responsible for our tendency to overlook the important ethical dimension of our work.

The first line of argument begins with the premise that teaching is an art. Since it is an art, questions concerning what to teach, how to teach, how to evaluate, and how to advise students are similar to questions about how to paint a canvas or sculpt a piece of clay. Each of us should answer them relative to our own personal "aesthetic" sense. There are no important ethical issues here, only matters of personal taste.[5]

Yet, surely the decision of whether to use the power and prestige of being a professor to attract an undergraduate into a sexual relationship is not simply a question of personal taste; neither is the decision of whether to condone cheating on exams, nor the decision of whether to prepare for class. The mistakes in the argument are clear. Teaching is not an art in the general sense of an activity aimed at the production of forms, colors, movements, or other elements so as to affect our aesthetic sense; the professor's aim is not to create beautiful students out of unformed hunks of "student clay." Teaching may be an art in the narrow sense that, when practiced with excellence, it involves an intuitive ability that cannot be taught, but its status as an art in this narrow sense in no way implies that the basic questions about how to do it are questions of taste to be answered in whatever way a teacher feels appropriate. Medicine and law have equal claims to be "arts" in this way, but no one doubts that doctors and lawyers face important ethical issues.[6]

A second argument for denying the ethical dimension of being a professor is based on the idea that very little hinges on a professor's decisions. Our decisions about what to teach, how to teach, how to advise, and so on are not matters of life and death. The closest we come to the physician's decision of whether or not to terminate life support is the decision of whether to drop a graduate student from our program. The closest we come to the lawyer's decision of whether to defend a killer who is likely to kill again is the decision of whether to pass a marginal student on to take the next course in the program. The ethical duties, rights, and dilemmas of physicians and lawyers provide fare for popular TV dramas; not so ours. So, if there's an ethical dimension to being a professor, it is a pretty trivial one.

It is a mistake to confuse a lack of immediate and dramatic impact with a lack of importance. The ethical issues facing professors are not the stuff of TV dramas; professors do not make immediate life or death decisions. Nonetheless, we make important ones with the potential to greatly benefit or harm others.[7] We need only listen to students to discover what is at stake. The positive reports are generally found in letters of support for teaching awards, the memories of returning alumni, and, perhaps most frequently, in thank-you notes from students to their favorite professors. They tell of knowledge gained, opportunities discovered, confidence found, and self-esteem generated. They talk of turning points at which a professor's advice provided crucial guidance. Indeed, many of us remember one or two professors who had a great positive impact on our life; that impact is often what inspired us to become professors. The negative reports are less common. Students seldom write letters against teaching awards, disappointed alumni seldom return to visit, and students seldom write notes of disappointment to their professors. Students who are harmed by a professor often don't even realize it; they are so unsure of what they should receive by way of an education. Yet only a fool would believe that, while those of us who honor our obligations do so much good, those who neglect them do no real harm, and the negative testimony is there. Consider just one of many surveyed responses from women concerning the impact of sex discrimination on their educational experience:

> You come in the door . . . equal, but having experienced the discrimination—the refusal of professors to take you seriously; the sexual overtures and the like—you limp out doubting your own ability to do very much of anything.[8]

The third argument for the view that there is no important ethical dimension to being a professor begins with an observation already made: each professor is engaged in a cooperative venture with others. Our ethical duties are specified by the agreements that define that cooperation, which are generally spelled out in our contract and in the university's regulations. The agreements can change over time. As universities become more concerned about sexual harassment and cultural sensitivity, the institutional arrangements may change to give us a new duty to refrain from consensual sexual relationships with our students, as well as one to refrain from certain types of speech within the classroom. The important point is that any issue concerning teaching not covered by the duties thus assigned falls within the scope of academic freedom; it is the individual professor's to decide. So, other than to read our contract and the university's regulations, there is nothing for professors to think about under the heading of professorial ethics. Anything not covered by the institutional arrangements is a matter of personal judgment—if not taste—after all.

This reasoning falsely assumes that all our ethical obligations are determined by the explicit provisions of our contract and the university regulations. Does the professor who engages in sexual harassment or racist humor only act unethically if the university has a rule against it? Professors have ethical obligations that exist independently of the university's regulations. Sometimes an ethical duty arises from considerations of justice. Sometimes it arises from the good that will be produced or the harm that will be avoided. Sometimes it stems from the need to treat students, colleagues, or the subject with the respect they deserve. All these considerations exist independently of being codified in our contract or the university's rules. Indeed, they are prior to such documents in that we expect the documents to provide explicitly for the most important ones.

Consider the analogous relationship between our ethical and legal duties. Each of us has ethical obligations that exist independently of the legal system. I am ethically obligated to give to charity and to keep my promise to get my daughter a cat, even though the law does not require me to do so. The law makes some of our most important ethical obligations legal ones as well, thereby backing them with the government's persuasive and coercive power. The same is true of our ethical obligations as professors in relation to our contract and the university's regulations.

There is an important point to appreciate here about the right of academic freedom. Each professor has an ethical right to the liberty needed to pursue our vision of the truth and to communicate that vision through publication and teaching. It does not follow from this, however, that we have no ethical duties with regard to what and how we teach. Our right to academic freedom does not excuse us from ethical duties with regard to how we communicate our vision of the truth through publication and teaching, any more than the right to free speech excuses anyone from the ethical duty to tell the truth and avoid saying gratuitously hurtful things to others. Indeed, when we accept the right to academic freedom, we take on ethical obligations with regard to how we choose to exercise it, just as we do with the right to free speech.[9]

In all, professors have serious ethical obligations. We cannot slide out from under the fact by claiming that teaching is an art, that our decisions are unimportant, or that we are only obligated to do what our contract and the university regulations require. To acknowledge that we have important ethical obligations is the first step, to discover their content and source is the next, and to determine how best to encourage professors to honor them is a third. My concern in what follows is with the second step. I shall provide an initial map of the content and source of some of our obligations in teaching.

Our ethical obligations arise at different levels. Just as there are ethical issues about how individual professors should use their power and discretion in deciding what to teach and how to teach it, so too there are ethical issues about how a department or college faculty should do so. It is sometimes impossible to address the issues fully at one level without raising issues at the other. To determine our individual obligations in selecting material for a course, we must consider the course's role in the department's curriculum, and that leads to a consideration of the ethical obligations and rights of the department faculty in designing the curriculum. I shall concentrate on our ethical obligations as individual professors, though the issues will sometimes force me to at least refer to those of department, college, or university faculties.

It is also important to distinguish the task of determining our ethical obligations as individual professors from the related task of determining how a department, college, or university can best encourage fidelity to those obligations. To decide that we have a certain obligation as professors is not necessarily to decide that we should codify that obligation in a department, college or university rule or that we should adopt a particular way of monitoring performance with regard to it. I shall generally hold aside the issue of how we can best encourage fidelity to our obligations. The issue is a pressing one, especially at a time when our profession, like others, is being held to increased demands for public accountability, but we cannot successfully address it until we first determine what our obligations are.

Two final points deserve mention. First, the ethical dimension of teaching is not the only important one. There is more to being a "good" professor. It is certainly possible for two professors to be equal in ethical behavior, but unequal in talent. The ethical dimension concerns how responsibly we use our talents. The quality of our talents themselves is another matter. Second, the ethical dimension of teaching, like the ethical dimension of any activity, is not completely defined by our obligations. Our obligations define a moral minimum: what we must do to avoid acting unethically. They leave us with a great deal of room to move. Most of us honor our ethical obligations in such a way as to be decent, responsible teachers; others go further and, by giving more than duty demands, display a superior form of virtue in their professional life. Although I shall concentrate on the moral minimum defined by our obligations, we must never forget that we have the opportunity to achieve more.[10]

Notes

1. The connection between certain moral values and intellectual inquiry was brought to my attention by Alan Gewirth in "Human Rights and Academic Freedom," in *Morality, Responsibility and the University,* ed. Steven M. Cahn (Philadelphia: Temple University Press, 1990), pp. 15–16. Consider how he puts the point: "[T]he pursuit of intellectual knowledge requires certain traits of personal and social morality: such traits as honesty, truthfulness, freedom of inquiry, public communication of results, and willingness to subordinate one's own selfish desires to impartial acceptance of the facts."

2. Some may object that I have just gone beyond making points so obvious as to need no argument. If so, see Chapter 4 for more discussion of, and argument for, the points presented here.

3. I owe this way of putting the point to Brand Blanshard, "Current Issues in Education," *Monist* 52 (January 1968), p. 21: "But surely a teacher of philosophy should himself be a philosopher, not simply a purveyor of other people's notions."

4. Edward Shils, *The Academic Ethic* (Chicago: University of Chicago Press, 1983), p. 44, puts the point nicely: "A university in which teachers shirk their pedagogical obligation in order to advance 'their own work,' as if their sole obligation is to do research, infringes on the academic ethic. Properly understood, 'their own work' includes teaching."

5. I owe this suggestion to David D. Dill, "Introduction," *Journal of Higher Education* 53 (1982), pp. 247–48.

6. Note too, that the most important skills in good teaching—from the best way to use examples to the best testing techniques to the best ways to use class time—clearly can be taught. Here again, the comparison to medicine and law is appropriate.

7. David Dill, "Introduction," pp. 247–49, speculates that we tend to underestimate our ethical obligations as professors because we fail to appreciate the impact we can have on the moral development of students. I suspect he is right, but the important point is a more general one: we underestimate the general impact we can have on students.

8. This quote was initially reported in "Harvard Women Protest Unequal Job Opportunities," *The Washington Star,* October 24, 1980. It can be found,

along with a host of similar reports, in Roberta Hall and Bernice Sandler, "The Classroom Climate: A Chilly One for Women?" *Project on the Status and Education of Women* (Washington, D.C.: Association of American Colleges, 1982).

9. John Searle puts the point nicely: "Any healthy human institution— family, state, university, or ski team—grants its members rights that far exceed the bounds of morally acceptable behavior." See John Searle, "Reply to Gerald Graff," *New York Review of Books,* May 16, 1991, p. 63. For a valuable discussion of the relation between academic freedom and ethical issues in teaching, see John Martin Rich, *Professional Ethics in Education,* Chap. 4, "Teaching and the Protection of Student Rights" (Springfield, Ill.: Charles Thomas, 1984).

10. We could indeed take a different perspective on the ethical issues in college teaching by concentrating, not on the basic teaching obligations that go with being a professor, but on the basic ethical virtues that characterize an ethically good teacher. Some philosophers have argued that, in ethics generally, more is to be gained by an account of the moral virtues than by an account of moral obligations. An important and influential work in this regard is G. E. M. Anscombe's "Modern Moral Philosophy," *Philosophy* 33 (1958); see too the collection, *Midwest Studies in Philosophy, Vol. XII: Ethical Theory: Character and Virtue,* ed. Peter A. French, Theodore E. Uehling, Jr., and Howard Wettstein (Notre Dame: University of Notre Dame Press, 1988).

CHAPTER TWO

What to Teach

Professors decide what students get a chance to learn. We decide what topics they study, at what level, for how long, and by what texts. We do this with little supervision and evaluation. No one approves the syllabus beforehand; seldom does anyone review it afterward. There is usually a course description in the college catalogue, which we are expected to honor, but seldom does anyone check, and most catalogue descriptions have been so severely cut by space-hungry editors that they limit our freedom to design the course as little as they inform our students' decision to take it.

The appropriate amount of supervision and evaluation in college teaching is a controversial topic, but there is general agreement on one point: each professor must have a great deal of discrction in deciding what to teach. This fundamental requirement of academic freedom enables each of us to represent the truth as we see it. It gives students the security of being guided toward the truth, as seen by someone with appropriate expertise, as opposed to the truth as seen by those who lack expertise but have enough political power to control the curriculum. Yet, what ethical obligations define the proper use of our discretion in deciding what to teach? What is their basis? How do they relate to each other?

The Audience's Knowledge and Abilities

In one department I know, a professor's teaching assignment in an introductory course changed from teaching twenty-five honors students to teaching 140 students, only about ten of whom were honors students, with two teaching assistants to help. The professor retained the advanced text and kept her lectures the same. Her need to prepare remained low, and her time for other activities remained high. Three weeks into the semester, most of the students had stopped reading the text and were complaining to one another that they couldn't understand it. In class, they were passively hearing lectures they couldn't follow. Four weeks into the semester, the professor tried to liven things up by asking questions, found the students unprepared, and responded with a surprise quiz at the next meeting. The students were outraged at what they saw as a punishment. The professor was irate at the students' failure to prepare for class. In defending her actions, the professor mentioned that the surprise quiz had been a teaching assistant's idea. Five weeks into the semester, the teaching assistant complained to the department head that she was being made into a scapegoat.[1]

Where did things go wrong? The source of everyone's distress was that the professor forgot or just ignored the fact that we teach people and are obligated to choose our material relative to their knowledge and abilities. Are they honors students or nonhonors students? Are they first semester freshmen or more advanced undergraduates? What are their reading and writing skills? What is their prior knowledge of the subject and related areas? We must consider all these points in selecting material. Fitting the subject to the students' knowledge and abilities requires knowing the audience and selecting material they will find demanding yet be able to understand and evaluate with assistance.

Our obligation to fit the subject matter to the students' knowledge and abilities derives from the university's commitment to intellectual advancement and knowledge. Each university is founded on a commitment to this good, and having made this commitment for itself, each makes a related one to students. When it admits them and takes their tuition, it promises them the opportunity to advance intellectually and attain knowledge. We make the university's two commitments our own when we accept a faculty appointment, and we can honor them only by selecting material that is demanding for students but within their grasp.[2] Students never advance significantly without being confronted with a realistic challenge. They never attain knowledge by being presented with what they already know or what is beyond their comprehension.

Violations of this obligation are not limited to cases in which we keep a course the same despite changes in the students' knowledge and abilities. We violate it when we make an introductory course as easy as yawning. The students understand the material and our teaching evaluations may even contain high marks for mastery of subject and clarity of presentation, but the students are cheated of the chance for intellectual advancement. In upper-level courses, we can violate our obligation by teaching material from a current research project. We may hope that our teaching and research will be combined and that our excitement about our research will carry over to our teaching, but, quite often, the material is so beyond the students' abilities and prior knowledge that they can't understand and evaluate it even with help. Teaching and research are then combined to the exclusion of teaching, and our excitement about the topic conveys little content to our students.

We cannot use the claim that students are not interested in intellectual advancement and knowledge to slide out from under the obligation to teach demanding but accessible material. "They don't care, so why should I?" has no force here. First, most students want to advance intellectually. Second, even if students were only interested in the outward signs of academic achievement—building up credit hours, receiving high grades, and gaining a diploma—and even if all students announced a lack of interest in attaining knowledge and so attempted to release the university from its commitment to them, the university's, and so our own, foundational commitment to intellectual advancement and knowledge would still bind us. Indeed, it would give us an obligation to recruit new students interested in pursuing the university's defining goal. Whatever the interests of the particular students at hand, each university, by its very nature, is committed to intellectual advancement and knowledge, and to accept a faculty position is to join in the commitment.

Some may think that I have lost touch with reality. The mix of abilities and knowledge among students in the same class makes it impossible to select material they will all find demanding and be able to understand and evaluate with assistance. The students in an introductory class may vary from marginal admission cases on academic probation to National Merit Scholars on the dean's list. How do we "pitch" the course? Aim too high and we lose the bottom; aim too low and we fail to challenge the top. Aim for the middle and we fail to provide a realistic challenge to students on the top and bottom. Since the mix of students prevents us from picking material that is challenging and accessible to all, we are not obligated to do so.

This objection overestimates the student mix and underestimates the ability of professors to adjust for what mix there is. Generally, we can find material accessible to all with assistance and, to the extent necessary, challenge the best students through additional readings, paper assignments, and exercises. More importantly, if the range of students' abilities truly does keep us from offering demanding and accessible material to all, it is because another obligation has not been met. Something is wrong with the admission requirements for the course if the spread of the students' abilities outstrips our ability to provide a realistic challenge to all. The admission requirements should be designed so that each student admitted has a reasonable chance of success, where success is not simply receiving a passing grade but is being intellectually challenged and attaining knowledge. If the admission requirements do not do this, and we have the power to correct them, we must do so. If the power lies elsewhere, we must work to get them changed. The university that admits students to a class without a reasonable chance of success is like a medical clinic that offers bogus treatments for incurable illnesses. A professor who goes along is like a quack doctor in on the scam.[3]

The Purpose of the Course

Students come to a university for all sorts of reasons, but the reason for which they are admitted is to advance intellectually and gain knowledge, and they are supposed to accomplish that through their particular degree program. Their individual courses are supposed to contribute to their program. Every university has courses that stretch this understanding. The physical education department offers tennis, scuba, golf, and yoga, and my favorite is my own university's now-defunct course in "power entertaining." Intended to prepare the student leaders of today to be national leaders of tomorrow, it was taught by the director of student life and came complete with dinner at the professor's home (one cocktail per student) in a session devoted to social skills. Such exceptions aside, universities establish degree programs and offer courses within them on the general premise that each program, and each course within it, is designed to lead students to knowledge in a particular area. The university tells this to students when it sends them the catalogue with degree options. It says it again when it approves each student's choice of a major, and still again when it hands each graduate a diploma. It is quite appropriate, then, for students to ask of each course, "What has this got to do with my education as a candidate for my degree?"; and it is quite obligatory that the course be designed so that there is a correct answer relating the material in the course to the general goals of the student's program.

This obligation arises out of the university's commitment to provide each student with the opportunity for intellectual advancement and knowledge, but it ultimately falls on the professor who selects the course material. The course is supposed to give students the opportunity to gain some piece of what they need for their overall education. The professor is obligated to discover what this piece is and to design the course so the students have a chance to learn it. In what areas is the course supposed to provide knowledge; is it a course in calculus, Shakespeare, or ancient religions? At what level is the course supposed to cover those areas? Is it a general survey course for students unlikely to do further work? Is it a required course to prepare students to move on to other courses, and, if so, what must a student learn in this course to be prepared for the others? If it is not a required course, is it still part of an *ad hoc* sequence of courses for most students, and, if so, what do they need to cover in this course to get the most out of the sequence? In short, we are obligated to design each course to fit the educational purpose assigned to it within the curriculum in general. As Alan Gewirth puts the point, if "hired to teach quantum mechanics or molecular biology, the academic may not spend all her or his class time discussing the novels of Jane Austen."[4]

We cannot honor our obligation to select material that respects the purpose of the course unless the course has a purpose in the first place. The task of assigning a purpose to each course belongs primarily to the department faculty as a whole. The faculty of each department are obligated to define the educational goals of their program and to design the curriculum to serve them. As individual professors, we are obligated to help define the appropriate educational goals and curriculum, and then support those decisions in our teaching.

How much does this obligation limit our choice of course material? It is unethical to turn an introduction to quantum mechanics into an introduction to Jane Austen, but what of less obvious cases? Suppose the philosophy department adopts a required ethics course for all graduate students. The course is intended to teach graduate students the main topics currently occupying center stage in that area. Professor Edge works in a new, developing area of ethics. The topics that interest him are not yet receiving much attention from others, but he firmly believes they soon will and that the topics that interest his colleagues and the rest of the profession are yesterday's news. Edge is assigned to teach the required ethics course. The course description, past syllabi, and his colleagues' expectations direct him to teach the topics of importance to his colleagues. He wants to teach, and believes graduate students should learn, the topics that interest him. Is he ethically obligated to limit his academic freedom by bowing to his colleagues' judgment? Is he ethically permitted to teach the course so it doesn't serve its assigned purpose in the curriculum?

A tempting but mistaken response is that, since Edge is not obligated to bow to his colleagues' judgment of what is important in his research, he is not obligated to do so in his teaching. The tempting kernel of truth here is that the obligations that limit a professor's teaching are similar to those that limit his research, when the teaching and research situations are relevantly similar. The mistake is the assumption that the teaching and research situations are usually similar in a relevant way. Teaching involves cooperation with one's colleagues in a way research often does not. To consider a research situation relevantly similar to Edge's situation in his teaching, suppose Edge is a partner in a joint research project. He is not then permitted to devote his research efforts to whatever interests him most, for he has made a commitment to his colleagues to work in a certain area as part of the project. So too, in his teaching, he has made a commitment to his colleagues to teach the course so as to honor the purpose assigned to it.

Yet, won't we seriously threaten the development and communication of new areas of knowledge, if we require professors like Edge to bow to their colleagues' judgment and subscribe to the party line as soon as they enter the classroom? No. Edge has an obligation to his colleagues to honor the intended purpose of the required ethics course. His colleagues have an obligation to him to let him teach the material that interests him in some other course. They will hinder the development and communication of new knowledge if they fail to honor their obligation, but they certainly won't do so by having Edge honor his.

Edge may not have the same access to graduate students if he is forced to teach his preferred material in some other course, for that other course will not be required and may be viewed as out of the mainstream of the department's program. Yet, this is part of teaching in a new and developing area, just as it is part of teaching in a traditional but very specialized one. The course material is not yet central enough to the discipline to be required. If Edge is a good teacher and his material is challenging, students will be attracted to his course. If Edge's colleagues are responsible, they will encourage students to step out of the mainstream. If the subject matter is important, it will make its way into the mainstream and the department's required course.

That the faculty of each department and college are obligated to define the educational goals of their programs and to design a curriculum that serves them does not imply a lock-step curriculum in which one required course leads to the next and ultimately to a diploma. Nothing I have said implies that the curriculum should be an assembly line, that courses should be work stations, or that students should be treated like processed cheese. We should, however, reject the casual attitude recently expressed by Daniel Albright, a University of Rochester professor:

> Let good teachers teach what they want to teach, which is whatever is interesting to them at the moment. Let the students learn what they want to learn.[5]

The interests are not likely to match. What most interests a full professor of mathematics at midcareer is not what freshman students want to learn in mathematics, let alone what they are prepared to learn or need to learn. Moreover, when it comes to learning, most students lack specific wants. They want to study great literary works, but they don't want to study *Paradise Lost,* for they don't know it exists. Students come to a university looking for guidance about what they need to study to satisfy a general conception of what they want to learn. It is the faculty's obligation to provide that guidance through the curriculum and then to give students the chance to follow it by teaching courses as intended in the curriculum.

Writers on this topic generally warn against giving students responsibility for the curriculum.[6] The warnings are appropriate and should also be made with regard to state legislators, business leaders, and any other group beyond the faculty. These groups all have a great stake in the curriculum's being well-conceived—students who want to learn to design airplanes, companies that want to build them, workers who want to sell tickets on them, and anyone who plans to ride in one all have a stake in the engineering curriculum—but they all lack the requisite knowledge by which to plan it. We should keep in mind, though, that what these groups often want most is not control of the curriculum for themselves, but the appropriate exercise of that control by the faculty. During the student upheavals of the 1960s, a New York University professor, Robert Gurland, correctly described the source of much student dissatisfaction over the curriculum.

> Students do not genuinely want the responsibility of academic self-determination, for they realize that they are not in a position to make

vital decisions about which courses are needed in order to pursue certain goals. But students do want the administration and faculty to be responsive to their complaints and needs, and to consult with them in good faith. They must feel that their recommendations will be considered seriously and have the potential to move the institution to positive action. In short, they recognize the distinction between authority competently exercised and authority that is abusive. Their unrest represents a protest against the latter and should be construed as a plea for the former.[7]

Gurland's description remains, I believe, generally accurate today.

Others warn of a danger from within the professoriate in the form of a movement to politicize the curriculum by designing it to teach a particular set of political values.[8] I shall consider this issue shortly in terms of the permissibility of designing a course to teach the values one holds dear. At this point, I want to point out a different, and to my mind more serious, danger within. If we lose control of the curriculum or unwittingly substitute inappropriate values for educational ones, it will most likely be due to our own inattention and neglect. We too easily forget our obligation to design the curriculum to serve appropriate educational goals, and we too often honor it by accident. Too many professors in too many departments concentrate on teaching their own courses and working on their own research projects; too little attention is given to developing a common view of the curriculum and its purpose. Ask these questions for each department: How many times has the faculty engaged in a discussion of the general purpose of their program and the role of each course? To what extent does the training of those graduate students likely to be the next generation of professors include a consideration of what it is to be educated in the field and to be an educated person in general? In most of the departments I know, the answer to the first question is seldom. The answer to the second is very little. The result is that when we are forced to examine the curriculum with regard to such issues as the balance between the traditional Western canon, on the one hand, and the intellectual and artistic achievements of other cultures on the other, we have no well-developed, shared conception of what higher education is supposed to accomplish by which to guide our debate to a correct, rationally based outcome.[9]

Truth, Excellence, and Knowledge

As already emphasized, each university, and so each professor, has an obligation to serve the goal of intellectual advancement and knowledge. Professors in the sciences have an obligation to guide students to knowledge of true theories in the sciences. Professors in the arts have an obligation to guide students to knowledge of excellent works in the arts. Note the reference to true theories in the sciences and to excellent works in the arts. Note too the reference to knowledge. Several important points are contained in each.

To write of an obligation to truth and excellence these days is to risk being interpreted as committed to teaching the Western classics in exclusion to the works of any other tradition. Champions of the Western canon have appropriated the banner of truth and excellence in an attempt to gain the argument's high ground, just as those who would exchange some Western classics for works from other cultures have appropriated the banner of diversity. So, let me emphasize three points that should be obvious. First, an obligation to truth and excellence is not an obligation to one particular intellectual tradition in opposition to all others. No particular tradition has an exclusive franchise on these values. Second, to maintain that students should be presented with works from different traditions is not to escape the obligation to select works both from and across traditions relative to their truth and excellence. Indeed, we are awarded discretion in designing courses on the dual assumptions that our courses should guide students to knowledge of what is true and excellent and that we are best qualified to judge what that is. To accept the position of professor in a particular discipline is to buy into this understanding; it is to claim to know the standards for truth and/or excellence appropriate to the discipline and make a commitment to design courses on the basis of this knowledge. Third, our obligation to truth and excellence is limited by our obligations to honor the intended purpose of the course and the abilities of our students. A physics professor may present Newtonian mechanics to undergraduates not yet prepared to understand the general or special theories of relativity. An English professor teaching a course devoted to certain literary periods must select works in terms of the sometimes competing considerations of both their individual excellence and their ability to represent the periods under review. The question of what to study in a particular course is not the question: What works are true and/or the most excellent? It is: What works are most appropriate relative to the standards of truth and excellence in conjunction with the limited purpose and level of the course?[10]

Our obligation is to guide students to *knowledge* of what is true and excellent. Knowledge is not just a set of beliefs or even a set of true beliefs. To have knowledge is to have true beliefs on the basis of justifying evidence. Professors in the sciences have an obligation to guide students to true beliefs backed by justifying evidence in the sciences, and professors in the arts have an obligation to guide students to true beliefs backed by justifying evidence in the arts. What ethical obligations flow from the commitment to knowledge?

It is too simple to say that we are obligated to teach what is true and not what is false. What we believe to be, and teach to be, the truth today, we or others may discover to be false tomorrow, and while that discovery may imply that we were mistaken in what we taught, it will not imply that we acted unethically. Let's forget as well the idea that we are obligated not to present material we know to be false. I am confident I know certain philosophical theories to be false, but other respectable philosophers believe them to be true, and given that the theories are accepted by creditable philosophers and backed by reasonable arguments, I do nothing wrong when I present them to students.

We are obligated to teach those views generally accepted by experts working in the area, along with their supporting evidence. These views are students' current best bets for knowledge, and they need to be exposed to the supporting evidence if they are to gain knowledge as opposed to mere true beliefs. Where the experts disagree, we are obligated to teach the various sides, along with their strengths and weaknesses. The professor who teaches only one of the options—even if it happens to be the true one—will not lead students to knowledge. Students can only gain the justifying evidence knowledge demands by examining and assessing the competing theories for themselves. No one has put the point better than John Stuart Mill.

> [T]he only way in which a human being can make some approach to knowing the whole of a subject is by hearing what can be said about it by persons of every variety of opinion, and studying all modes in which it can be looked at by every character of mind. No wise man ever acquired his wisdom in any mode but this; nor is it in the nature of human intellect to become wise in any other manner.[11]

Sooner or later, most students encounter a professor who seeks to avoid teaching the competing sides of an issue by announcing at the start of the course that the treatment will be one-sided and encouraging students to take another section if they want a more balanced approach. An economics professor might announce that he teaches his introduction to the field as a course in Marxist economics. A philosophy professor might announce that she teaches her introduction to ethics as a course in utilitarianism. Such announcements do nothing to release these professors from their obligation, though they warn students of their intent to violate it. The students who remain in class do not give their informed consent to the professor's arrangement, for they do not know what they will and will not learn by accepting the terms. Indeed, the arrangement even deprives them of the chance to get that knowledge. Moreover, the obligation to teach the competing sides of issues is not simply based in a commitment to students from which students may release professors by informed consent. It is based in the university's commitment to intellectual advancement and knowledge and each professor's acceptance of that commitment upon accepting a faculty appointment.

While our obligation to teach the competing options cannot be removed by a mere announcement, it can be limited by our obligation to honor the course's purpose and the students' abilities. An advanced seminar often focuses on the details of a single position or theory. Students in a low-level course are often unprepared to study the more advanced options in a dispute. In these cases, our obligation to teach the competing views becomes an obligation to inform students of their existence and to ensure that they are taught elsewhere in the curriculum.

A second implication of our obligation to guide students to knowledge is our duty to teach certain intellectual skills and values to students. The successful search for knowledge requires the ability to analyze a line of reasoning and evaluate a work of art. It requires honesty, the willingness to question one's beliefs, and the willingness to subordinate personal desires and preconceptions to the dictates of logic. Students often lack these prerequisites of study. The content of our courses should include not just the scientific theories or works of art, but the skills needed to analyze, appreciate, and evaluate them. The values are best taught by example. We have an obligation to exemplify them in our teaching and to communicate and hold students to the expectation that they display them in their work.

Finally, the obligation to guide students to knowlege implies a duty to limit our teaching to those areas in which we have sufficient expertise. Like any professionals, we are obligated to confine the limits of our practice to the limits of our competency. Everett K. Wilson states the underlying ethical principle well:

It is not appropriate for a teacher to make unsupported, or unsupportable, claims for his or her teaching.[12]

An interest in fields other than our own may quite naturally and properly inform much of our research and teaching, yet we should never take on the task of guiding students to knowledge in an area where we are not appropriately knowledgeable ourselves.

When obligations multiply conflicts arise, and it is not always clear how the conflicts should be settled. Suppose Professor Edge is assigned to teach a course where the material specified in the course description and past syllabi is out-of-date, and the material he wants to teach is up-to-date. He tries to get the department to modify the course, but his colleagues are unwilling. They haven't kept up with the advances in the field; they are caught in their own fears of being left behind. What should Edge do? If he teaches the theories the course is intended to cover and advertised as covering in the course description, he will violate his obligation to teach the views currently accepted by experts in the field. If he teaches the course so as to concentrate on the currently accepted views, he will violate his obligation to honor the course's purpose. Should he just refuse to teach the course? Should he teach the course as it is intended to be taught but tell the students that the material is out-of-date? Should he teach the course so as to concentrate on the current views and explain to students why he is departing from the course description?

A few points are relatively clear. First, it is too simple to say that, since students register for the course with the understanding that the course description will be followed, Edge should honor the description. Students also register with the understanding that the course's content will guide them to knowledge, and Edge will violate this understanding if he honors the course description. Certainly, at a minimum, if Edge decides to honor the course description, he should inform students that they are not studying the most current work in the field. Second, Edge's ethical conflict is based in his colleagues' failure to design a curriculum that best serve students' educational needs. The basic question is at what point does his colleagues' failure to honor their obligation relieve him of his obligation to honor the course's role within the curriculum? Just as public servants charged with applying an unjust social policy must determine when the policy's failure to serve the common good relieves them of any obligation to apply it, Edge must determine when the course's failure to guide students to knowledge relieves him of any obligation to teach it as described.

Values

Professors sometimes find that students lack important values. They have strong racial or sexual prejudices, they are overly materialistic, they are too self-centered, they don't respect the environment. May we, as individual professors, select the material for our courses with an eye toward teaching students the values we think they should have? We can take the question up a level: May we, as the faculty of a department, or even of a college or the university as a whole, adopt the goal of designing courses to teach the values we think students should have? Andrew Ross, a Princeton English professor, seems to think the answer is yes.

> I teach in the Ivy League in order to have direct access to the minds of the children of the ruling class. Whoever the politically correct are, it's about time some of them were in the universities.[13]

If we ignore the negative connotations currently associated with talk of what is "politically correct," this is a fairly plausible position. The correct political values are likely to include such values as democracy and freedom of the press, which graduates of Princeton or any other college ought to know. Yet, is it the proper business of a university to teach them?

It is important to keep some preliminary points in mind from the start. First, we are talking about *teaching* certain values to students, not simply discussing or debating them. In a philosophy course in ethics, the professor and students discuss and debate values—pleasure is the only intrinsic good, human life is more valuable than nonhuman life—but the values are not taught, and there is no interesting ethical issue of whether the discussion or debate is appropriate. To talk of teaching values is minimally to talk of presenting them as being correct and designing the course to guide students to the justified, true belief that they are correct.

Second, to endorse the teaching of certain values is also, short of a general rejection of all testing and/or grading, to endorse testing students to see if they have understood and accepted the values, at least for the purpose of the exam, and making their grade depend on their performance. It is *ad hoc* at best to maintain that it is right to design a course to teach students certain values along with some nonnormative content, but only right to test and grade for the nonnormative content. If it is appropriate to teach it, it is appropriate to test for it. So too, if we select the material for a course with the teaching of certain values as one of our central aims, then this aim should be part of the course description. It is again *ad hoc* to maintain that while the other central aims involved in the selection of course material should be part of the course description, the goal of teaching certain values may be left out.

Third, the issue at hand cannot be settled by an appeal to each professor's academic freedom. It is a mistake to argue that, since each of us has a right to academic freedom, we may each teach whatever we believe to be most appropriate, whether it is a particular set of values or a particular scientific theory. Our right to academic freedom does not excuse us from ethical duties with regard to what we teach, any more than our right to free speech excuses us from ethical duties about what we say (e.g., the duty to tell the truth). The right of academic freedom is certainly relevant to whether we may be required to teach or not to teach certain values, but it is not directly relevant to whether it is permissible for us to teach those values.

A fourth and last preliminary point is that we cannot settle the issue by the observation that no university education can ever be value free. The observation is, of course, correct. We cannot help but communicate to students the values contained in the standards of truth and excellence by which we choose our course material. We are even obligated to teach students the intellectual values necessary to the search for truth. Professional schools quite properly offer professional responsibility courses in which students are taught the values in their profession's code of conduct and how to relate those values to actual situations. None of this settles the issue of whether it is ethically permissible for a professor to teach some further values (e.g., the endorsement of certain social policies that are not contained in the discipline's standards of truth and excellence, are not necessary for the search for truth, and are not part of the profession's code of conduct).

The suggestion that professors may teach some values beyond those necessary to the search for truth, embedded in standards for truth and excellence, or associated with their particular profession is often met with a rhetorical question: Whose values are we to teach? Like most rhetorical questions, it is loaded with an argument: any attempt to justify one professor's teaching a value we hold dear—say, the rejection of racism—once generalized, will justify another professor's teaching exactly the opposite value, racism; since we don't want to endorse the teaching of the latter, we had best not endorse the teaching of the former.

It is not this simple, though. Two plausible arguments support the teaching of some values without supporting the teaching of any values whatsoever. The first appeals to the university's social responsibility.

Whenever the university can use its teaching activities in a way that will benefit society, it has an obligation to do so. The university can benefit society by teaching students certain values; it can, for example, benefit society by teaching students to reject racism and sexism. Hence, the university has an obligation to teach students those values, and professors who design their courses so as to teach them are simply doing their part to honor the university's obligation. Their actions are both ethically permissible and obligatory.

The second argument appeals to the university's character as a just community.

Every member of the university has an ethical obligation to honor and promote certain values essential to the existence of the university as a just community. All members, for example, are obliged to accept and promote the proposition that individuals are to be judged on the basis of individual merit, independently of considerations of race and sex; so too, all are obliged to accept and promote the proposition that everyone is to be treated with a basic degree of respect. Professors who design their courses so as to teach these values are simply honoring their ethical obligation to promote them within the university. Their actions are both ethically obligatory and permissible.

Neither argument tries to show that individual professors are ethically permitted to design courses so as to teach whatever values they hold dear, be it the rejection of racism and sexism, on the one hand, or the adoption of those attitudes, on the other. The first argument is limited to values the teaching of which will benefit society. The second is limited to values essential to the existence of the university as a just community. For this reason, the arguments do not provide equally strong support for teaching the acceptance of racism as for teaching its rejection. Premises that are true with regard to the rejection of racism (it benefits society; it is among the values essential to a just university community) are false with regard to the acceptance of racism (it doesn't benefit society; it is not among the values essential to a just university).

We can, then, argue plausibly for the teaching of some values, without thereby arguing for the teaching of any values. And isn't this what we would expect? A major reason why it is wrong to teach racism and sexism but (perhaps) permissible to teach their rejection is simply that the latter activity promises to benefit society and support the university's status as a just community, while the former promises to do the opposite.[14]

The arguments contain two important limitations, however. First, they only concern the teaching of very general values: the rejection of the view that individuals should be judged by their race or sex; the endorsement of the principles of individual merit and respect. These general values do not entail many of the more specific ones some may wish to teach under their banner, such as an endorsement of quota-based affirmative action programs, and so the permissibility of teaching the general values does not automatically establish the permissibility of teaching the more specific ones. If we restate the arguments, replacing the general values with the more specific ones, the central premise often becomes quite doubtful. It is far from clear, for example, that society will benefit from the university's teaching the acceptance of quota-based affirmative action or that that form of affirmative action is among the values essential to a just university community.

Second, neither argument establishes the permissibility of teaching even the general values it mentions without serious qualifications concerning our other obligations as professors. To see this, let's take a closer look at each argument, beginning with the first.

The argument's initial premises are true. Just like General Motors and the Boy Scouts, the university as a social institution has an ethical obligation to take advantage of its opportunities to benefit society. This obligation is behind many of our expectations for the university, from the expectation that it pursue its commitment to intellectual excellence to the expectation that it have a recycling program. So, too, the university can teach students to reject racism and sexism. If we can teach students to judge a scientific hypothesis by the evidence rather than by whether it is consistent with their personal preconceptions and desires, we should be able to make some progress at teaching them to judge individuals by their merits rather than by their personal preconceptions about race and sex. Any progress the university makes in teaching students to reject racism and sexism will certainly benefit society.

These premises imply the argument's first conclusion that the university has an obligation to teach students to reject racism and sexism, but they don't straightaway imply the further conclusion that any professor who designs a course with that aim is simply doing what is ethically obligatory. The university can honor its obligation in a variety of ways, some curricular and some extracurricular. We can design the content of courses in an attempt to teach against racism and sexism; we can also teach against racism and sexism through workshops offered by the office of student life, through the student conduct regulations, and through the university's employment practices. The argument does not provide any reason to believe that the university's obligation to teach against racism and sexism is in turn an obligation to do so through its course offerings.

Even if the university's obligation carries over to the regular curriculum, it doesn't follow that professors who design courses to teach against racism and sexism always act permissibly. It is wrong to convert topology into topics in social oppression, for the change violates fundamental obligations linked to the course's place in the curriculum. In short, we cannot settle the issue of teaching values just by considering the university's obligation as a social institution. The crucial question is how, if at all, we can design courses to teach socially worthwhile values without violating more stringent obligations.

Similar points apply to the second argument's appeal to the university's existence as a just community. The premises are true. Members of the university are obligated to accept and promote those values essential to a just community, and those values include honoring individual merit and respect for persons. This obligation has clear implications for how professors conduct their daily relationships with colleagues, students, and staff. Yet again, the premises do not warrant the further conclusion that it is always permissible for professors to design courses to teach these values. The question remains of whether any other more stringent obligations will be violated.

We've come to the question on which the issue turns: Can we teach socially worthwhile values, such as the rejection of racism and sexism in our courses, without violating more stringent obligations? I've argued that we have primary obligations in three areas when choosing the material for a course: (1) to fit the course to the knowledge and abilities of the audience, (2) to honor the intended purpose of the course, and (3) to guide students to knowledge of what is true and/or excellent. Attempts to teach certain values need not conflict with the first obligation, but they may conflict with the second or third. Let's reformulate the question: Can we teach such values as the rejection of racism and sexism without violating our obligation to honor the intended purpose of the course and to guide students to knowledge of what is true and/or excellent?

Surely, we can. Suppose I am concerned about the sexism of my students. It is clear that the vast majority have a higher opinion of the intellectual abilities of men than of women, and several blatantly sexist incidents involving students have occurred on campus. I decide to work against this sexism in a small way in my introductory course in philosophy. I replace several works by men with equally excellent works by women. When the class gets to the new works, I take the time to point out that they are by women and talk about the ways in which women have been handicapped in their pursuit of academic careers, in general, and philosophical careers, in particular, by the prejudice that sex is relevant to intellectual ability. The rest of the course remains the same.

I have done nothing to violate the obligations we've considered. The changes in the course have not detracted from its ability to guide students to a knowledge of basic philosophical issues and excellent philosophical works. Someone might object that I have not honored the intended purpose of the course, since I have tried to teach students something that the course was not created to teach and something that is not part of the course description. Yet, why assume that professors have an obligation not to teach students more than what the course was created to teach? The attempt to teach against sexism is not a central part of the course, but the course description might be modified to include the course's additional purpose and content. Someone might object that I have not honored my obligation to teach the competing sides of the issue since I have not presented the view that philosophical ability is linked to sex, but the obligation to teach competing sides only extends to alternatives that are reasonable as represented by the endorsement of acknowledged experts in the field. The view that philosophical ability is linked to sex fails to meet this standard. There would even be nothing wrong with my testing and grading students on their acceptance of the value I teach. A student who argues in an exam essay that a philosophical theory is mistaken because it is held by a woman should lose some points for giving an *ad "hominem"* argument.[15]

At the same time, it is easy to conceive of cases in which the attempt to teach certain values is impermissible. Suppose a professor of English composition is disturbed by the racist attitudes of students. The professor structures the composition course around a set of readings that deal with the racist nature of major social institutions. Students are assigned expository and evaluative essays on the readings. The class sessions regularly give much more attention to the issues raised in the readings and the arguments they contain than to points of composition, and the professor is quite open about the lack of emphasis on writing skills. Students are warned from the start that the course is as much or more a course in social values as one in writing. They are told that the English department offers other sections that concentrate more on writing.

This professor violates the duty to honor the intended purpose of the course. It is supposed to teach students the fundamentals of English composition, and the professor cannot be spending adequate time doing that if extensive attention is given to the philosophical topics raised in the essays. The initial warning to students about the nature of the course and the advice to take a different section if they have reservations do not let the professor off the hook for reasons we have already considered. The professor may also violate part of the obligation to guide students to knowledge. The obligation to teach within the limits of competency applies here, as few professors of English are experts in social philosophy or sociology; so does the obligation to teach the competing sides of controversial issues, if the professor takes a one-sided approach to issues debated by experts (e.g., the injustice of certain employment practices, the social consequences of certain affirmative action programs).

What if the professor's department introduces a new course in the oppression of women and persons of color with the purpose of teaching certain values to students? We no longer have to worry about whether the professor is honoring the intended purpose of the course. Yet, many of the other issues remain. There is still the issue of whether the professor has the expertise to teach the course. So, too, there is the question of whether the course materials and lectures provide a balanced treatment of controversial issues, and, if they do not, whether some alternative course is offered to give students a balanced presentation. If the materials and lectures do not provide a balanced treatment and no alternative course is available, the professor teaching the course violates the obligation to provide students with all reasonable sides of a controversial issue. The irony in this sort of case is that the professor does not, after all, teach values to students. To teach is to guide students to justified true beliefs. Students cannot form justified beliefs without examining all the reasonable sides of a controversial issue.

A series of questions can thus provide guidance as to whether a particular attempt to teach values is ethically permissible. First, what values are to be taught and will society and/or the university community benefit from the teaching of these values? The two arguments we have considered for teaching values assume that the values to be taught are socially worthwhile, and it is important to distinguish those very general values, (e.g., the rejection of racism and sexism, for which the arguments are quite strong, from more specific ones, for example, the endorsement of particular affirmative action programs, which may be associated with the general values but for which the arguments are not nearly so plausible). Second, will the attempt to teach the material selected prevent us from honoring the purpose of the course? Third, will it prevent us from honoring the obligation to guide students to knowledge? If the answer to one of the last two questions is yes, our attempt to teach values conflicts with one of our fundamental obligations as professors. Even if the values are socially worthwhile, they are better conveyed to students in some other way.

Notes

1. Some of the examples I present as based on my own experience are actually based on the reports of other professors in other departments at my own or other universities. In some cases, I've changed such details as the level of the course or the sex of the professor.

2. See Joan C. Callahan, "Academic Paternalism," *International Journal of Applied Philosophy* 3:1 (1986) pp. 21–31. Callahan's essay is also part of this collection.

3. The adjustment of admission requirements, even for a single course, is often a major issue. Suppose the students in a mathematics class are too varied in their prior work in mathematics, and the professor adds one course in basic algebra as a prerequisite. Since the university is admitting a large number of students without basic algebra, the mathematics department should now offer basic algebra, to give those students a chance to meet the expectations now set for them, or the university should increase its admissions requirements to include basic algebra. Yet the mathematics faculty may be reluctant to offer basic algebra since it is not a college-level course. The university may be reluctant to increase its admissions requirements, because a large segment of the population believes its children should be able to attend the university even if they have not had basic algebra. Who is obligated to do what? There is no clear and specific answer. But one general point is clear: so long as the university presents itself to each student as providing an educational program devoted to intellectual achievement and knowledge, it is fundamentally obliged

to set admission requirements for courses and degree programs in such a way that, once the dust has settled, professors can design courses so that every student in every course is confronted with a realistic intellectual challenge.

4. Alan Gewirth, "Human Rights and Academic Freedom," in *Morality, Responsibility and the University,* ed. Steven M. Cahn (Philadelphia: Temple University Press, 1990), p. 16.

5. *Rochester Review,* Summer 1991, p. 13.

6. See, for example, Steven M. Cahn, *Saints and Scamps: Ethics in Academia* (Totowa, N.J., Rowman and Littlefield, 1986), pp. 8–9, and Robert H. Gurland, "Teaching Mathematics," in *Scholars Who Teach,* Steven M. Cahn, ed. (Chicago: Nelson-Hall, 1978), especially pp. 77–82.

7. Robert H. Gurland, "Teaching Mathematics," p. 82.

8. Consider, for example, Roger Kimball, *Tenured Radicals: How Politics Has Corrupted Our Higher Education* (New York: Harper and Row, 1990); Charles J. Sykes, *The Hollow Men: Politics and Corruption in Higher Education* (Washington, D.C., Regnery Gateway, 1990) and Dinesh D'Souza, *Illiberal Education: The Politics of Race and Sex on Campus* (New York: Macmillan/Free Press, 1991).

9. The point is well made by John Searle, "Storm over the University," *New York Review of Books,* December 6, 1990, pp. 34–42.

10. This point is sometimes overlooked by opponents of attempts to make some course offerings more representative of non-Western cultures. It is a mistake to look at the course syllabus, see that some Western classic is missing but that some non-Western work has been included, and object: "They are not studying so-and-so but they are studying such and such; surely, such and such is not as excellent as so-and-so." Even when the judgment of excellence is correct, the objection is not to the point. It overlooks the fact that, since one purpose of the course may be to consider different works representing different cultures, the standard for what should be taught is not simply what is most excellent. It is what is most excellent and most in keeping with the intended purpose of the course.

11. John Stuart Mill, *On Liberty* (New York: Bobbs-Merrill, 1956), p. 25.

12. Everett K. Wilson, "Power, Pretense and Piggybacking: Some Ethical Issues in Teaching," *Journal of Higher Education* 53, 3 (1982), p. 274.

13. Professor Andrew Ross, as quoted in "Deciphering Victorian underwear and other seminars: or how to be profane, profound and scholarly—all the while looking for a job—at the Modern Language Association's annual convention," by Anne Matthews, *The New York Times Magazine,* February 10, 1991, p. 58.

14. Yet, won't professors who want to teach racism and sexism claim that the teaching of those values will benefit society; won't they claim that adopting those values will support the university's existence as a just community? Most likely, they will. They'll also be wrong, and we can give good arguments to show that they are wrong. If we think we cannot give such arguments on the

ground that all value judgments are matters of personal taste and preference, we ought to quit wasting our time discussing the ethics of teaching.

15. Note that I would violate one of my ethical obligations if I replaced works by male philosophers with substantially inferior works by women. I am obligated to provide students with the most excellent philosophical works I can relative to my other obligations regarding the course's level and intended purpose. So, too, I would violate one of my ethical obligations if I redesigned the course so that students did not receive an introduction to the various areas and methods of philosophical inquiry, but just an introduction to the works of selected feminist philosophers. My selection of material for the course would conflict with its intended purpose.

CHAPTER THREE

How to Teach

Just as what we teach determines what students get a chance to learn, how we teach determines how great their chance will be. The analogy to other professions such as the law is obvious. A court's decision to hear my case and an attorney's decision to represent me give me a chance at justice, but how the court hears my case and how my attorney represents me determine just how great my opportunity will be. If the court is biased or my attorney unprepared, my prospects for justice are slight. When professors are biased or unprepared, their students' prospects for knowledge are slight. What basic obligations must we honor to give students a significant chance to learn?

Preparation

Students remember their best and their worst professors. I remember my psychology instructor. Each class was an improvisation exercise. He always began with, "What did you think of the reading assignment?" and the class took any direction our replies gave it. If a reply concerned the assigned reading, we discussed the assigned reading. If a comment came out of left field, our discussion went out to left field. If someone raised issues we had already considered, we considered them again. While priding himself on his ability to create each class from the same question and telling us he was making us take responsibility for our education, the professor was actually obstructing our education by shirking his duty. To be a professor is to assume the role of guiding students to knowledge, and the role includes providing the structure and content relative to which students can best learn. Providing the necessary structure and content entails preparing the course and each class in it.

What does the obligation to prepare demand? Suppose I pick the texts for my course, and I decide what topics I will cover, in what order, and for how long. I set the course requirements and office hours. I outline my lectures, anticipating questions and noting possible discussion topics. Prior to each class, I practice my presentation so I'm minimally dependent on my notes. Have I honored my obligation to prepare the course as a whole and each class in particular? Perhaps not.

The obligation to prepare the course includes more than giving it a definite structure of topics to be studied and assignments to be completed, and the obligation to prepare each class includes more than having enough material for the allotted time period. We are obligated to prepare the course and each class so as to establish a structure *in which students can best proceed, as free inquirers, to form their own rationally based true beliefs about the subject.* We have, after all, made a commitment to guide students to knowledge. Adequate course preparation includes all the activities mentioned above—picking the texts, choosing the topics, setting the course requirements and office hours—but it also includes doing these things so as to honor our commitment. Topics must be selected in terms of what students need to learn to progress, rather than our personal interests. Assignments must be made in terms of what will best guide students, help them develop the necessary skills, and provide effective measures of their progress, rather than how much time we wish to spend on grading. We seldom violate the duty to prepare by failing to provide any structure or content. We more frequently violate it by making preparations with an eye on something other than our role as an intellectual guide.

The ethical issue here involves more than an obligation to subordinate our own interest to that of our students. Teaching is only one of a professor's roles, and we must often balance conflicting demands. Many of us believe, for example, that students need to improve their writing ability and that they can best do so through written assignments in a variety of courses and extensive feedback on those assignments, yet we continue to rely on "objective" tests and at best assign only one paper, which we make due at the last class meeting, knowing most students will never claim it to read our corrections. We cite conflicting obligations, not self-interest or laziness, to justify our action: we have too many students to correct several written assignments for each and still prepare for each class; if we spend all our time correcting papers, we will not honor our research and service obligations.

For each activity we take on as professors, we are obligated to do the things that define what it is to do that activity well, and if we are engaged in too many activities to do each well, we should put some aside. Hence, so long as we are going to invite students to the university with the understanding that we will guide them to knowledge—so long as we are going to teach—we must prepare our classes so as to teach well. If we can't do that, because we have too many students to teach, too many grants to submit, too many manuscripts to write, or too many committees on which to serve, then the number of students to be taught, grants submitted, manuscripts written, or committees served must be decreased. Insofar as we determine these expectations—and quite often we do (either as individuals or as a department or university faculty)—we are obligated to adjust them so we can meet our fundamental teaching obligations. If someone else determines them, we must work to get them changed.[1]

Once we prepare our course, we have a duty to share our plan with our students in a syllabus, and we must be ready to explain the reasons behind it. It's not that students are so incompetent as to need written instructions from day one. It's not that they are buying the course and are entitled to a written description of its content to protect them as consumers. The basis of the obligation rests in three other considerations. First, we have a duty to respect our students' status as autonomous inquirers; we must give them the information they need to make informed decisions, not only about what to believe but also about what to study.[2] Second, since the plan for a course should reveal the structure and demands of the material to be studied, we miss an important opportunity to teach students about the general nature of the material, if we keep the plan to ourselves; explaining the course outline is an excellent occasion to present the major parts of the subject and their interconnections, and explaining the requirements is a chance to start teaching the discipline's standards of excellence. Finally, students function more effectively when they know where they are being led and why. They study best for an exam when they know its format and the material it will cover, and they get the most out of a reading assignment if they know the basic topics and questions related to it.

May we change the course plan, after we share it with students? There is a very strong presumption against doing so; the syllabus represents a commitment to the students announcing where we intend to lead them and how, and they often base a decision to remain in the course on that commitment. Nonetheless, we may change our plan for good reasons, which is generally to say reasons related to the students' educational welfare. Doctors who tell patients what course of treatment they intend to pursue may change their plans for reasons that concern their patients' health but not for their own preferences and interests. We are similarly obligated. We may not cancel the final exam, or make it optional, because we would rather end the course in a more enjoyable way. We may change the topics we plan to cover because we find that all our students lack the necessary skills to study them. The line between permissible and impermissible changes is not easily drawn. What should we do if we find that some, but not all, of our students lack the necessary preparation? Our obligation to teach the course as described must be balanced against our obligation to do the best we can to teach the students actually before us. The correct choice depends in part on the number of students with varying abilities and the availability of remedial courses. If only one student out of thirty is adequately prepared and no remedial course is available, the best option is to revise the course and offer the prepared student additional instruction. If only one student is unprepared, the best option is to advise him to withdraw. There is no formula, though, and the real solution is prevention: avoid the dilemma by honoring the prior obligation to know the course's likely audience and design it accordingly.

We most certainly should be ready to change the syllabus from one offering of the course to the next. It is not just a matter of staying current with the field. Each course should fit the needs and abilities of the students, and as these change so should the course. Good professors don't simply bemoan the declines and rejoice over the improvements in their students' abilities. They adjust their courses accordingly. If the students can't follow a complex argument, they devise assignments to teach that skill. If the students have improved writing skills, they capitalize on the improvement.

Accurate Representation

What we teach has generally been created by others who cannot be present to explain their work, and when we assume that task for them, we assume a duty of accurate representation. Accurate representation never precludes criticism. It always precludes ignoring what the material is and presenting it as what it is not. Plato, Cervantes, Maxwell, the Hopi Indians, and so on all have an interest in being interpreted accurately and taken seriously, and we wrong them if we fail to do so.[3]

Students introduced to new material need a correct understanding of what it is and a clear sense of why whoever had those ideas had them in the first place, so they can make their own informed judgments. We must also represent the material accurately to teach such intellectual values as a commitment to truth and objectivity.

One way to violate the duty of accurate representation is to teach what we don't know. Since we are regularly allowed to teach new courses without first showing that we have the requisite knowledge, it is often tempting to learn a new area by teaching it, especially in upper-level courses. We combine our teaching and our research. We expand our teaching repertoire. Teaching becomes more exciting. Our on-the-job training cheats both the material and the students, however. Our ignorance keeps us from accurately representing the former to the latter, and, although we gradually learn from our mistakes as we teach the course again and again, the students who take an early version never do. The initial development of a new course belongs to the research activity meant to supplement and support our teaching. Once we have mastered the material as part of our research, we may take it into the classroom.[4]

We also violate the duty of accurate representation if we ignore the material or bend it beyond recognition to pursue an alternative agenda. Mind-body dualism, a standard topic in introductory philosophy courses, is often taught through the work of René Descartes, a seventeenth-century French philosopher famous for his defense of the view that our bodies and minds are distinct entities, one material and the other immaterial. Suppose I introduce students to Descartes's claim that the mind and body are distinct, and then set the details of his position aside to present several concerns of my own. I dismiss Descartes's view as containing a "negative" attitude toward the human body. I engage the students in a discussion of their own attitudes toward their bodies and the social basis for those attitudes. I parlay this into a discussion of possible social causes of bulimia and anorexia. I never misquote Descartes; I never falsely attribute claims to him. I still violate my obligation of accurate representation. By ignoring the details of his position, I fail to present it as what it is—an attempt to demonstrate a certain view of human nature—and the students never get to make their own informed evaluation of it. To them, Descartes is never more than a long-dead philosopher who thought bodies were dirt.

None of this is to say that we may never use material to teach views that lie beyond it. Certainly, we may use the course material to generate discussion on other topics and to make points, including value judgments, about the historical tradition it represents. The point is twofold: first, insofar as we set out to teach some particular material, we are obligated to present it accurately; second, we must teach the material itself accurately before we can profitably use it to get at topics beyond it. We must not try to teach students certain opinions we have reached about the material without ever guiding them through the detailed examination by which we reached those views in the first place. Professors who do so are like mathematicians who try to teach a result without teaching the reasoning by which it is derived. They may convince students on the authority of their testimony, but they never lead them to knowledge.

Promoting Intellectual Inquiry

Students must go through the same activity to gain knowledge through our teaching that we must go through to gain knowledge through our research. They must question, reason, and experiment. Knowledge, as opposed to mere belief in half-understood propositions, requires individual, intellectual inquiry. Arnold Arons, a physics professor at the University of Washington, makes the point well.

> Virtually any student can tell you, with an ingenuous smile, that the Earth is spherical and that it and the other planets revolve around the sun, but if you ask how he knows these assertions to be true, on what evidence we believe such statements, his smile turns to dismay and embarrassment—in all cases except, perhaps, for a very few physics majors. In terms of our vaunted goals for "higher education," do these students really hold any significant knowledge? Are they in any way better educated than their medieval counterparts who would have given what we now consider the "wrong" answer on exactly the same basis that modern students give the "correct" one—an end result received from authority?[5]

We are obligated to promote intellectual inquiry, to aid those students who attempt it, and to make success in it a necessary condition of success in our course.

Intellectual inquiry takes time. There often seems to be a conflict between allocating enough time to examine each topic adequately and covering all the topics we should. As Rita Cooley, a political science professor at New York University, observes,

Teachers are often torn between what they deem adequate coverage of content and use of methodologies which require time for an examination of propositions, a review of evidence, reflection, and an appraisal of the proof on which knowledge claims rest.[6]

If we examine the reasons behind all the bits and pieces, we won't cover all the material assigned to the course; students will not learn what they are supposed to know and may need to know for the next course.

Confusion is at work here. Adequate coverage of content is defined by how much we lead students to know, not by how many topics we mention in class or how many claims we get them to believe. Achieving adequate coverage does not conflict with leading students through a critical examination of the material. It requires it. Consider Arons's way of making the point.

> When I urge, as I do here and continue to do at every turn, that we back off, slow up, "cover" less, give students a chance to think and understand, someone invariably demurs: "But if we stop way back here, if we do not cover our subject, the students will never know about this matter," or that, or the other "which is so profoundly important," or which is so "fascinating" because it happens to be modern or topical! To this I can only respond that the demurral constitutes a terrible prostitution of the word "know." What did the students reading the methods text "know" as a result of having read it and memorized the phrases?[7]

If promoting the intellectual inquiry necessary to guide students to knowledge requires that a sixteen-week course be devoted to three topics instead of five, we should devote the course to three topics or extend the course beyond sixteen weeks; the rest of the curriculum should be arranged accordingly. Decisions about what to teach and for how long—by an individual professor or by a department or college faculty—must be made relative to the basic obligation to teach so as to provide each student with a reasonable chance at knowledge.

The same holds true for decisions about how many students to teach in a class. Appropriate class size varies from one course to another, but, in general, the larger the class, the more difficult it is to promote intellectual inquiry. There are obvious ways to mitigate the problems of a large class: give assignments that require students to investigate the material outside of class; supplement the large lecture with small laboratory or discussion sections taught by graduate students. New technologies promise additional measures. Yet even with such modifications, mass lectures of 300 to 500 students promote inquiry as poorly as mass trials promote justice. What judge would try 300 people at once because they were charged with the same crime, even if every group of twenty-five defendants was assigned its own law student for legal counsel?

The reasons for large classes have nothing to do with educational quality. We don't increase class size to teach better. We increase it to teach more. The noble goal is to make higher education more accessible. The not-so-noble goals include gaining more tuition dollars and shifting the "hands-on" teaching to graduate assistants. Whatever our goal, any decision about how many students to teach must honor the obligation to teach so we have a reasonable chance of engaging each student in the kind of intellectual activity required for knowledge. When our class is too large to honor this obligation, we should decrease it insofar as we have the power to do so, and work to get it decreased insofar as the power lies elsewhere.[8]

To promote intellectual inquiry, we must avoid appeals to authority and give students reasons for the material we present. We must actively encourage them to demand justifying reasons from us, from those whose work they study, and from themselves.[9] Our presentations and questions should engender debate and discussion. Our assignments should require students to display the results of their own critical examination of the material. We must continually direct students away from the question, "What must I know in this course?" to the question, "How do I know the material in this course?" All these activities must be performed within the structure we have established for the course. Our duty is to spark intellectual inquiry and then to structure it so students who engage in it gain knowledge.

Note the reference to "sparking" intellectual activity. Although students are admitted to a course to study the subject matter, they often select it for a variety of nonacademic reasons: it's offered at a convenient time, a friend is taking it, it's a requirement, the professor is known as a "nice guy," it's located near a previous class. Students often don't know enough about the subject to have a strong interest in it, and when they do, they do not walk in each day brain cells ignited and ready to have at it. Their intellectual interest needs to be stimulated. It is the professor's obligation to do so.

Some may think that I've got the obligations reversed. It's not the professor's job to motivate intellectual inquiry by the students; it's the students' duty to be self-starters: "I just present the material; if they aren't interested in it, that's their problem." This too-common view misses a basic point. How we present the material greatly determines the students' interest. Good presentations create and nurture interest; bad ones kill it. It is no excuse to claim that students can only be inspired by the kind of "showman" that we are not, could not be, and do not care to become. Teaching techniques that promote student interest do not require us to turn our class into a circus, and they can be learned. Robert Gurland, a mathematics professor at New York University, gives one example.

A professor who walks into his classroom, sketches an irregular blob on the blackboard, and asks his class, "How do you think we can go about finding the surface of this amoeba?" may well be on his way to generating a discussion that will lead to a clear grasp of what the definite integral is, and what integral calculus is all about. On the other hand, the professor who marches into the class and states, "Today, we define the definite integral," while slathering a definition on the board that involves least upper bounds, greatest lower bounds, Riemann sums, limits convergence and so on, will more likely than not leave all but the best students in limbo. The first professor will get to the definition presented by the second, but not before he has his class playing with the problem of finding the area of irregular closed figures and the area under a continuous curve.[10]

The first professor does not forsake Socrates for P. T. Barnum, and the second can learn his technique.

Students will not take the risks necessary for knowledge—ask questions, try on different positions, challenge one another—unless the classroom environment makes them comfortable in doing so. Professors must be encouraging and demanding, critical and constructive, all at the same time. We should put students on the spot by expecting them to perform; they are, after all, in class to participate. We should call attention to their misunderstandings and weak arguments, along with their insights and cogent reasoning. Professors who never find fault with their students' work give them a false impression of their abilities and never effectively urge them to strive further or rethink their positions. (Why move beyond or rethink a position your professor has said is fine?) Criticisms must always be based on standards relevant to the course content and goals, however. A literature professor may not criticize a student's literary interpretation on the ground that it endorses the wrong social values. A history professor may not criticize a student's historical interpretation on the ground that it contains a negative assessment of the professor's favorite historical figure. Irrel-

evant criticisms direct students away from the intellectual purpose of
the course toward some alternative goal, such as adopting the right
social values and displaying them in one's work. Those who follow the
misdirection do not learn. Those who resist are alienated by their
discovery of the hidden agenda.

We must never treat students or their work as objects of ridicule or
pumps for our egos. There is no better way to discourage students
from taking intellectual risks than to encourage them to see mistakes,
or even questions, as personal failures: "Jim's question clearly shows
that he did not work hard enough on the assignment." We must not
make students feel as though their own worth is questioned whenever
their position is: "The point of today's reading is that Libertarians,
like Tom, are insensitive to human needs." We must not saddle
students with the responsibility of representing groups to which they
belong but for which they do not speak: "Tell us, Cindy, what is the
woman's perspective on this novel?"; "Andrew, what do you Chris-
tians think about evolution?" It is difficult enough to try on positions
for oneself and to challenge one's own views, without being expected
to speak for others or to conform to a preconception of what people of
"one's kind" think.

We must create an environment conducive to inquiry for all students.
Racist and sexist attitudes can lead professors to behavior that so
effectively discourages students as to deny them opportunities technically available to them. A student recently told me of how her ethics
professor routinely illustrated his lectures with comments on her
attractive appearance and examples that featured her as his wife or
lover. Quite uncomfortable, she spent more time wondering what the
professor was trying to tell her and what the other students were
thinking than she spent wondering about the course material. She
refrained from visiting the professor to discuss her term paper where
she would have visited another professor.

Racism and sexism can also cause professors to be more supportive
of the work of some students than others, and other causes can have
the same effect. It is easy to be less attentive to a student with an
annoying or sullen manner and more attentive to one with an engaging
personality. It is easy to "play to" students who look attentive,
volunteer answers, and ask good questions. They seem to appreciate
the course and our efforts so much. Nonetheless, every student deserves equal attention and support.

This is not to say we should treat all students in exactly the same
way. We may treat students differently just when some relevant differ-

ence between them justifies the difference in treatment, and, within the professor-student relationship, the relevant differences do not include race, sex, or social skills; the only relevant differences are those directly related to the goal of guiding each student to knowledge. Differences in ability may require us to give students different kinds or amounts of feedback on their work. Differences in preparation between graduate and undergraduate students in a "mixed" course may make different demands and expectations appropriate. Differences in personality may require us to adjust how we phrase criticisms. Justified differences in treatment are necessary to an environment conducive to inquiry for all.

The obligation to maintain an appropriate environment includes a duty to control and guide our students' conduct, as well as our own. Students should not be allowed to engage in private conversations or other activities that distract the class. None should be allowed to monopolize the discussion or to intimidate others into repressing their views. There is certainly no obligation to keep students from criticizing one another's positions—they gain much by analyzing and evaluating one another's ideas and hearing one another's objections and discovering that an attack on their personal beliefs is not an attack on their person—but we must teach students the rules of argument that govern intellectual exchange.

Offensive Conduct

Muslim students at the University of Pennsylvania reportedly lobbied to remove *The Satanic Verses* from a course reading list because it was offensive to their religion.[11] Many universities are concerned to discourage various kinds of insensitive behavior—my own university has a "Protocol on Gender Awareness" discouraging "gender insensitivity"—and insensitive and offensive behavior are often equated. When people offend us we generally think that they are insensitive to our views and values. What obligation, if any, do professors have to avoid offending their students?

We have no obligation to avoid offensive conduct per se. Consider an analogous case. Physicians cannot practice medicine without making at least some patients anxious, and the mere fact that a medical procedure, comment, or question will make a patient anxious does not obligate the physician to forgo it. Some unethical conduct by physicians certainly makes patients anxious, but we must not confuse the by-product anxiety with the real ethical mistake; if a physician knowingly tells patients without cancer that they have it, the ethical error resides in the lie, not in any anxiety produced, and the lie remains wrong even if a patient takes the news calmly. An adequate medical ethics code must certainly include sections on truth telling and informed consent, but not patient anxiety. A physician's one obligation concerning anxiety-producing conduct per se is to seek to guide patients past their anxiety to a point where they can appreciate their condition and participate in its treatment.

Analogously, professors cannot teach without offending some students in some ways. Teaching requires exposing students to new and different ways of thinking, and new and different ways of thinking often offend. Students can be offended by the theory of human evolution, criticisms of government's policy, conservative social institutions, various forms of art and literature, and the practices of other cultures. Some students are offended by teaching styles that challenge them to develop and defend their own views. Some are offended by criticism of their work. The mere fact that conduct will offend does not, in and of itself, obligate us to avoid it. Some unethical conduct certainly offends students, but we must not confuse the by-product offense with the real ethical mistake. The use of cultural, racial, or sexual stereotypes offends, but the ethical error lies in the fact that the stereotypes undermine self-esteem and reinforce false beliefs, and their use would be wrong even if they did not offend. Those who refrain from using the generic "he"/"man" simply to avoid giving offense do the right thing for the wrong reason. Roberta M. Hall of the Association of American Colleges puts the right reason quite simply.

> Some contend that concern about the use of the generic "he"/"man" is a trivial matter. However, research indicates that the "generic" "he"/ "man" is not generic in people's perceptions and that it can limit girls' and women's self-perception—especially when it occurs in a classroom context. . . .[12]

Offensive conduct per se is not an appropriate category for a code of teaching ethics, any more than anxiety-producing conduct is an appropriate category for a code of medical ethics. Our one obligation concerning offensive conduct per se is to guide students beyond any feelings of offense to an honest, objective appreciation of whatever they find offensive.

While we have no obligation to avoid offensive conduct per se, we are obligated to avoid conduct that, through its offensive nature, has further, negative consequences for our teaching and no redeeming educational value. The medical analogy works again. If conduct makes reasonable patients so excessively anxious as to avoid treatment, yet honors no ethical obligation such as truth telling, we expect physicians to avoid it; not because of the patient's anxiety, but because the patient's anxiety gets in the way of successful treatment. If our conduct so offends reasonable students as to alienate them from learning and serves no redeeming educational purpose, we must avoid it—not because it offends, but because, by offending, it gets in the way of education.

The caveats concerning "reasonable" students and the lack of "a redeeming educational purpose" are all-important. A student who is offended to the point of educational distraction by the color of the professor's tie has unreasonable expectations for the conduct of others and the professor has no duty to meet them. The professor who plays devil's advocate by arguing strongly for a particularly offensive view and alienates students along the way can actually be employing the best way to challenge them to explain why they find the view so clearly mistaken. If the professor can combine devil's advocacy with strategies for guiding the students past their initial feelings of offense to serious critical thought, their education may be well served.

The caveats can be met. Consider a student who skips lectures she would otherwise have attended, partly because the professor routinely makes offensive "dumb-blond" jokes. Certainly, the student has reason to be offended, and the jokes have no redeeming educational value.

Our obligations concerning our own behavior are matched by ones with regard to controlling and guiding our students' behavior in class. We've no obligation to restrict students' offensive behavior per se. Nonetheless, those whose actions so offend reasonable students as to damage the class environment, while serving no redeeming educational purpose, must be instructed on the limits of acceptable conduct, just like those who insist on speaking when others have the floor. The caveats concerning "reasonable" students and the lack of "a redeeming educational purpose" are again crucial. We have no obligation to accommodate the student who cannot concentrate because he finds sitting next to students of a particular race offensive. The student whose argument for racial superiority disrupts the class must, when the argument is relevant to what is being studied, be allowed, even encouraged, to present it, and our job will be to lead students past any feelings of offense to an objective evaluation of the argument.[13]

All these considerations refer to *how* we teach, not *what* we teach. We must avoid offensive conduct that needlessly interferes with a reasonable student's learning, but we may certainly teach works that offend reasonable students to the point of distraction. Those who have difficulty seeing the distinction might consider a related point: we must not lie to students, but we may teach works we know to contain false claims. Our obligation in teaching works containing false claims is to display the falsehoods and show why they are false. Our obligation in teaching works that greatly offend is to guide students past any feelings of offense to an understanding of what they find offensive and why and from there to an objective evaluation of the work. We must never drop any work from a course simply because it offends.

Neutrality

Does the obligation to maintain an environment conducive to learning require professors to be neutral when teaching controversial material, especially to undergraduates? Elias Baumgarten, a philosophy professor at the University of Michigan–Dearborn, believes it does.

> [T]here is no lack of ideologues vying for each person's acquiescence. . . . The proper role of the university teacher is not to join the competition but to help others reach a critical understanding of the history of human creative expression and thereby to escape some part of the human ignorance that is escapable. . . . For an instructor to present one position as being "strongest" shortcuts the process of questioning that is the essence of humanistic study; and it may deprive students of the creative anguish that comes with having to think through an issue and come to a conclusion purely by assessing opposing arguments, not knowing in advance what the "correct" position is supposed to be.[14]

A professor should present the various alternatives in a neutral way, encouraging and assisting each student's own evaluation of the options relative to the evidence. To shun neutrality is to encourage students to avoid their own rigorous investigation by simply accepting "the professor's view." High Wilder, a philosophy professor at Miami University, disagrees.

> I have often presented in class several different answers to a question, suggesting that they could all be true; I would present the case for each as strongly as possible, hoping that my students would buy only the truth

in this marketplace of ideas which I had set up. However, my plan often backfired; rather than buying the truth, my students often rejected all answers. They appeared to reject them and often to reject reasoning itself. . . . Because each answer had been presented so seductively, they concluded that there must be something wrong with reason itself. . . . The cure is to give up liberal tolerance, which means, concretely, to stop presenting all sides of an issue as persuasively as possible, and to stop encouraging students to think that all answers to all questions can be correct. We now know the answers to some questions, and we will be fostering misology if we do not teach these as clearly and unequivocally as possible.[15]

A professor's neutrality seldom encourages students to study all the options; it often encourages them to mistrust reason. According to Wilder, we often know the right answer, and when we do, we should teach it as such.

The truth lies between these views. We may not, contrary to Wilder, stop presenting the different sides of controversial issues as persuasively as possible, even when we know the right answer. We may, contrary to Baumgarten, reveal our own position and explain why we adopt it. Indeed, we often must.

As discussed in the preceding chapter, we must teach the views generally accepted by the experts working in an area, since they are students' best bets for knowledge; when there is significant debate among the experts, we are obligated to teach the different options, representing each one fairly and accurately. A fair and accurate presentation includes putting forth the best, most persuasive, evidence available, so students can understand why those who adopt the view do so. Even if one option is true and we know it to be true, we will not lead students to knowledge by teaching it alone. To gain the evidence they need for knowledge, they must examine and assess the competing theories for themselves.

A balanced presentation need not make frustrated students distrust reason. Controversy, even enduring controversy with strong competing arguments, does not imply the absence of a right answer, or that reason cannot settle disagreements or even that it cannot ultimately settle the one at hand. It does not even imply that individuals cannot make their own informed judgment about which arguments are strongest. Our job is to help students learn that these implications do not hold; it is not to avoid whatever behavior might encourage them to draw them.

We can teach by example here. By explaining our own view of which option is superior, we can show that the existence of controversy does not warrant the attitude that reason cannot support one view over others. We can communicate to students that individuals who work their way through the tangle of arguments can gain evidence that entitles them to believe a particular option and, perhaps, even leads them to know it. Revealing our own position need not make students accept our view as "correct" in lieu of their own investigation. Students who have this reaction to hearing what we believe are again making a mistaken inference. When controversial issues are correctly taught, the professor's endorsement of a position has no independent weight but simply echoes whatever strength is contained in the arguments behind the position. Students must be directed to those arguments and taught to assess them in relation to the competing ones. Here again, our job is to help students see that a reliance on authority is incorrect, not to avoid any behavior that might encourage them to fall into it.[16]

Examinations and Grades

No part of being a professor contains as many unattractive chores as evaluating students' work: correcting endless attempts at an elementary exercise, listening to complaints about grades, judging woeful requests for make-up exams, outsmarting acts of academic dishonesty. Worse than the chores is watching the very students we had hoped to lead to knowledge reveal their true, unswerving devotion to The Grade, as we cease to be intellectual guides and become mere taskmasters. These unattractive chores tempt us to minimize examinations and grades as much as possible and to delegate what remains to graduate assistants, who need to learn what they are getting into anyway. Being reduced to a taskmaster makes us question the place of exams and grades in education in the first place. Everett Wilson, a sociology professor at the University of North Carolina, doesn't seem far off in his answer.

> The testing-grading process . . . pits impotent student against instructor and taints every other interchange between the two. The disparity of power represented in our customary testing-grading practices creates an adversary diad. This diad perpetuates a compliant dependence, engenders higher levels of deception, subverts the goals of learning, and ultimately has the effect on the master that slavery always has.[17]

Martin Rich also seems to be on target, however, when he notes that we take on an obligation to examine and grade our students when we accept a university apppointment.

> The teacher will comply with regulations regarding the administering of examinations and the submitting of grade reports. In accepting a position in the system, the teacher in effect agrees to comply with institutional policies, rules and regulations, even though by [*sic*] accepting the position does not mean that the teacher believes that each of these regulations is wise or sensible. Should the teacher believe that the rules governing examinations and grade reports are unsound, then he would have the right to make these known to the proper authorities and thereby seek to rectify them.[18]

What, then, are our basic obligations when it comes to examining and grading students? Must we trudge through the chores as dedicated members of the institution? May we cease the activity entirely?

Let's start at the beginning. We are to guide students to knowledge. We cannot guide them as we would a mechanical toy, flipping a power switch, setting a speed control, and pointing it in the right direction. Students are autonomous, rational inquirers. We guide them by telling them where they stand relative to mastering the material and how they can best attain that goal. They must adjust their efforts and plot their course accordingly, just as we must use information on their progress to adjust our plans. To guide students, then, we must obtain and share with them regular information on their progress, and this requires an effective system of evaluating their work throughout the course.

An effective evaluation system does not require an extensive use of grades as we know them. We can evaluate students' progress and guide them by an exam that we return covered with remarks concerning strengths, weaknesses, and areas needing more attention; we need not declare some exams to be A exams and others B exams, and we need not label some as passing and others as failing. In a course where adequate knowledge of one section is presupposed in the next, we must tell students whether they are ready to advance, and so whether they have "failed" or "passed" at mastering the material covered so far, and at the end of any course, we must tell students whether they are ready to progress to courses that presuppose it. That's as close as we must come to giving grades in our role as guides.

An effective system for evaluating students' progress must provide the right information, at the right times, without conflicting with other essential aspects of teaching. More specific obligations fall under one or more of these general elements.[19] Consider our general obligation to design assignments that provide the right information. We need to know what our students have learned, what they have not learned, what they should focus on next, and how we should modify our own efforts. We should, then, test only for what is relevant to the course. We should not test for such factors as the ability to follow insanely complex directions or the ability to write quickly. We should emphasize the various parts of the material in relation to their varying degrees of importance. We should return exams and assignments with comments and explanations that tell students how to proceed. We must tell students when and how their progress will be evaluated, so they can prepare properly.

In terms of timing, we should schedule evaluations for the points at which students and we can best assess and redirect our efforts. The appropriate number and frequency of evaluations varies from course to course, but they must occur throughout the semester. Professors who only give a final exam or term paper only learn how many students mastered the material with a minimum of help. Evaluations must be returned to students in time to be of maximal use to them. Students do not learn from midterms returned on the day of the final.[20]

Perhaps most important of all, our evaluation system must not undermine our other efforts as teachers. We cannot avoid the additional inequality it brings to our relationship with students. We set the task, they are challenged to meet it, and we evaluate their performance. Being a taskmaster is part of being a professor. We should not encourage students to see us as nothing more, however, or allow our evaluations to alienate them from the material, learning, or both. When we give assignments as punishments, when we use our evaluations of students to embarrass or belittle, or to curry favor or promote increased enrollments, we use our evaluation system in a way that conflicts with our reason for having one.

These obligations are often violated. The requirements in an introductory course commonly consist of a midterm exam, final exam, and term paper due on the last day of class. Only the midterm can guide the students while the course is in progress, and sometimes it is returned too late with too few comments to be helpful. Once the enrollment in a course gets above seventy-five or so, a graduate assistant often does all the grading. The professor does not read the exams and may never know how well the class is doing or may at best get grade distribution reports—how many students received A's, B's, C's, and so on—which say little about how to fine-tune one's teaching.

Consider, too, how frequently professors return papers with no comments except for a one-liner tailored to the grade: ''A—excellent work; well written and some original ideas too''; ''B—very good job; you present your ideas well, but several need more development''; ''C— good work, but you fail to consider some important points''; ''D— your presentation of the material contains fundamental errors''; ''F—I'm afraid you missed the point of the assignment.'' It is no surprise that students who receive such comments are primarily concerned with their grade; that's the only solid information they get.

A standard defense against this criticism is to complain that we have too little time to devote more attention to evaluating students' work. We are, after all, expected to do other things: get grants, publish research, serve on committees. Another defense is that our classes are too large to allow us to be more involved with each student's progress through the course. No professor assigned to teach 300 students can make frequent assignments; carefully read, evaluate, and make extensive comments on each one; and then return them promptly. Both arguments are partially correct: we are expected to do a wide variety of things and, if we try to do them all, we may not have enough time to evaluate students' work properly; the number of students we are assigned to teach can conflict with our obligations about how to teach. Yet, let me go back to a point I made earlier. What professional activities we perform and how much we do of each must be adjusted so we can honor the basic obligations that define what it is to do each well. We—as individuals, a department, or a university faculty—often determine those expectations, and, when we don't, we generally have opportunities to get them changed.

A partial cause of our failure to evaluate students properly may be that we, like students, become preoccupied with grades. We must report a grade for each student at the end of the semester; it is the one institutional requirement we are under. We are under no similar institutional requirement with regard to giving them regular evaluations of their work, extensive comments on their papers, and so on. So, we design a set of assignments that will give us a basis for assigning grades, and we evaluate each student's work primarily with an eye to determining where it fits on the grading scale. If the assignments are few and far between or evaluated by someone else, it doesn't matter; we still get a grade for each student. We fall into thinking that so long as we give enough graded assignments—enough so students don't complain about an insufficient number of chances to raise their grade but not so many that we or they are overworked—we are doing all we are supposed to do. We forget that our basic reason for evaluating our students' work is not to give each a grade, but to guide each to knowledge.

Should we, then, have a grading system in the first place? When we grade a student's work we relate it to some measure of achievement and make a judgment about where it stands relative to the different categories defined by the measure; grading, thus, involves ranking students' work into higher and lower categories. I have already noted that a simple form of grading—telling students whether they have done well enough to proceed to the next level in the course or to the next course in the sequence—is essential to our role as guides. Yet, we generally grade students in a more extensive way, using some variation of the A through F scale. Should university education involve so extensive a form of grading?

Robert Paul Wolff, a philosophy professor at the University of Massachusetts–Amherst, claims that grades serve no educational purpose and are actually harmful to education, especially undergraduate education.

> Once a teacher has shown a student how he can state an argument more cogently, express an insight with greater felicity of phrasing, or muster evidence more persuasively for a conclusion, nothing is gained educationally by adding the words "good" or "bad." . . . The true rationale of evaluation is not educational but professional. When a candidate seeks admission to a profession on the basis of some performance, the judges must ascertain whether he has qualified. For prospective professors, lawyers, or doctors, "pass" means admission to the profession with the legal right to practice and make a living thereby; "fail" means exclusion, and if second chances have been exhausted, the necessity of looking for some other career. . . . By requiring a bachelor's degree as a prerequisite for work toward "higher" degrees, the professional schools force the colleges to take on a grading task which is irrelevant to education and sometimes positively harmful.[21]

Wolff also believes that, in their ranking aspect, grades serve a primarily economic function: helping to facilitate the allocation of scarce resources.

> Up to a point, as I have noted, professional schools use college grades as evidence of minimal qualifications; but those schools with more applicants than places rely upon relative rankings, together with such ranking devices as objective tests and letters of recommendation, to establish an

order of priority among the candidates. Here again, no other purpose is served by cumulative grade averages, class rank, and all the other devices for the making of efficient invidious comparisons among students.[22]

Wolff clearly has some points right. Grades—and degrees—are tickets to further study and ultimately to certain careers with associated social and economic benefits. Grading has harmful educational consequences: students become fixated on grades and forget about learning; professors concentrate on grading students and forget to teach them; the professor's power to dispense grades carries opportunities for abuse.

Nonetheless, grades serve an important educational purpose. Wolff believes that once we have corrected a student's work and shown how it can be improved, we do not add anything of educational value by labeling it with a grade of A or B or calling it "good" or "bad." He is right in that the grade does not give the student any more information about how to improve at the assigned task. He is wrong in that the grade does give the student and others educationally valuable information. Every coherent course of study requires the grouping of students by ability, knowledge, and interest. Not every student is ready to take the accelerated version of a foreign language course; not every student is best served by the standard paced introduction to college algebra. Grades indicate to the student, professors, college advisors, and the like where a student best fits. Professors who advise students on their career choices gain valuable information about their interests and abilities from their grades. A hard-working student who is passing an elementary mathematics course with a low D is well advised to reconsider his plan to become an engineer. Instead of being obligated to do away with grades, we are obligated to use them in ways that support rather than subvert our attempts to teach. I shall not discuss our specific obligations in detail, as they are generally well-examined elsewhere, but I do want to raise two important points.[23]

In many courses, we use the very same assignments to guide our students as we do to assign them a grade for the course. The conceptually distinct activities of guiding students through an effective evaluation system and assigning grades to indicate their levels of achievement are collapsed into one. We should do more to separate the two by increasing our use of ungraded, but required, exercises to evaluate students' progress. The use of ungraded but required exercises will help us to concentrate, not simply on assigning grades, but on actually determining how far each student has progressed and how each can best direct his or her future efforts. It will help students to be concerned not simply with their grades, but with what they have and have not learned. There is, of course, the concern that students will not take ungraded work seriously. In a context where education is sometimes similar to animal training and grades are used as rewards and punishments, saying an assignment will not be graded is likely to communicate that it is unimportant. We can, however, show that the assignments are important by taking them seriously ourselves. If we design them so they measure each student's progress and return them promptly with useful comments, most students will see their importance and treat them accordingly, and some who do not give them all the attention they deserve will learn from them, nonetheless.

Like all professionals, we must eliminate conflicts of interest or at least minimize them and guard against their negative effects, and, as George Schurr of Eckerd College points out, we are ensnared in at least two conflicts when we evaluate and grade students' work.

> First, it is in the interest of instructors to show that they are effective teachers. A favorable evaluation of their students gives evidence that they have been well taught. Why should instructor-evaluators be self-condemned by not making a favorable evaluation of those who study under them? . . . Second, it is in the interest of instructors to attract students who will pay tuition and generate credit hours. It is in the interest of students to be evaluated favorably, and thereby get degrees, jobs and admission to professional schools. What could be more natural than collusion between students and instructor-evaluators? The word gets out—take professor A, or go to college Z and get good grades.[24]

Every professor who has ever contemplated adjusting the grades for a course to avoid student complaints knows what Schurr has in mind. The conflict is especially strong for junior faculty whose promotion and tenure cases depend on favorable teaching evaluations. Moreover, as Schurr notes, there is reason to believe we are not doing well at resisting these conflicts of interest through mere strength of will: "Grade inflation and the national scandal of illiteracy cannot be separated from the conflict of interest built into giving responsibility for instruction and evaluation to the same people."[25]

Schurr mandates a "separation of function between instruction and evaluation" and claims that a proper code of ethics for teachng must include the injunction: "Evaluation of learning shall be performed by those who have no vested interest in the certification of competence," but exactly how to develop his proposal is unclear.[26] A few independent evaluation procedures already exist. In some fields (e.g., law, account-ing, and engineering) a professional competency exam provides an independent evaluation of students' course of study. Graduate pro-grams generally require doctoral candidates to be examined by a committee that includes department faculty other than those directing the student's work as well as a faculty member from outside the department. Some universities give general assessment exams to un-dergraduates at various times in their academic careers. Most of these measures are of limited value. Professors on doctoral examination committees are often reluctant to be too hard on a colleague's stu-dent—after all, that colleague was fairly easy on their own student last time around—and the outside member of the committee is often unqualified to make an independent judgment. My own university requires all undergraduates to take a general education assessment exam midway through their course of study, but nothing requires those who take it to take it seriously.[27]

There are other possibilities. We can monitor our grading practices by comparing the grades we assign to those of other faculty teaching similar courses. We can ask colleagues what grades they would assign to some of our students' exams and then check their unbiased judgment against our own. Departments can agree on what basic areas of knowledge and what basic skills their majors should have at graduation or at some other point in their study and then develop independent ways to test for them, perhaps—in universities where the administra-tive travel budget has been redirected to teaching—by using external referees. We can also eliminate some of the underlying causes of the conflicts of interest. While all professors want to be liked by their students and giving high grades helps make one be liked, we can limit the extent to which simply being liked becomes important to a profes-sor's success in such matters as tenure, promotion, and salary in-creases. We can evaluate teaching by methods that are independent of whether professors have bought students' affection with grades (e.g., peer reviews by other faculty). We can avoid the hasty inference from the premise of high enrollment and high grades to the conclusion of good teaching.[28]

Confidentiality

We learn a great deal about our students. We learn of their abilities in certain areas of study; we learn whether they are self-disciplined, tenacious, and objective; we learn about their career plans, hopes for the future, and insecurities. Even the most casual or ordinary questions can yield information about a student's personal life. I once asked a student if she had enjoyed the semester break and learned that she had had an abortion; I asked another why he wanted to work on a particular paper topic in ethics and found out that his father was on trial for embezzlement. The American Association of University Professors points out that each professor must respect "the confidential nature of the relationship between professor and student," but it is often unclear what information falls under this requirement or what respect for its confidentiality demands.[29]

It is important to distinguish between information we solicit or use as part of our teaching and academic advising and information only incidental to the activity, since only the former is subject to the demand of confidentiality set by the professor-student relationship. When we elicit information on students' academic abilities to better teach and advise them, the information falls within the professor-student relationship and its confidentiality is protected by the requirements of that relationship. When, in a context unrelated to teaching and advising, a student volunteers that he was once hospitalized for psychiatric reasons, the information does not fall within the professor-student relationship. If we have a duty to protect its confidentiality, the duty is based in something other than our position as a professor, such as the need to avoid harming another. The same information can fall in either category, depending on the context in which it is obtained and the use to which it is put. If a student refers to his marital problems to explain why an assignment is late, the information is within the professor-student relationship; if he does so as part of a casual, nonprofessional conversation, it may be outside it.

Two major considerations determine the extent of our obligation of confidentiality with regard to information within the professor-student relationship. The first is the student's stake in controlling the information. When information is innocuous or trivial, students have no stake in controlling it, and we have no serious duty of confidentiality. When information is more significant—and especially when it is likely to determine how others will behave toward them—students have an important stake in controlling it, and we have an important duty of confidentiality. The second major consideration is the purpose for which we have access to the information. Generally, it is to guide students through a course of study. Students may not have this purpose in mind when they provide the information—some move through their education so unthinkingly as to never contemplate what it involves and why—and we may not have it in mind when we seek it—some professors perform their duties with a similar lack of self-awareness—but it is the justification for the institutional arrangements that give us access to the information, and it helps determine our obligation of confidentiality. Where information falls within the professor-student relationship and the student has a stake in controlling it, we must share the information only with those who have a legitimate claim to it relative to the goal of guiding the student to knowledge. Any more extensive sharing of the information is permissible only when our duty of confidentiality is waived by the student's actual consent (or the reasonable expectation of it) or overridden by a more powerful obligation.[30]

Consider some of the information we typically obtain in teaching a class: grades, our assessment of students' general intellectual abilities, and our judgments of their character. Students clearly have an interest in controlling access to this information; thus we have a professional obligation to share it only with those who have a legitimate claim relative to the goal of guiding them to knowledge. The registrar and the advising staff qualify for much of it, since it can be essential to their attempts to advise students and place them in appropriate classes. Departmental advising and review committees qualify as well.

Other students do not qualify. It is unethical to tell one student another's grades or to share our general assessment of one student's talents with another. We violate this obligation by posting grades with readily accessible identifiers and by leaving graded papers outside our office door for students to pick up. None of us would want our physician to leave our medical history in a stack to be sorted through by every other interested patient, and our students' position is no different.

Parents do not qualify. When they ask how their son or daughter is doing in our course, we must advise them to ask their son or daughter. It is unethical to tell them more without the student's permission, and if they point out that they are paying the tuition bill, we should point out that their financial arrangements with their child create obligations for their child but not for us.

Other professors may not qualify for confidential information about our students. Even department colleagues are not entitled to it without a need to know based in the student's educational welfare. A doctor-patient analogy may again make the point clearer: My curious neighbor is my physician's colleague but that does not make it appropriate for my physician to give her the results of my last physical exam. It is only appropriate for my physician to share that information with my neighbor if my neighbor becomes involved in my treatment and so has a need to know based in my well-being.

A student's potential employers do not automatically qualify for confidential information. If a friend at another university calls to get our opinion of a graduate student who is applying for a teaching position there, we must restrict our comments to information outside the professor-student relationship, unless we have the student's permission to be more revealing. Our friend's interest in knowing more is not a compelling professional need based in the student's educational welfare.

Some may find these claims too extreme. They certainly conflict with a lot of common practice. We often leave graded term papers and final exams in a public place for students to pick them up. When we meet the parents of outstanding students, we unhesitatingly describe how well their son or daughter is doing in our class. When colleagues ask, we freely share our assessment of our students. When potential employers, especially ones who are our friends, ask about an ex-student, we freely share what we know.

Some of these practices do not conflict with the principles I've presented, since they are based on the reasonable expectation that the student would consent to our sharing the information. It is reasonable to assume that outstanding students would consent to our singing their praises to their parents; it is reasonable to assume that ex-students would consent to our giving a *favorable* review of their performance to a potential employer. Other common practices are, I suggest, just plain wrong. The loose way in which graded papers are often returned is an excellent example; so is the free and easy way in which we share information about students with colleagues who have only their curiosity to justify their request. Some of these practices are so prevalent that students do not expect us to do otherwise. Yet, that students do not actively expect certain information to be kept confidential neither implies that they have consented to its release nor makes it reasonable to expect that they would.

Obligations of confidentiality can be overridden. Certainly, if we learn information of grave importance to the physical safety of the student or others, we should share it with the appropriate parties. When a student we know to be in counseling tells us he plans to commit suicide as part of his explanation for why he is dropping our course, we should call his therapist. When he makes serious threats against the life of his sociology professor while explaining why he dislikes that discipline, we should warn the professor. Our obligations of confidentiality can also be overridden by an obligation to promote or protect other elements of the academic enterprise. We must report academic dishonesty to the required administrative authorities, not because they have a compelling need to know based in the particular student's educational welfare, but because we have an overriding obligation to support institutional policies designed to promote academic integrity.

Notes

1. I do not assume that every professor should be engaged in exactly the same activities to the same degree. Teaching, research, and service duties vary, and should vary, across faculty and time.

2. This is not to say that students should not be subjected to course requirements to obtain a degree, any more than it is to say that they should not be required to study certain material to receive credit for a particular course. It is to say that we should provide them with the reasons behind the requirements we set; indeed, we should encourage them to be the sort of inquirers who instinctively ask why we have the requirements we do.

3. This is, of course, to assume that we can have obligations to those who existed in the past just as we can have them to future generations.

4. The situation is very different when we work with some advanced students on a joint project with the understanding that the material is as new to us as it is to them and we will be learning it together. We no longer serve as the subject's representative to the students; we are using our skills to help the students master the material as we do so as well.

5. Arnold Arons, "Teaching Science," in *Scholars Who Teach*, ed. Steven M. Cahn (Chicago: Nelson-Hall, 1978), pp. 101–30.

6. Rita W. Cooley, "Teaching Social Science," in *Scholars Who Teach*, p. 144.

7. Arons, pp. 112–13.

8. Decreasing the size of a class can require other modifications as well. Suppose a department decreases the size of its introductory course by distributing the students among graduate teaching assistants who are now given primary responsibility for their own classes. There is no improvement if the graduate students are not qualified to teach the course, so the department must now make sure they are prepared. How can it do this, if it can no longer break graduate students into teaching by having them assist in large lectures? It can assign them to assist professors in smaller classes, and it can develop a graduate curriculum that includes training in teaching. This will not be as cost effective as the previous large lecture format, but the faculty will honor their

obligation to their students, as well as teach graduate students the skills they will need to do the same in the future.

9. As noted by Kenneth Strike, the obligation to provide reasons for the beliefs we expect students to form is also based in our duty to teach in a way that recognizes each student's status as an autonomous rational agent. See Strike's *Liberty and Learning* (New York: St. Martin's Press, 1982), especially pages 41–53; or see the selection from Strike's work included in this collection.

10. Robert H. Gurland, "Teaching Mathematics," in *Scholars Who Teach*, pp. 89–90.

11. Reported in *The Chronicle of Higher Education*, xxxvii, 12, November 21, 1990, p. 1.

12. Roberta M. Hall and Bernice R. Sandler, *The Classroom Climate: A Chilly One for Women?* Project on the Status and Education of Women (Washington, D.C.: Association of American Colleges, 1982), pp. 18–19.

13. Some may think I am splitting hairs by claiming that offensive conduct per se is not objectionable, while admitting that it can have objectionable effects on the classroom environment. The distinction is important. Those who object to a professor's conduct must do more than say it offends them. They must explain its negative impact on learning and its lack of any redeeming educational value. Moreover, while a claim to academic freedom is a substantial defense against attempts to require faculty to act inoffensively, it is significantly weaker as a defense against attempts to require faculty to avoid acts that detract from the educational environment while serving no redeeming educational purpose. Similarly, universities should not concentrate on such categories as "offensive behavior" and "insensitive behavior" in drawing up codes of conduct, since these categories of action per se are not objectionable. The focus should be on determining the best features of an educational environment and just what activities threaten them.

14. Elias Baumgarten, "Ethics in the Academic Profession: A Socratic View," *Journal of Higher Education* 53 (1982), p. 288, pp. 290–91. Baumgarten's essay is also part of this collection.

15. Hugh T. Wilder, "The Philosopher as Teacher," *Metaphilosophy* 9 (July/ October 1978), pp. 320–21. Wilder's essay is also part of this collection.

16. This is not to say that we may evaluate students on the basis of whether they adopt our position. Even if we have a well-evidenced belief, better yet knowledge, that a particular view on a controversial topic is correct and we share that belief with our students, it may be inappropriate for us to evaluate them on the basis of whether they adopt it. The belief may not be part of what the course is supposed to teach. I know the answer to some controversial philosophical issues I teach in my introductory courses, but those courses are not intended to teach those particular answers. Given the controversy that exists, they are intended to teach the issues and the different answers available.

17. Everett K. Wilson, "Power, Pretense and Piggybacking: Some Ethical Issues in Teaching," *Journal of Higher Education* 53 (1982), p. 273.

18. John Martin Rich, *Professional Ethics in Education* (Springfield, Ill.: Charles Thomas, 1984), p. 68.

19. See Steven M. Cahn, "The Uses and Abuses of Grades and Examinations," in *Scholars Who Teach,* for a detailed discussion of various specific obligations. An updated version of Cahn's essay is included in this collection.

20. If we are primarily interested in evaluating our students' work so we can guide them to knowledge, why bother with a final exam? The course is over; they have made it or they haven't. We have no more guiding to do. One reason is that even at the end of the course, the students and the professor can still learn from the results of the final. The students can learn how well they have mastered the whole course, the final section, or whatever part of the material is on the exam; the professor can learn more about how well he or she has taught. Final exams are also important for another activity closely related to evaluating students' progress: assigning grades, which I shall discuss shortly.

21. Robert Paul Wolff, *The Ideal of the University* (Boston: Beacon Press, 1969), pp. 64–65.

22. Wolff, pp. 66–67.

23. Cahn's "The Uses and Abuses of Grades and Examinations" contains a much fuller discussion of both the educational value of grades and the specific obligations we have with regard to assigning them.

24. George M. Schurr, "Toward a Code of Ethics for Academics," *Journal of Higher Education* 53 (1982), p. 327.

25. Schurr, "Toward a Code of Ethics," p. 328.

26. Schurr, "Toward a Code of Ethics," p. 328.

27. In some cases, there are worries about the reliability of the assessment tests themselves as well as a concern that the rush to adopt them is the outcome of a political agenda rather than a carefully considered educational judgment. Nonetheless, it is important that we separate these concerns from the basic issue of how we can best respond to the conflicts of interest that exist in our present way of evaluating and grading students. Even if all the assessment tests are in fact unreliable, even if they are often pushed into place by university administrators or politicians out to build a reputation for educational reform, the conflicts of interest remain and we are obligated to address them.

28. Take none of my remarks to suggest that every unpopular professor is in fact a fine teacher who has nobly traded popularity for maintaining high standards. I have never met such an individual, though I have met several poor teachers who try to dismiss their students' low opinion of them as sour grapes stemming from poor grades rooted in the students' own lack of ability and motivation. My own experience has been that demanding professors *who are also good teachers* generally gain their students' respect, and while their demanding approach may keep them from being extremely popular, the respect they gain keeps them from being unpopular and often gains them a following among the best students.

My comments on the evaluation of teaching raise the general issue of our obligations concerning the evaluation of teaching performance. There are two basic issues here: our obligation as individual professors to evaluate our own performance on a continual basis and adjust our efforts accordingly; our obligation as a department, college, or university faculty to establish a systematic way of evaluating teaching and giving appropriate weight to the results in decisions concerning tenure, promotion, and salary increases. I have touched on the first issue in my discussion of our obligations concerning preparation and examinations. I have not discussed the second; it is best left for an examination of the more general topic of how we can best encourage ourselves to honor our professional obligations as teachers. As noted in Chapter 1, that topic is beyond the scope of my discussion.

29. "Statement on Professional Ethics," *Policy Documents and Reports of the American Association of University Professors*, December 1969, p. 40.

30. Even if students consent to our making certain information public, we may retain an obligation not to do so. If all the students in my class consent to my publicly listing their midterm grades by name, I still have an obligation not to do so if my university, in accord with the Buckley Amendment, prohibits my doing so.

CHAPTER FOUR

Beyond the Classroom

Teaching-award testimonials praise professors for being friends with their students; my own award from the student government is inscribed "Docére est amáre." Yet, as we have become more sensitive to sexual harassment and learned more of "the lecherous professor," we have become more concerned about maintaining a professional relationship with our students. Professor Billie Wright Dziech and Linda Weiner express the concern well.

> When a professor assumes or is told that he should foster the moral, social, and spiritual as well as intellectual development of students, he can lose sight of the proper limits of his interest and authority. The distinctions between his professional jurisdiction and the student's private life become blurred, and a faculty member can readily convince himself that he is acting appropriately when he may in fact be violating the parameters of proper relations with students.[1]

What does a "professional" relationship require? Must we avoid friendships and romantic involvements? What of more casual, but still clearly nonprofessional, relationships (e.g., racquetball partners)? What of the areas where the professional/nonprofessional distinction is unclear, such as advising that mixes both academic and personal concerns?

Those same teaching awards often cite the ways in which good teaching is informed by research, and when pressed to justify the time we spend on research, we cite our need to be active scholars to be accomplished teachers. Critics, such as Charles Sykes, find an apparent inconsistency between our principles and practice, however.

> The academic establishment insists that only professors who do research can be good teachers, so they need to spend most of their time outside of

the classroom; and because they are off researching (to become better teachers, remember), they are replaced by part-timers or temporaries who may do little or no research at all. Academia has an almost infinite capacity for ignoring such contradictions, especially when the payoff is so high.[2]

Do we have an obligation as teachers to be active scholars?

Relations with Students: What's Not Obligatory

We seem to be in a bind, when it comes to extracurricular relations with our students, and an engineering professor describes it well.[3]

> I think I ought to spend time with students. Most of us seem so aloof and remote to them. So when they invite me to an organizational function, like a skating party or a potluck, I'll go. And I think it's good for them to feel free to talk about their problems—their coursework is pretty demanding and the job market is very competitive. But it gets a little crazy sometimes, and I find myself being asked to advise them about their girlfriends or views about religion. I barely know what to do with my own daughters, let alone their problems. But I at least think I should listen.[4]

A sense of obligation leads us to become involved with students outside of class; once involved, we are drawn into areas where we don't seem to belong. At a minimum, we are asked for advice on matters where we have no expertise. In more serious cases, we develop personal relationships that corrupt the professional relationship we are supposed to serve.

Let's start, then, with the first point: Are we obligated to interact with students beyond our courses? Are we obligated, for example, to accept invitations to advise student organizations or to attend skating parties and potluck suppers they sponsor? Are we obligated to advise students—at their request or our own initiative—on such personal matters as romantic relationships, family problems, religious beliefs, and finances?

Certainly, professors who work with students beyond the classroom in ways that support learning are advancing the university's obligation to create a supportive educational environment. They contribute their free time, giving up evenings and weekends, and often donate their own funds. Their behavior is permissible, indeed laudable. It does not follow, however, that every faculty member is obligated to be involved with students in this way, and professors who decline invitations to advise student organizations and excuse themselves from student-sponsored social functions may be doing what is best, rather than shirking a professional duty.

Consider an analogous case. Professors who serve on campus committees and are appropriately involved in the political life of the institution clearly support the principle of faculty governance, but it does not follow that we must all be similarly involved. Some have little interest or talent for university governance, and they do not act unethically when they decline nominations to elected committees to pursue research or teaching more intensely. So, too, professors with little interest or talent for extracurricular relations with students do not act unethically when they decline to advise student organizations and to attend their social functions. Every professor has a general obligation extending beyond the classroom to support the university's activities, but that obligation allows for a great deal of individual adjustment. The university is best served when professors play to their strengths and interests. Short-tempered faculty seldom advance faculty governance by working with administrators. Self-involved faculty seldom advance education by advising student groups.

What about advising students on nonacademic issues such as their love life, parent problems, or finances? The solution to a student's academic crisis often lies in the resolution of a personal one, and we often have the chance to intervene. Yet, here again, there is no general obligation for professors to give students personal advice, even when the personal matter is related to an academic concern, beyond simply referring them to an appropriate university counseling service. Nonacademic counseling is not among the expectations associated with a faculty appointment. When we appoint professors, we don't request evidence of their psychological or financial counseling skills; when we train graduate students to be professors, we don't try to give them such skills. We don't, because we don't expect professors to be personal counselors. We have no reason to change our expectations. The strongest reason for a change—students' personal problems often directly affect their academic performance—at best implies that universities should have trained counselors on staff and that those without the proper training should refer troubled students to those with it. Universities have wisely and appropriately responded to this obligation, not by trying to turn professors into personal counselors, but by adding professional counseling services.

There is, then, no general obligation for professors to interact with students beyond their courses—for example, by advising student organizations and attending their social functions—even though professors who do so often strengthen the university's educational environment. There is no general obligation to assist students in making personal adjustments related to their academic goals, even though professors who do so often help students academically. The next question is when are such activities permissible? Are some forms of involvement with students beyond the classroom not only generally nonobligatory, but also just plain wrong?

Relations with Students: What's Not Permitted

We must not cause needless harm, we must not break promises without sufficient justification, and we must not violate any moral rights.[5] These and other standard ethical principles govern our relations with students just as they do our relations with anyone. Since these principles are universal, they do not carve out any special restrictions on how we, as professors, may interact beyond the classroom with those who are our students. The special restrictions come from two additional principles based in our professional status. First, we must forsake any relationship with students that detracts from our ability to honor our obligations as their professors; not only do our obligations not include extracurricular relations with students, they also restrict the form such relations may take. Second, we must renounce any relationships in which our power over students serves an end other than the educational purpose for which it is granted. These two principles define the limits of a professional relationship, and the limits are severe.

We must not be friends with our students. By the very nature of friendship, friends exchange otherwise private information, enjoy each other's company, value each other's welfare because of whose welfare it is, and acknowledge their affection through a series of shared expectations and mutual commitments. Friendships are intrinsically valuable relationships. Friendships with our students, however, conflict with our fundamental obligations as professors.[6]

We are fundamentally obligated to give all students equal consideration in instruction, advising, and evaluation. We may treat students differently only when a relevant difference justifies doing so, and the only relevant differences are those directly related to guiding each student to knowledge.[7] Any friendships we establish with students are likely to prevent us from honoring this obligation. If we become friends with our students, we will become friends only with some—even if we try to be friends with all, some won't be interested—and so we will have a special concern for, and a special commitment to, the welfare of some students but not others. We will treat students differently on the basis of the irrelevant fact that some are our friends while others are not.

Requests to hand in a late paper, take a make-up exam, or receive a letter of recommendation are much more compelling when made by a friend in need. When grading exams, we will be more inclined to be sympathetic to a friend's efforts and more inclined to work hard to appreciate what a friend is trying to say. We will be inclined to use professional contacts to aid student friends, even though we do not use them to aid students who are not friends but equal our friends in interest and ability. We will be likely to give student friends extra advice about their course of study and career. Our conversations with them are likely to include the subject matter of the course, and so contain instruction we don't give other students. These are some obvious ways in which student friendships are likely to conflict with our obligation to give all students equal consideration in instruction, advising, and evaluation.

It is foolish to think we can monitor our behavior to ensure that our friendship for some students does not keep us from giving equal consideration to all. We don't attribute such powers of self-control to other professionals; we don't even grant them to ourselves in other contexts. We require the most respected jurists to excuse themselves from hearing cases that involve the interests of a friend, because we doubt their ability, if not their willingness, to control the strong inclination to favor a friend. We require letters in support of promotion and tenure to be solicited from professors who are not friends of the candidate; we treat letters from the candidate's friends, even from friends who claim to be giving an objective evaluation, as likely to be biased.

Some may object that friendship is a relevant consideration justifying different treatment, perhaps not when we evaluate students, but at least when we offer instruction and advice. As long as we give all students the basic level of instruction and advice to which they are entitled, we are permitted to give extra to our friends. We do nothing wrong if we use our professional connections to help friends but not otherwise equal students who are not our friends. When we instruct and advise students we are providing a service, and so long as we provide this service to a certain agreed upon level to all, we may make an extra effort for our friends. Having agreed to give five people a place to sleep, we may certainly give the best bed to our friend and the remaining beds to the four strangers; so too, we may give extra instruction and advice to student friends, so long as other students receive an appropriate amount.

This objection misses the basic point. Even if we are sometimes permitted to favor student friends simply because they are friends (and in a moment I will argue that we are not), there are still cases in which we should not, and professors who become friends with students are likely to violate the obligation of equal consideration in those cases. Being the professor's friend is clearly irrelevant in the evaluation of students' work. Suppose I have my teaching assistant grade all the exams, and I then add ten points to each exam written by a friend; having assured each student of an initially objective evaluation, I make an "extra effort" for my friends. My extra effort is clearly wrong.

It is also a mistake to think that we are simply providing students with a service when we instruct and advise them. Our students are competing for class rank, honors, and job opportunities, and we are running the competition. We both evaluate their performance and prepare them to perform. The fairness of the competition rests not just on how much preparation—instruction and advice—each gets, but also on how much each gets relative to the others. Being the professor's friend should not gain a student a competitive advantage in preparing for the competition any more than it should in the competition itself.

Finally, the objection makes the mistake of assuming that professors act as independent contractors permitted to distribute our instruction and advice in whatever way best fits our own personal commitments. We do not. We act for the university, not ourselves, and from the university's perspective the fact that some students are our friends is irrelevant.

Student friendships conflict with more than our obligation of equal consideration. We must refrain from conduct that will lessen the credibility, and so the worth, of our evaluations, and when we become friends with students we give others a good reason to doubt our evaluations; namely, that we are friends with some but not all we have evaluated. We need not actually favor some students over others. The appearance of favoritism is enough to lessen our credibility.

We risk misusing our power even in trying to establish friendships with students. We misuse our power, if we intentionally use it for an end other than the educational purpose for which it is granted. It is unethical, for example, to use our power over students to get them to join extracurricular activities they would rather forgo, be it a social engagement or chauffeuring us to the airport. We also misuse our power by creating situations in which, no matter what our intentions, reasonable students are likely to feel compelled to engage in extracurricular activities against their will. Power carries both an obligation to avoid its intentional misuse and an obligation to prevent situations in which others, no matter what our intentions, quite reasonably experience it as inappropriately compelling. Requests that students join us in the social activities from which friendships arise—no matter how innocently intended—are necessarily calls from someone with a substantial amount of power over their lives. We may make them as innocent invitations to be declined or accepted freely, but students often receive them as summonses to be declined only at risk: "I have to go; he is grading my midterm tomorrow." The danger that students will reasonably experience invitations in this way is small when the invitations are directed to a group in relation to some obvious occasion, as when we invite an entire class out for pizza to mark the end of the semester. The risk greatly increases when we repeatedly invite particular students to the exclusion of others for no particular purpose other than to share their company, which is just what we do when we try to start a friendship.

Every argument against friendships is matched by an equally strong argument against romantic relations. Being a professor can provide the opportunity and temptation for romantic involvement with students, but the fundamental obligations of the position do not allow it. We cannot be romantically involved with one student and provide equal consideration for all. Those who doubt this would do well to consider whether they would like their spouse's lover to be the judge at their divorce hearing. We cannot become romantically involved with a student and maintain a credible system of evaluations. Few faculty-student affairs remain secret, and once they are public, it is simply assumed—no matter whether rightly or wrongly—that the professor's affection infects his or her evaluation of the student. The potential for the abuse of power is always present and substantial. Even when professors do not intend to use their position to gain sexual favors, students are likely to experience their overtures quite reasonably as inappropriately compelling.[8]

What of more casual social relationships that do not involve the same levels of affection, trust, and exchange of confidences as friendship and romance? Is it wrong to become regular racquetball or lunch partners with some of our students? It all depends on the relationship. Even casual ones can involve inappropriately favoring some students and create reasonable doubts about our evaluations. Robert Audi of the University of Nebraska puts it simply, using "friendship" to cover a variety of social relationships.

> If I play ball, lunch out, and regularly socialize with my students, I will find it hard to give them low grades or, even more, to decline to recommend them for certain opportunities they want to pursue, or to rank them below others who are appreciably better but not my friends. I can, to be sure, face such conflict between friendship and professorial duty and still act professionally. But how do I know that when I am in such a situation I will always face the conflict?[9]

Casual relationships can also involve an abuse of power. A student recently told me of how advising sessions with one professor regularly led to talk about life in general and from there to an update on the professor's personal problems. To the professor, it was just a friendly conversation; to the student it was being a captive audience for a middle-aged male's tale of woe. She was uncomfortable hearing it and uncomfortable having to make up an excuse to leave early.

We must assess each case, and we should keep two points in mind as we do. First, as Audi suggests, we may easily overestimate our ability to maintain our objectivity and impartiality, and we may fail to appreciate how coercive our invitations can be to a student. Second, the costs of erring on the side of restraint—we deprive ourselves and a student of a casual relationship beyond class—are substantially less than the costs of erring on the other—we violate our fundamental professional obligations. In cases of uncertainty and high risk, the best strategy is often the most conservative: forgo the social relationship and ensure the professional obligations are honored.

To maintain the sort of professional distance I am urging is not to be so cold, formal, and insensitive to students' needs that we cease to be good teachers. Good teachers act toward students in a warm and friendly manner and are sensitive to their educational needs and concerns; they value and give special consideration to each student's educational welfare simply because it is the welfare of one of their students. None of this requires that we be friends, lovers, or even casual social companions with our students.

We must discard at least one model of graduate teaching, however. Some professors view graduate teaching, especially at the Ph.D. level, as a process in which they identify the students most worthy of their efforts, woo them to their specialty, and train them as representatives of their intellectual approach and views. At graduation, each goes forth as a "Professor X student." The selection of the favored students involves more than intellectual considerations. Only students sufficiently attractive in intellectual skill, temperament, and personality merit a chance to carry on the tradition. Ideal candidates often remind professors of themselves in graduate school, and a difference in sex or race can keep a student from fitting the image. Professors who follow this model of graduate teaching see students as potential clones, and they face the same ethical risks as those who see students as potential friends or lovers. The selecting, wooing, and training involve acts of individualized attention both in and out of class—from special attention to the favored student's work to invitations to dinner—that violate basic professional obligations concerning equitable treatment, credible evaluations, and the appropriate use of power.

Ethical risks are also present, though not as great, in a form of graduate teaching Robert Audi calls "the collegial model."

> Its motto might be: Be my junior colleague. . . . It is in seminars, laboratories, and individual consultations with students that this model is most influential. In these informal settings, students are drawn out, treated as if their ideas are worth taking seriously, and corrected without an authoritative tone or, more subtly, by such devices as the gentle suggestion of an alternative. They may be invited to criticize the professor's work and may be asked to serve as coauthors on papers in their joint areas of specialization.[10]

As Audi notes, it is often difficult to teach in this way without establishing extracurricular relationships that violate our professional obligations.

> If, in the collegial relationship as imagined here, there is already a personal connection and a sense of shared role, the dangers that friendship with students will supplant the professor's faculty obligation loom up. . . . It is not just that we may do too much for our friends relative to those to whom we owe similar obligations; consciously or unconsciously, we may also exploit their understanding of our own preoccupations and thereby do too little for them.[11]

The need to maintain a professional distance also has implications for how we advise students. All our obligations concerning equitable treatment and the abuse of power apply, and those concerning the latter take on an additional form. No matter what its content, our advice to students derives a hefty weight from our position. It may concern applying to graduate school or getting married and our words may be informed by knowledge or filled with hot air, but we still speak from a position of authority. We must caution students that our authority in academic matters does not carry over to areas where it has no justification. If we give advice on matters beyond our professional expertise, we must point out that we are doing so, and if professional nonacademic advice is needed, we must direct students to the appropriate university service.

Scholarship in Support of Teaching

Fine teaching, active scholarship, and regular publishing are ideally connected in each professor's career: teaching is informed by scholarship, which is shared with the community of scholars through publications and presentations at professional conferences. We use this ideal to justify teaching loads, research leave policies, and tenure and promotion standards. The arguments behind the ideal are generally sound, but in several ways they contain both more and less than meets the eye.[12]

Two arguments establish an obligation to engage in scholarship in support of teaching, leaving aside for a moment any obligation to present the results through professional publications and presentations. The first appeals to our duty to make informed choices about what we teach, and Theodore Benditt, of the University of Alabama–Birmingham, states it well.

> [A] professor has an obligation to engage in research and scholarship because these are integral to conscientious teaching. A professor at the very least must make choices about what set of ideas is most nearly correct and therefore worth teaching, and research and scholarship are required in making such choices.[13]

Steven Cahn of the City University of New York makes the same case by an analogy.

> When we seek legal counsel, we have a right to expect that our attorney is knowledgeable about recent court decisions and does not rely solely on cases studied during law school. Analogously, students are entitled to assume that their instructor does not merely repeat stale ideas, but is able

to provide an informed account of the most promising lines of recent thought. A Ph.D. signifies that, as of the date awarded, the recipient has mastered a discipline. The degree does not entitle the bearer to a lifetime exemption from scholarship.[14]

We have an obligation to know the areas we teach so we can make informed choices about what to teach and so we can teach the material accurately. The material changes with developments in the field, and we must continually know it to the point where we can represent each view to students as though it were our own.[15] We can't remain appropriately knowledgeable just by reading the table of contents in a few journals. We must maintain an intensive program of scholarship; we are, therefore, obligated to do so.

The argument is sound, but at least three of its most important aspects are routinely overlooked. First, the obligation established is an obligation to engage in *scholarship that supports our teaching by maintaining and increasing our knowledge of what we teach.* We do not honor this obligation by engaging in scholarship ten, twenty, or thirty times removed from our teaching, and we cannot justify time spent on such scholarship by appeal to it. Our teaching and scholarship are to be interwoven aspects of one activity, not opposed or even separate enterprises.[16] We frequently miss this point when we evaluate each professor's teaching and research. We consider the teaching evaluations for each course. We consider the number and quality of publications. We don't consider whether the publications have anything to do with what is taught. Yet we certainly should, if a major reason for the scholarship is that it is needed to support the teaching. As Kenneth Eble puts it, there should be a "vigorous and specific examining of the intellectual activities of a faculty member as they have outcomes in teaching."[17]

Second, our obligation does not apply in elementary courses in which the material remains constant. I need not study the *Journal of Symbolic Logic* to make informed choices about what to teach in my next section of Introduction to Logic.[18] Commentators on higher education, like Charles Sykes (consider his statement quoted earlier in this chapter), miss this point when they cry "hypocrisy" at the assignment of graduate students with no scholarly credentials to teach introductory courses.

Third, since we are obliged to engage in scholarship that informs our choices of what to teach, we are also obligated to engage in scholarship that informs our choices about how to teach. We must study the

journals devoted to different teaching strategies, just as we must study
those containing the latest research. This obligation even covers elementary courses. I need to study the journal *Teaching Philosophy* to
prepare my introductory logic course. Those who criticize the extensive use of graduate students and other nonregular instructors to teach
introductory courses may have a strong point here; our principles and
practice are inconsistent, unless these instructors know how to teach
and get the chance to keep that knowledge current.

The second common argument for an obligation of scholarship
appeals to a duty to show students how knowledge continually develops through the contribution of people like themselves. Benditt puts it
as follows.

> [S]tudents should be shown as part of their education, how knowledge
> advances, and the best way for professors to do so is to demonstrate it,
> to show themselves to students as engaged, in small and appropriate
> ways, in the advancement of knowledge. . . . Students should be shown
> where and how ideas really come from and that they can be developed
> not only by giants but by people not unlike themselves. In order to do
> this kind of teaching, professors must be engaged in research projects.[19]

The argument's force does not lie in its appeal to our duty to show
how knowledge advances. We can effectively show this without ever
showing ourselves to students as engaged in scholarship. Physics
professors can teach the development of modern physics without ever
presenting their research as their own; so too philosophy and psychology professors. Benditt says that presenting ourselves as engaged in
scholarship is the "best way" to show students the developing nature
of knowledge, but having presented students with the various changing
positions on a topic and given exercises to help them appreciate the
reasoning involved, we add nothing important by showing them a
publication of our own. The only thing they learn that they couldn't
learn from other readings or by reading the publication under someone
else's name is that we too contribute to the field. They do not need to
know that to appreciate how the field develops. The argument's
strength lies in its appeal to the duty to be a scholarly role model: as
Benditt puts it, students should be shown that ideas "can be developed
not only by giants but by people not unlike themselves." To be
scholarly role models, we must present ourselves to students as
engaged in scholarship; we are, therefore, obligated to do so.

The obligation to be a scholarly role model only exists in certain
situations, however. We are obligated to model an activity only when

we are teaching students how to engage in it. We have no obligation to model Shaker religious beliefs for students we are not preparing to adopt that way of life; we have no obligation to be scholarly role models for students we are not preparing to be professional scholars.[20] The obligation to be a scholarly role model primarily applies, then, when we are teaching doctoral students. We must present ourselves as actively engaged in scholarship to give them an ever-present example of their goal and how it can be attained.

Once again, the source of our obligation to engage in scholarship demands that our teaching and scholarship be interwoven. Our scholarship must be closely enough related to the specializations of our advanced graduate students to allow us to be effective role models, and we must display our scholarly activity to them through our teaching. Any evaluation of our teaching or scholarship must consider the extent to which the former is informed by the latter.

Publishing

The role-model argument for a duty of scholarship in support of our teaching also supports a duty to present the results of our scholarship for professional review through publications and presentations at professional conferences. If we are training advanced students to be scholars or researchers, the positions for which we are training them generally include the expectation that they will engage in professionally reviewed research, and we cannot be effective role models unless we engage in that activity ourselves.

Moreover, if we develop theories of our own that we would teach as alternatives of equal standing to the other major views adopted in the field, we must first present our theories for expert evaluation. Most of us can only do this by submitting our work for publication and presentation at professional conferences. Our theories do not equal the other alternatives in standing until they too have undergone expert review, and we may not present them to students as though they have. We may certainly present them as our "hunches" concerning where the truth lies, but we must then be quite explicit about their status as untested.[21]

It is no answer to this point to cite the standard objections to the professional review system. Studies—such as one in which already accepted work was rejected when resubmitted under different authors and university affiliations—do indicate difficulties in the system.[22]

Nonetheless, the bottom line is that we need to test theories of our own that we would teach as creditable views and submitting them for publication and professional presentation is generally our best available option. Given this, the problems with the review system do not remove our obligation to use it. They give us a duty to improve it.

The considerations I have presented do not apply to some professors. They do not train advanced students to be professional scholars or researchers. They do not develop theories of their own that they would present to students as alternatives of equal standing to major views in the field. Their scholarship is restricted to remaining current with the work of others so they can best represent it to students. These professors may be able to meet all the conditions for teaching well— e.g., remain appropriately knowledgeable, model the relevant roles, maintain their ability to think through the material carefully and critically, and so on, without submitting creative work of their own for professional review. A program of professional publications and presentations can certainly help them meet some of these conditions— nothing encourages careful scholarship like the anticipation of sharp peer review—but it may not be required. These professors, then, may have no teaching-based duty to maintain a program of professional publications and presentations. Any expectation that they do so must be based on considerations beyond their teaching (e.g., their commitment to the university's research mission or the university's interest in having reliable indicators of the quantity and quality of each professor's scholarship). These considerations deserve investigation, but they lie beyond the territory I have been mapping: each individual professor's ethical obligations in teaching.

Notes

1. Billie Wright Dziech and Linda Weiner, *The Lecherous Professor: Sexual Harassment on Campus,* 2nd edition (Urbana: University of Illinois Press, 1990), pp. 40–41.
2. Charles J. Sykes, *Profscam* (New York: St. Martin's Press, 1990), p. 46.
3. In this section and the following, I take each professor's students to include those the professor is likely to teach in the future as well as those he or she is currently teaching.
4. Dziech and Weiner, p. 41; the professor is identified simply as "David G."
5. Some of the material in this section is taken from my "Professors,

Students and Friendship,'' *Morality, Responsibility and the University,* ed. Steven M. Cahn (Philadelphia: Temple University Press, 1990), pp. 134–49.

6. Steven M. Cahn, *Saints and Scamps: Ethics in Academia* (Totowa, N.J.: Rowman and Littlefield, 1986), and Sidney Hook, *Education for Modern Man* (New York: Dial Press, 1946), also pursue the line of argument I present here, though neither develops it to the extent I do. The relevant part of Hook's work is contained in this collection.

7. See my discussion in Chapter 3, especially the section, ''Promoting Intellectual Inquiry.''

8. Dziech and Weiner *(The Lecherous Professor)* provide a host of anecdotal evidence in support of this point. Discussions of particular cases often focus on the issue of whether the student entered the relationship as a consenting adult and soon get caught up in the difficulties of determining when consent is uncoerced and what to say of students who, after the fact, come to believe (realize) that they were pressured into the relationship. It is important to note that, while the student's consent is a necessary condition of the relationship being permissible, it is certainly not sufficient. That two people engage in an activity by mutual, uncoerced consent does not make the activity ethically permissible. The professor's obligations are not simply to the student; the student's consent cannot remove them. Whether or not the student has consented, the relationship is likely to lead the professor to violate the obligation of equitable treatment and the obligation to maintain a credible evaluation procedure.

9. Robert Audi, ''The Ethics of Graduate Teaching,'' in Cahn, *Morality, Responsibility and the University,* p. 127.

10. Audi, ''The Ethics of Graduate Teaching,'' p. 121.

11. Audi, ''The Ethics of Graduate Teaching,'' p. 127.

12. My only concern here is the extent to which our obligations as teachers generate an obligation to engage in scholarly activities. It goes without saying that many professors are obligated to maintain an active research program independently of considerations linked to teaching, simply because they have agreed to do so in accepting a faculty appointment at an institution with an important research mission.

13. Theodore M. Benditt, ''The Research Demands of Teaching in Modern Higher Education,'' *Morality, Responsibility and the University: Studies in Academic Ethics,* p. 103. Benditt's essay is included in this collection.

14. Steven M. Cahn, *Saints and Scamps: Ethics in Academia,* p. 42.

15. See my earlier discussions of these points in Chapter 2 and Chapter 3.

16. This is not to say that we are never obligated to also engage in research far removed from our teaching; we often are as a result of the general commitments we have made in accepting a faculty position. The point is that the scholarship we engage in to honor the particular obligation of scholarship that arises from our teaching must be closely related to our teaching.

17. Kenneth Eble, ''Conflicts between Scholarship and Teaching,'' *The*

Aims of College Teaching, Chapter 5 (San Francisco: Jossey-Bass, 1983), p. 83. Eble's essay is included in this collection.

18. See too Benditt, pp. 104–5.

19. Benditt, p. 103.

20. We are, however, obligated to model those basic values associated with learning in general (e.g., honesty, objectivity, and a willingness to follow wherever the evidence and correct reasoning may lead). See my earlier discussion of this point in Chapter 2.

21. Benditt, p. 106, makes a similar point. As I understand him, though, he endorses a more general obligation than I do here: all professors must submit the results of the scholarship they do in support of their teaching for professional review. I give my reasons for not endorsing this more general obligation in what follows.

22. See Eble, pp. 77–78.

PART TWO

The Professor-Student Relationship

The Good Teacher*
Sidney Hook

> *"If the modern teacher will think of himself not so much as a schoolmaster but as a lifemaster doing from another angle what the social worker does in his sphere, then he will be striving for all the knowledge available which could help him in his task. He will try to educate a generation of youth which combines emotional stability with a flexible mind; yet he will only succeed if he is capable of seeing each of the problems of the new generation against the background of a changing world."*
>
> KARL MANNHEIM

All plans for educational reforms depend on the teacher for their proper realization. Unless carried out by a personnel sincerely imbued with the philosophy animating the reforms and trained in the arts of effective teaching, they are doomed to failure. Everyone who remembers his own educational experience remembers teachers, not methods and techniques. The teacher is the kingpin of the educational situation. He makes and breaks programs. The initial difficulties and growing pains of progressive education were primarily caused by a scarcity of competent teachers. It still remains a source of great difficulty. The recruitment of good teachers has bogged down partly because hasty *ad hoc* programs have been adopted to meet the urgent needs created by the post-war population explosion. In the main it has been due to the downgrading of the teaching profession itself, both by the detrac-

---

* This selection is chapter ten of Hook's *Education for Modern Man* (New York: Alfred A. Knopf, 1963), reprinted here with the permission of his family.

tors of current education and by the impersonal mechanisms of the market which rewards talent in other professions much more handsomely.

The major role of the teacher in the educational process has led some writers to the conclusion that, once students have been assembled for purposes of instruction, the good teacher is all-sufficient. Given a good teacher, they assume, further concern with educational content and method is unnecessary. He has an unfailing natural sense of what it is right to teach and how to teach it. He does not even need a well-appointed classroom. One end of a log will do. Invariably someone will recall an individual of whom he will say: "He did not know anything about pedagogy but he was a great teacher."

Such a position is understandable as a reaction to the view that anybody can be educated to be an educator. It manifests a healthy skepticism toward the overdeveloped curriculums of professional schools of education in which courses are needlessly proliferated. But there is little to be said for it as a serious response to the problems of instruction. If *what* a student learns depends altogether on *who* his teacher is, the result is sure to be a disorderly cross-patch pattern. The traditions and knowledge and skills which our age requires as a common soil in which to cultivate individual variety could hardly be developed. The diversity in temperament of these uniquely endowed persons, and in the direction of their interests as well as ideas, is much greater than among those who cannot spin an entire educational curriculum out of their innards. Such diversity within limits is desirable, provided students are exposed to the varied stimuli of several outstanding personalities. But this is not likely to be the case. For the number of these extraordinary teachers is not large enough to go around. And what the educational system of America needs is at least a million good teachers.

Teaching is an art and like all arts it can be learned with varying degrees of proficiency. Some are so gifted by nature that they can perform as good teachers without learning the arts of teaching, just as some singers can have brilliant musical careers without studying voice culture. On the other hand, there are some individuals who are naturally so handicapped for a teaching career that instruction in the teaching arts can do as little for them as musical study for the tone deaf. Most teachers fall between these two extremes. It is a crime against students to permit individuals of the second kind to enter the ordinary classroom as teachers, no matter how great their gifts may be in other respects or in other fields. Whatever teaching is, it should at least not be an obstruction to learning. But it is certainly no crime, it is not even a hardship, to require of naturally gifted teachers—those who are to the teaching manner born—that they learn the formal rudiments of the art of teaching. They can always improve their skills. An enormous amount of time can be saved by familiarizing oneself with teaching devices and techniques even if one already possesses the educator's insight and an adequate educational philosophy. No one who has not actually attempted to teach the details of a curriculum can properly appreciate the great difference that mastery of specific ways and means can make in motivating interest, facilitating communication, and starting in students a train of thought which runs its course to the click of understanding. There are some things that are best learned *not* on the job. And although we can rely on any teacher to learn by trial and error experience, why should the students pay the price for that experience?

The most satisfactory teaching in American education is being done on the most elementary levels wherever plant facilities are adequate. The least satisfactory teaching is being done on the highest levels. By the "highest" level I mean, not the university, which is or should be primarily an institution for the study and publication of new truth, but the liberal arts college. If we must tolerate a disparity in effective teaching, it is, of course, preferable that the best teaching be done on the lowest level, at the most susceptible age, rather than on the highest, when habits have already hardened. But there is no justification for the disparity, and were the public aware of the actual volume of bad teaching on the college level something would be done to remedy a scandalous situation. Practices are countenanced in colleges which would not be suffered for one moment in any good elementary or secondary high school, and I am not referring here to lecturing and unsupervised study which are sometimes assumed to be the distinctive procedures of college instruction. That some college instruction is excellent does not gainsay the fact that the quality of most of it is bad. Exceptions do *not* prove the rule; neither do they disprove it when the rule is true for the most part.

There are many causes for the comparative deficiencies of college teaching. First is the failure to clarify the function of liberal education, and the dual role the faculty is expected to fill as teachers and research workers. The second is the absence of any training in college teaching, indeed in any kind of teaching, despite the fact that there are certain common psychological and philosophical principles which hold for all varieties of instruction. The third is the indifference, almost hallowed now by tradition, to pedagogical questions. Officially many college teachers, especially if they feel secure because of length of service or publication, profess not to care whether they are good teachers or not. Little serious effort is made to evaluate how well the aims of college instruction are being carried out.

Before discussing the qualities which make for good college teaching and which should serve as criteria in the selection of teachers, I wish to say a brief word about each of the causes of the present state of college teaching.

The historical association between the college and the university has led to administrative confusion about the prerequisites of teaching in both institutions. Insofar as a university is an institution of research, it can use anybody—the blind, the deaf, and the halt—provided only he has a brain. Capacity or incapacity to teach is strictly irrelevant. The only relevant question is whether this man or that can make a contribution to truth. University students are, or should be, mature men and women who are in a sense co-operating with their professors in the quest for truth. They should be expected to discount the personal and superficial mannerisms in those who are guiding their research, and fend for themselves.

The primary function, on the other hand, of the liberal arts teacher is to help young men and women to achieve intellectual and emotional maturity by learning to handle certain ideas and intellectual tools. This requires scholarship, and *familiarity* with current research but not necessarily the capacity to engage productively in it. It is alleged that the good liberal arts teacher will also be interested in doing creative work in his field. This is true for many but cannot be held true for all save by peculiar definition. It is certainly not true—and no one will be bold enough to make it true even by definition—that the good research worker will be an effective undergraduate teacher. Consequently, in selecting college teachers, once scholarly competence in the subject matter has been established, the primary consideration should be whether they give promise of being good teachers—and not, as is the case now, of whether they give promise of being good research workers. There is no necessary connection between a gift for discovery and a gift for lucid explanation, nor even between a gift for discovery and a gift for teaching which evokes the desire for discovery in others. Until the liberal arts college is emancipated from its tutelage to the university, it will not find the teachers it needs.

It is notorious that most college teachers have never taken a course in methods of teaching, even in their own subject matter—and are proud of it. In most institutions, after an instructor survives a preliminary three-year teaching period he can stay put for life. Whether he survives depends basically on his contributions to the world of research—and this world, particularly in the humanities and social sciences, may be served in many curious ways—and only incidentally on his skills as a teacher. Only incidentally—because in few colleges does there exist an established method of evaluating teaching. Hearsay, student popularity, enrollment figures build up a picture, as often false as reliable, of what transpires in the classroom. Teaching is rarely supervised and, when it is, the credentials of the supervisor do not always pass critical muster. In most institutions, visits to the classrooms of one's colleagues are not considered good form. This hypersensitiveness to observation increases when departmental lines are crossed. There are exceptions, of course, but they must not blind us to the general rule.

The indifference and professed contempt of the liberal arts teachers as a group to problems of teaching is partly a reaction to the activities of schools of education. Standards of scholarship are lower in these schools. Not infrequently subject matter courses in the liberal arts are offered in schools of education by individuals who would not qualify on academic grounds for teaching in liberal arts colleges. And yet, when no subject matter courses are offered and instruction is given in *methods* of teaching, these courses are characterized as vapid and empty. In other words, there is a tendency for liberal arts faculties to damn schools of education not only for what they do poorly but for what they do well. There is a legitimate place for schools of education as teacher training institutes, not as rivals to the liberal arts colleges. In addition to stress on methods and techniques, strong curricular emphasis should be placed on the philosophy and psychology of education—themes that are, however, much too important to be left only to schools of education. A more genuine co-operation between liberal arts colleges and schools of education might begin at a point which enables the latter to serve the former by taking over the pedagogic training of its candidates for teacher's posts, leaving certification, on the basis of mastery of subject matter, strictly alone.

The function of the teacher is among the most important in our culture. He not only transmits essential knowledge and skills but, when he takes his calling seriously, strongly influences the formation of habits and the development of a philosophy of life. Yet this high calling is not valued at its true worth by the community nor, ironically enough, by teachers themselves. "Schoolmaster," "professor" are epithets of derision, and the odor of genteel poverty is repellent even to those who regard it as a sign of election. In boom periods the profession is deserted by a scramble for better-paying jobs; in times of depression it is swamped by those who hanker for security. Social disesteem has operated as a principle of selection and bred a type noted for timidity. On paper, college faculties are responsible for all matters pertaining to educational policy and organization; in fact, until recently they have exercised less authority than their glorified clerks. Faculty participation in democratic control of colleges is a favorite theme—for discussion. Here and there in the better-known colleges, faculties have played significant roles in determining educational policy and in providing leadership, but in most situations they are inadequately represented on the governing board.

The first step towards much-needed reforms in the selection of teachers is stabilization of the economic conditions of the profession. This should take place on a plane high enough to liberate teachers from gnawing worry about making ends meet. Once this is achieved, the democratization of the college would be much easier to carry out. For the timidity of teachers grows largely from the knowledge that they face a restricted market for their services in which competitive bidding is only for a few, that administrators fight shy of "troublemakers" even in a good cause, and that the price teachers pay for independence may be loss of a vocation—the only one for which they are trained.

This first step, however, must be accompanied by a rigorous revision of the process by which teachers educate and select their successors. The revision cannot be accomplished overnight, for we must begin where we are and educators themselves must undergo some re-education. What is needed is the *will* to begin, since the knowledge of what constitutes a good teacher is widely distributed. The formulations of the traits which identify the good teacher vary, but it is possible to list those that are observable wherever there is agreement that a good teacher is in action.

A good teacher is not good for all purposes and in all circumstances. In the army, in the church, in the political party, in the penitentiary, as they are presently constituted, a good teacher as we shall define him cannot be used. What makes a good teacher, like what makes a good education, must be considered in relation to certain values. What we are seeking are the criteria of a good teacher in a democratic society whose educational system has embraced the fundamental aims we have previously outlined.

(a) The first criterion is intellectual competence. By this I mean not only the truism that the teacher should have a mastery of the subject matter he is teaching and that he should keep abreast of important developments in his field, but that he should have some capacity for analysis. Without this capacity, he cannot develop it in his students. There are different levels and types of analysis, but what they have in common is an understanding of how to approach problems, of how to take ideas apart, of how to relate our language habits to our intellectual practices. Capacity for analysis is something different from mere possession of the dry-bones and heaps of knowledge. Insofar as the distinction can be made, it is bound up more with method than content. Whatever information a teacher imparts, he must know (and wherever relevant be able to explain) how it is reached, what its validity depends on, and the role of empirical and conventional elements in the answer.

Another element in intellectual competence is a sense of relevant connection. The good teacher should be well oriented in some other fields besides the one in which he may claim to be a specialist. He should be able to follow the thread of an argument or the ramifications of a problem without concern for what a subject is called or for departmental non-trespass signs. I have heard a professor of political science bitterly complain that the economics department was teaching government, too! If the teaching was good, he should have applauded it. On the other hand, not everything in the world is interrelated; and if it were, not all of it would be equally relevant to a specific problem. The most obvious evidence of bad teaching is classroom "thinking by association," in which by a series of grasshopper jumps topics are dwelt on that have no logical connection with each other. The usual result is that the original problem, where there is one, is lost sight of.

Related to intellectual competence is the willingness to countenance, if not to encourage, rational opposition and spirited critical dissent by students. The inquiring mind even among youth sometimes probes deeply. Only a teacher unsure of himself will resent embarrassing questions to which the only honest reply must be a confession of ignorance. Intellectual independence is such a rare virtue that the good teacher positively welcomes it, despite the occasional excesses of youthful dogmatism and exuberance. For many years I refused to believe that any liberal arts teacher would actually penalize a student for intellectual disagreement. But the evidence is overwhelming that in many colleges this is far from exceptional, and that students are often fearful of venturing a defense of ideas and attitudes incompatible with those held by their teachers. In one institution, a teacher of philosophy did not conceal from his students his conviction that to embrace the metaphysics of materialism was to reveal a moral deficiency in character. Anyone who expected a recommendation from him was warned to look to his philosophy. In another institution, a bright member of the Young Communist League bitterly complained to his English teacher who had given him the lowest possible passing grade. In answer, he was told that anyone who believed in dialectical materialism deserved nothing better. A few years later, a young woman who had a perfect record in all her subjects took the same course with the same teacher and received the only C in her college career. On inquiring the reason she was told that no student who *disbelieved* in dialectical materialism deserved anything better. The teacher had become converted and had changed his mind about dialectical materialism—a speculative doctrine really irrelevant to the subject matter of his course. But he had not changed his intellectual ways. He was sincerely convinced that he had the truth on both occasions, but lacked the wit to realize that the students' *reasons* for embracing truth or error were far more important, in their educational experience, than the question of the validity of dialectical materialism. In the last decade, more than one class of students has been punished for the tortuous intellectual pilgrimages of their teachers—particularly at the hands of a certain school of militantly doctrinaire teachers who, despite the fact that their opinions veer as if by order from year to year, regard themselves as qualified to settle the most delicate problems of economics, politics, history, philosophy, and religion with a zeal and confidence that specialists, handicapped by genuine knowledge, shrink from assuming.

Some teachers seem to be constitutionally incapable of tolerating disagreement. Most often their views are deeply conservative. But there are also radical teachers, advanced thinkers about all subjects from sex to salvation, who are just as intolerant of disagreement as the most extreme reactionaries. If anything, their unction and hypocrisy makes their failure a more painful experience. Both types have chosen the wrong profession. In the classroom, the crusader must always play a subordinate role to the teacher and the inquirer. Otherwise he becomes a persecutor in behalf of the old gods or the new.

(b) Intellectual competence is necessary but not sufficient for good teaching. It must be accompanied by a quality of patience towards beginners which accepts as natural the first groping steps towards understanding by the uninitiated. The "simple" and the "obvious" are relative to antecedent skills and knowledge. Failure to see and act on this is responsible for intellectual browbeating by otherwise competent teachers and for the air, deliberately only half-concealed, of suffering the hopeless stupidity of those who are stumbling their way forward. The intellectually quick, and all teachers should be quick, have a tendency towards intellectual impatience. The impatience but not the quickness must be curbed. Patience is something that can be learned, except by certain temperaments who should never be entrusted with a class. Good teaching is not found where a star teacher holds forth for the benefit only of his star pupils, but where some participating response is evoked from every normal member of the class. Nothing is easier than to yield to the pleasures of colloquy with the exceptional students of a class—and nothing is more unfair to the rest, in whom this builds up intense resentment, oddly enough not against the teacher but against their exceptional classmates. Special provision should be made for the instruction of superior students, but a good teacher does not let their special needs dominate the class to the exclusion of the legitimate educational needs of the others.

(c) The third characteristic of good teaching is ability to plan a lesson, without mechanically imposing it on the class, in those subjects where basic materials have to be acquired, and to guide the development of discussion to a cumulative result in subjects in which the seminar method is used. The bane of much college teaching is improvisation. Improvisation is not only legitimate but unavoidable in motivating interest and finding points of departure or illustration for principles. But it cannot replace the planful survey of subject matter and problems, nor provide direction to discussion. It is delightful to follow the argument wherever it leads. But it must be an argument. And it should lead somewhere.

Where improvisation is chronic and draws its materials from autobiography, teaching sinks to its lowest level. In my own experience I recall teachers who rarely knew what they were going to talk about before they came to class. Usually they would talk about themselves or their families. Over the years, when members of their successive classes came together, they were able to construct a fairly accurate composite family portrait. The personalities of such teachers rarely possessed a richness or power that might justify taking themselves as subject matter. The contempt in which intelligent students held them was checked only by the teachers' power to distribute grades—a power which they wielded with a whimsical irresponsibility.

Naturally, the responsibility of the teacher for the progressive organization of subject matter varies with elementary and advanced classes, and he will proceed differently in presenting a lecture and in conducting a tutorial. Nothing I have said suggests the necessity of a detailed lesson plan which is as often a drawback as an aid even in the secondary schools. What the teacher must aim at is to make each class hour an integrated experience with an aesthetic, if possible a dramatic, unity of its own. Without a spontaneity that can point up the give and take of discussion, and a skill in weaving together what the students themselves contribute, preparation will not save the hour from dullness. The pall of dullness which hangs over the memories of school days in the minds of many unfortunately envelops the whole question of education.

(d) Another important quality the good teacher possesses is knowledge of human beings. He is in a sense a practical psychologist. He knows something more about people than the laws of their learning curves, and what he knows he has not found in textbooks on psychology. The more one studies students, the more differences they reveal. These differences need not be relevant to what they are trying to learn; but sometimes they are. A teacher devoid of this knowledge cannot solve the problem of motivation or evoke full participation from his class. Nor can he tell when to temper the wind, when to let it blow, when to build up self-assurance in the pathologically shy, when to deflate the bumptious. Unable to diversify his challenges, he cannot teach with proper justice and discipline in a class of miscellaneous talents. He may have a standard for the group; he should have a standard for each individual in terms of his special needs—whether they be disabilities or advantages.

Except on the frontiers of knowledge, subject matter cannot be continuously fresh. The great bulk of what is taught to students in every institution except the graduate schools of universities is "old stuff" to their teachers. To stay intellectually alive as one traverses familiar ground year in and year out is not easy. It can be done, of course, by rotating assignments, by taking sabbaticals and, most important of all, by strong theoretical interests in one's own field and related fields. But to stay intellectually alive in the classroom is something else again. Yet for the sake of students one must be alive there if nowhere else. The new developments in one's field seldom bear upon the fundamentals of college instruction, and the minutiae of scholarship have meaning only to those who are already well instructed.

The secret of intellectual vitality in the classroom, when a theorem is being derived for the twentieth time or when an elementary point in the grammar of a foreign language is being explained or when the nerve of an old philosophic argument is being laid bare, lies in experiencing the situation as a fresh problem in communication rather than one in personal discovery. Or, putting it a little differently, it consists in getting the students to reach the familiar conclusion with a sense of having made their own discovery. The task is to make as many as possible see as much as possible of what they have not seen before. It is this perennial challenge, which cannot be adequately met without a knowledge of people, that keeps the good teacher alive. If he does not recognize it, he is a pedagogical automaton, and almost always a bore.

Where knowledge has not yet been won and the authority of method does not point to inescapable and well-tested conclusions, the love of truth can be relied on to generate its own enthusiasm. But where knowledge is already warranted by methods that are themselves warranted, and where originality is likely to be little more than a craving for attention or an expression of conceit, the love of truth by itself cannot be relied upon to make a lesson exciting. There is something suspicious about any mind that can be thrown into raptures of enthusiasm at stated intervals, and in pretty much the same language too, by the statement of truths he has been purveying to students term in, term out. Such enthusiasm is synthetic and the students know it.*

There is a crackle of interest always present in the classroom of a good teacher no matter how trite or timeworn the theme. It is supplied not merely by the teacher's love of truth but by the students' desire to discover the truth, and by the teacher's interest in that desire and in the arts of gratifying it. In the end, the good teacher makes himself superfluous and the good student learns the art of self-education. But it is literally in the end.

(e) He knows man best who loves him best. A teacher cannot love all his students, nor is it wise to love any of them. The knowledge appropriate for good teaching requires an emotion not so strong as

---

* There is a story told on the campus of an eastern college of an art teacher, now happily no longer teaching, who used to lecture by what might be called the method of sustained respiration. In treating a certain figure in the history of art, at a fixed point in his course, he would draw a deep breath and, in a mounting crescendo, declaim the artist's wonders. One day he began as usual. "He had no sense of form, he had no sense of color, he had no sense for religion or morals, he broke all the rules of good drawing . . ." and before he could finish, back chorused the class with his punch-line, "But my God! could that man paint!"

love but also not so irrational. This emotion is sympathy. The good teacher must like people and be interested in them as people, and yet he need not like or be interested in everyone. I am speaking of a general personality trait. It need not find universal expression in every action. But without it an intellectually competent teacher may do more harm than good. There is such a thing as sadism in educational life. Teachers have enormous powers to make students miserable; and, where they are chosen haphazardly, there will always be some who will visit their frustrations and disappointments upon those before them, usually under the guise of being strict disciplinarians. The incidence of insanity is higher among teachers than in any other profession, and the academic community is no freer from phobias like anti-Semitism than the rest of the community. It requires only one teacher to ruin a student's career.

Sympathy is a positive attitude of imaginative concern with the personal needs of others. Benevolent neutrality and mechanical application of rules, no matter how scrupulous, are no substitutes for it. If justice is based on understanding, then without sympathy there cannot be true justice. For understanding is never complete without the sympathy that awakens our organs of perception. Those who teach large numbers and never get to know their students have a tendency to regard all but a brilliant few as a dull, cloddish mass. Reduce the number in each class, shorten the perspective, and no one worthy of being a teacher will fail to see the interesting variety of potentiality in every group. Even outside the classroom it takes two people to make one bore. And, next to ideas, persons are the most interesting things in the world. In each person there is some unique quality of charm, intelligence, or character, some promise and mystery that invites attention and nurture. The teacher who seeks it will find it.

Students respond to sympathy for their special intellectual needs like plants to sunshine and rain. They undertake more and achieve more. A certain danger exists that they may at the beginning undertake tasks in order to please their teacher or not to disappoint him but, if proper guidance is furnished, their own sense of growing mastery of a task and of its increasing significance provides intellectual momentum. The function of the teacher at this point is unobtrusively to raise the stick of achievement higher and to offer criticism without killing self-confidence. Students rarely disappoint teachers who assure them in advance that they are doomed to failure. They do not, of course, always live up to the more optimistic expectations of their teachers but they invariably do the better for it.

It is easy to caricature what I am saying by pretending that this is a demand that the teacher be a nurse or a psychiatrist to his students or that he serve literally *in loco parentis*. It would be helpful, naturally, if a teacher were to know the chief relevant facts about those students who need psychiatrists or nurses, if only to put them in proper professional hands and thus prevent them from serving as a drag on other students. But the teacher should not essay the role of amateur psychiatrist or nurse. His sympathy must be primarily directed to his students as growing intellectual organisms in a growing intellectual community, in the faith that they will become integrated persons capable of responsible choice. He cannot cope with all their emotional needs or assume the responsibilities of family and society, priest or judge. He must be friendly without becoming a friend, although he may pave the way for later friendship, for friendship is a mark of preference and expresses itself in indulgence, favors, and distinctions that unconsciously find an invidious form. There is a certain distance between teacher and student, compatible with sympathy, which should not be broken down—for the sake of the student. A teacher who becomes "just one of the boys," who courts popularity, who builds up personal loyalties in exchange for indulgent treatment, has missed his vocation. He should leave the classroom for professional politics.

What I have said flows from the faith that imaginative sympathy towards the needs of the individual student, based on an intelligent appraisal of his equipment and achievements, will enhance his powers of growth. This faith may appear utopian or romantic. Those who are so impressed usually confuse two things: whom we shall teach and how we shall teach. If, at any level or for a specific purpose, a student is uneducable, a large assumption but sometimes obviously true, he should either be directed to a field in which he is educable or committed to an institution for the feeble-minded, for that is where people who are absolutely uneducable belong. But so long as a teacher finds himself before a class in which there are varied talents, varied capacities for educability, he is under an obligation to help each one develop the best within him. That is what he is there for. If he accepts his obligation gladly and not as a chore, he will find that the results are worth the effort.

What to teach and how to teach must be distinguished from the problem of certification of student competence. Competence is a relation not only to subject matter but to comparative performance and to a set of conditions, far from fixed, defined by the nature of the task for which competence is required. There is also something that may be called a "conventional" element in the determination of competence. This is clearest when, because only a certain number can be certified, all whose achievements fall below this number are failed even though their achievements surpass those of individuals who have been previously certified. Competence established by position on a comparative scale can be ascertained even by those who are not teachers. What the teacher alone can supply is testimony of intellectual and personal qualities which he is uniquely qualified to observe. This testimony together with other data of measurable competence should determine the educational decision to advance, to hold, or to transfer the individual student. The basic consideration should be: what action will educationally most profit the individual without too great a cost to others? Detailed rules cannot wisely be drawn *in abstracto*. For all sorts of factors, sometimes even the state of the nation, may affect their formulation.

To develop the best in each student, therefore, emphatically does not mean that the teacher believes that all students are equally good, or that when he must rate them he should rate them all in the same way, or that he must sacrifice "standards"—a blessed word which is the hardest-worked substitute for thinking on educational matters among college teachers. Those who mouth the word most loudly as soon as any proposal is made to liberalize liberal education do not know what "standards" actually are, their source, their history, and that "standards," too, must face a test which requires other standards. They usually maintain that their own standards are absolute and objective, but no two of them agree with each other. It is notorious that one college's *Pass* student is another's *cum laude,* and that even in the same college one professor's *A* is another's *C.* Time and again it has been experimentally proved that the same teacher, irrespective of subject matter, rates the same paper differently, when he has not identified it as such, depending on matters that have nothing to do with education. Those who talk in absolutes here are only absolutizing their own subjectivity. Those who are militantly self-righteous about the number of students they regularly fail rarely stop to ask whether the fault lies in their own teaching or in the kind of standards they are using. I have heard teachers urge the imposition of standards which would obviously have barred *them* from any possibility of a college education if the proposed standards had been applied in all fields when they were students.

The teacher's working standards in the classroom should be distinct from the rules that determine the next step in the educational career of the student, i.e., whether he is to pass or fail. These working standards cannot be adjudged "high" or "low," for they should be nothing else but the realization of the fundamental ends of the educational process itself through the use of the most appropriate means that will insure the maximum intellectual growth of every student entrusted to him. If these are his working standards, the teacher will never be satisfied that this maximum has been finally reached. For with every intellectual achievement new vistas of knowledge open before us.

(f) The good teacher, to close our inventory of his traits, possesses vision. It is the source of both his intellectual enthusiasm and his detachment in the face of inevitable failures and disappointments. Without vision he may become a kindly technician, useful in a limited way. But he cannot inspire a passion for excellence. The vision may take many forms. It may be a doctrine—but he must not preach it. It may be a dream—but he must not keep talking about it. It may be a hope, an ambition, a work in progress, so long as it is not merely personal and has a scope or sweep of some imaginative appeal. But it must not obtrude itself into the details of instruction. Its presence should be inferable from the spirit with which the instruction is carried on. It should operate in such a way as to lift up the students' hearts and minds beyond matters of immediate concern and enable them to see the importance of a point of view. Wherever an intellectually stimulating teacher is found, there will also be found some large perspective of interest that lights up the corners of his subject matter. If students catch fire from it, it should not be in order to believe some dogma but to strengthen them in the search for truth and to become more sensitive to visions that express other centers of experience.

The best teacher possesses all of the qualities we have mentioned to a pre-eminent degree. But the best teacher is to be found only in a Platonic heaven. Good teachers, however, who exhibit some or all of these qualities are to be found on earth. They can become, can be helped to become, and can help others to become, better teachers. If a resolute beginning is made by those who educate and select teachers, in time the community will discover that a new spirit and morale is abroad in the teaching profession. It will discover that a good teacher is a *dedicated* person, strong in his faith in what he is doing, worthy not only of honor in a democracy but of a place in its councils.

When educational laymen speak of the non-material rewards of good teaching, only too often their kindly observations are fumbling words of consolation for the presumed deprivation of careers isolated from the dramatic struggles of "real" life. There *are* deprivations entailed by the profession of teaching but these are not among them. Most teachers are not men of action by temperament and self-selection keeps them out of the forays and battles of daily life. And no matter what their temperament, a lifetime of exposure to immature minds unfits them for positions in politics or business in which risks must be run and quick decisions taken before all the evidence is in. Teachers unaware of the limiting effect of the very fact of pedagogic excellence upon their habits of mind tend to take themselves too seriously and to regard the world as a classroom waiting for the proper lessons to solve the problems of adult experience. A sense of humor about themselves is the best assurance of a sense of proportion in these matters—a safeguard against taking themselves too seriously as well as against vain regrets. When a man becomes a teacher it is extremely unlikely that the world has lost a great political leader or prophet.

Every choice among viable alternatives involves a sacrifice of some genuine good. Teachers, like others, make sacrifices in the selection and pursuit of their calling. To the individual who has found himself in teaching these sacrifices are far from galling. For if he has found himself in his calling, in all likelihood he has had a successful career. It is not the emoluments and social status or holiday words of community praise which are criteria of success for him. Rather is it a twofold satisfaction. First, he is aware of being a part of a continuing tradition which, no matter how humble his role in it, connects the great minds of the past with those of the present and future. Second, although the teacher like the actor is a sculptor in snow and can leave no permanent monument of his genius behind, he can reach the minds of those who will survive him, and through them affect the future. The lives of most people would have been pretty much the same no matter who their teachers were. But there are a sufficient number of men and women in the world who can truthfully testify to the determining and redetermining role which some teachers played in their lives. To very few is it given to exercise this influence. The opportunity to do so is a measure both of the power of the teacher and of his responsibility.

The Authority of Ideas and the Students' Right to Autonomy*
Kenneth Strike

The ignorance of the person just beginning the study of a subject has a special character. It is not just that the novice is ignorant of the facts and theories of the subject matter; the student is also ignorant of the principles that govern thought about the subject matter. He does not know what the problems of the field are, he does not know what approaches to take to solve a field's problems, and he does not know how to identify a reasonable solution to the problem.

Consider an example. It has been common to introduce the oxidation theory of combustion by means of an experiment in which students are asked to thrust the smouldering end of a stick of wood into an inverted test tube of oxygen. The stick will normally burst into flames. It is then explained that this is because the test tube contains a higher concentration of oxygen than does the air in the classroom and that this oxygen combines with the material in the wood, yielding carbon dioxide and water plus a residue of ash.

What issue is being addressed by this experiment? Note that the explanation is not focused on burning. No account is given of the flame or the heat. My ten-year-old car, like the stick of wood, has undergone considerable oxidation, producing a noticeable residue of iron oxide. It has not, so far as I have been able to see, burst into flame during the process. Why does the oxidation of the wood produce heat and light in

* This selection is chapter three of Strike's *Liberty and Learning,* published in the United States by St. Martin's Press and in Great Britain by Martin Robertson & Co., reprinted here with the permission of Blackwell Publishers.

large amounts? This is not explained. The reader might ponder the question of what exactly the explanation explains and how the experiment supports the explanation. One should come to the conclusion that the answer is not very obvious. Moreover, with perseverance it may also be observed that a grasp of the issues presupposes a knowledge of such fundamental ideas as the atomic theory of matter and the conservation of matter.

It might also be profitable to ask whether other accounts of the phenomena might be constructed. During the nineteenth century it was widely believed among chemists that heat was a substance that flowed from one place to another. Most phenomena concerned with combustion were explained in terms of the behaviour of this substance, called phlogiston. Could the experiment described above be explained in such terms? Phlogiston theorists were ingenious in explaining apparently difficult phenomena via the theory. Air was necessary for combustion because it was needed to absorb the phlogiston given off. Air in which combustion occurred rapidly (as in our experiment) was dephlogistated air, thus having a great capacity for absorbing phlogiston. Combustion ceased when the air had absorbed its capacity of phlogiston. The real ingenuity of the phlogiston theorists was demonstrated when they were acquainted with the fact that some substances gained in weight when heated. This problem was solved by assigning to phlogiston the property of negative weight. Thus, when the phlogiston was driven out, the object that lost its phlogiston gained weight. The theory has an odd ring to modern ears. But what is wrong with it? Does the combustion experiment described refute it?

I hope that these questions about such a commonplace experiment will be puzzling to the reader. They are meant to suggest how deeply our beliefs about oxygen and combustion are embedded in a complex set of beliefs about physical phenomena, how complex the reasoning is that supports the oxygen theory of combustion, and how unfamiliar most of us are with the principles of reasoning that function in the arguments. Those of us who have been blessed with only an introductory course in chemistry are a long way from being able to reason like a chemist. The novice and the expert differ not just in their knowledge of the facts of chemistry. They differ in their capacity for chemical reasoning. The novice is not in a position to have much of an understanding of even the most simple chemical experiment.

With this as background I want to argue two claims that I believe are central in understanding the students' rights and interests in the pedagogical relationships.

(1) Students as persons have a right to autonomy. This requires teachers both to give students reasons for what they are asked to believe, within the students' capacity to grasp them, and to teach so as to expand the students' capacity to comprehend and assess reasons.

(2) A variety of processes, which I shall collectively refer to as reason-giving, is essential to the development of the students' capacity to comprehend and assess the claims of any subject matter.

Persons have the right to autonomy. What does this mean? Fundamentally, it means that people have a *prima facie* right to be self-governing. Autonomy is complex; it contains at least three components. The first is psychological freedom: this is the capacity for independent choice, and it requires the capacity for rational judgment and for self-control. The second component is the right of self-determination in those areas of life that are properly left to the individual's discretion: individuals should have the right to choose their own beliefs and their own lifestyle, and they have a number of other rights that limit a government's or a society's authority over them. Finally, individuals have the right to participate in collective choices.

There is a great deal that might be said about the meaning and justification of these rights that cannot be said here. The following point is crucial. These rights are rooted in the value of moral agency. *Human beings are ends in themselves and are moral agents who are responsible to choose wisely on their own behalf and act justly with respect to others. They are morally responsible for what they choose and what they do.*

A moral agent who is responsible for his choices must demand both the opportunity and the resources to choose wisely. The opportunity for such choices is autonomy. Autonomy in its several forms specifies both the psychological and political preconditions of responsible choice. A person who is not free in these ways cannot freely choose and act.

The resources to choose responsibly are of essentially two sorts. First, responsible choice depends on information and evidence. One cannot consistently demand that a person make a responsible choice and at the same time withhold information relevant to that choice. Here, indeed, is another kind of argument for rights such as free speech or free press, which serve the function of making information freely available for moral agents who require it to decide responsibly.

A society that restricts the free flow of information denies to its citizens one of the conditions of responsible choice. In doing so, it in effect expresses a decision to refuse to regard its citizens as responsible moral agents.

Information is not, however, sufficient to allow people to make responsible choices. They must also have the will and ability to do so. Concerning the will to choose responsibly, I shall note only that it seems to me to require such virtues as a regard for and commitment to truth, honesty and fairness. There is, no doubt, much more to say, but I mention these ideals because they are intellectual virtues in the sense that they are presupposed by the commitment to have one's choices and actions warranted by available evidence. The central point about the ability to choose responsibly is that having information that provides a satisfactory base for a decision is not the same thing as being able to interpret or judge that information in a reasonable way. This is, of course, the point I have argued at length: concepts are tools. Two people with the same piece of information can differ vastly in terms of their capacity to draw reasonable conclusions from it. It follows that the cognitive resources necessary for responsible choice are acquired. The point is not that there is some particular set of cognitive skills that somehow defines the capacity for rational choice. The intellectual requirements for responsible choice will differ depending on the character of the issue. Nonetheless, the capacity for responsible choice depends on achieving a degree of intellectual sophistication. Education is a prerequisite of autonomy.

These observations have significant import for the view we must take of the rights of the student in the teacher-student relationship. They imply that *the teacher must see the student as more than a novice who is ignorant of the context and principles of the subject matter. The teacher must also see the student as a responsible moral agent who, because he is responsible for what he will believe and what he will do, must ask for and be given reasons for what he is asked to believe. He must also see the student as one whose capacity for understanding reasons must be expanded.*

Now this may seem paradoxical. I have, it would seem, argued both that the teacher has a moral duty to give reasons to the student and that the student is in no position to grasp these reasons. These claims are not, however, as inconsistent as might first appear to be the case. The argument I have given concerning the student's capacity to appreciate reasons shows that the student is not capable of viewing the subject matter from the perspective of the expert. This is a limit on the kinds of reasons a student can grasp concerning a subject, but it is far from showing that the student is altogether incapable of appreciating any reasons. The expert and the student will both approach any phenomenon with a set of concepts that they will use to assess the phenomenon or arguments concerning it. The concepts of the expert and the student will normally differ in scope and power, but the student does have a set of concepts that he can and will use to judge what he encounters in instruction.

These concepts are the students' court of appeal. They will provide the criteria by means of which the claims of a teacher will be judged and the context in terms of which these claims will be understood. The concepts of a given student may be more or less adequate to the instructional purposes of a teacher. A student, for example, who understands the atomic theory of matter is in a better position to understand the oxygen theory of combustion than one who does not. Students' concepts may also be dysfunctional. A student who sees matter as a continuous substance rather than as consisting of discrete parts cannot understand such phenomena as heat or the compression of gases, and the instructor will need to provide the student with reasons that suggest the inadequacies of this concept and the need for a different one.

We thus know two important things about the 'epistemic situation' of the student. We know that the student is not in the same position as the expert to assess the phenomena or the arguments of a discipline. We also know that the student has a position of his own from which the subject matter of a discipline will be assessed. Thus, the teacher cannot appeal to the student's epistemic situation as grounds for not giving the student reasons for what the student is asked to believe, although he may appeal to the student's epistemic situation as grounds for not giving the student the kinds of reasons that would be given to an expert. The teacher continues to have the duty to regard the student as a responsible moral agent, which entails the duty to give reasons within the student's capacity to grasp.

There is a second reason why the teacher has a duty to give the student reasons. The teacher has a duty to expand the capacity of the student for understanding and evaluating reasons. The giving of reasons is a necessary condition of a pedagogy that can expand this capacity. The meaning of the phrase 'giving reasons' should be broadly understood. It includes any device whereby a student can be made aware of the evidence for some claim. Verbal accounts of the reasoning for a claim are, no doubt, paradigmatic of giving reasons, but demonstrations, discussions, exercises or assignments that direct the student's attention to evidence are also included.

It is also to be insisted that reason-giving is an interaction between the teacher and the student that requires the student's active participation. Propositions that are objective evidence for some claim must be subjectively seen as evidence by the student. This requires the student to integrate reasons given by an instructor into the student's current concepts in such a way that they are structured as evidence within the student's cognitive structure. We must remember that a proposition or a phenomenon is only evidence for a claim in relation to a set of concepts that interpret it. The burning stick in our experiment is only evidence for the oxygen theory of combustion to the student with a proper set of prior assumptions. The suggestion that evidence is relative to the student's current concepts indicates a need on the part of the teacher to know what the student's current concepts are. There is, I think, no substitute for an active exchange between student and teacher in this regard. The clues to a student's concepts are the questions asked, observations proffered or counter-arguments produced. Reason-giving is thus not simply a process of transmission of ideas from teacher to student. It requires the participation of the student if it is going to succeed.

But reason-giving is far more than the way in which evidence is obtained by students. It is the way in which students come to understand what counts as evidence. It is thus the means whereby students come to internalize the concepts and criteria that are appropriate to thought in a given area. Reason-giving does this in at least two ways: it provides models and exemplars of what counts as a reason in a given area, and it provides practice in the use of relevant criteria and concepts.

To get a handle on the idea of an exemplar we may return to the combustion example and ask what its role in instruction is. One answer is that it is a way of providing the student with evidence for the oxygen theory of combustion. I have already suggested grounds for believing that this is not an altogether acceptable view. While it is the case that the student is being shown a phenomenon that can be interpreted as a piece of evidence for the oxygen theory of combustion, it is also the case that *as evidence* it is a remarkably weak piece, particularly from the student's point of view. The particular phenomena can be given a coherent interpretation within another theory, and the student is not in a position to assess the strength of the interpretation provided.

A more plausible view of the role of such demonstrations is that they are the means whereby students learn how the abstractions contained in the theories, formulae and concepts of a discipline are applied and manipulated. The concepts of a discipline come to have their meaning both in terms of how they are connected with one another and how they are attached to phenomena. A good exemplar exhibits both sorts of meaning. In such a way, the student can begin to get a feel for the criteria that govern the use of such concepts, not by having the criteria stated, but by seeing them employed. Students learn the syntax of scientific concepts much as they learn the syntax of their own language—by seeing it in use. Exemplars also perform the role of showing how the concepts and abstractions of a field attach to the phenomena with which they are concerned. This 'attachment' can involve several things. It can indicate the procedures by which abstract terms are given empirical meaning by showing how quantities are measured or experiments conducted. Simultaneously, an exemplar shows the student how to *see* a phenomenon through the concepts of a theory: the student is taught to see burning as oxidation. An exemplar may be part of the justification for some scientific theory, but its fundamental role in teaching is to allow the student to see the phenomenon in the way in which the expert can see it and in doing so to learn what counts as justification.

An exemplar need not be an empirical demonstration of the application of some scientific theory. What will count as an exemplar will depend on the problem or the field. It may be the analysis of a poem or painting, the diagnosis and treatment of a disease, or a paper that contains a classical treatment of a classical problem. The important thing is to exhibit the application of the concepts and techniques of a field to a representative problem.

The role of the instructor in transmitting the standards of a field is to be a model of competent performance. When a teacher gives the reasons for a given claim, he is giving the student a justification for it. But again, the point of the activity is not so much to justify the claim to the student, but to help the student to see what counts as a justification. The teacher does this by exhibiting the argument forms and criteria extant in a field in the process of giving reasons.

These ways of communicating or exhibiting the concepts and criteria of a field can be successful only when they elicit the active participation of the student. One reason is that the student's participation allows the instructor to see the student's view of the matter and to express a justification in a way appropriate to the student's current concepts. A second reason is that participation is a means of practicing the intellectual skills of a field.

People do not learn an intellectual skill merely by watching it employed, any more than they learn a language merely by listening to others talk. Part of modelling is practice. The learner attempts an approximation of what he has seen. The teacher will respond in a way that highlights how the student's efforts fall short of the standard. Practice is an essential part of bringing any action into conformity with a standard. It is impossible unless the student is an active participant in the process of learning.

These arguments should suffice to show that reason-giving is both a moral and a pedagogical necessity for teaching. They also imply much concerning what the pedagogical relationship should be like and the kinds of freedoms that should and should not be available to students. These arguments indicate that *the pedagogical relationship should be governed by two fundamental ideas:*

(1) there is a significant inequality between the student (as novice) and the teacher (as expert) in terms of their current capacity to understand and assess the ideas and arguments of a field;
(2) the student and the teacher are equally moral agents and owe one another the rights and respect due moral agents.

The expertise of the teacher conveys certain kinds of authority upon the teacher over the student. The teacher's competence generates the right to govern the intellectually rooted decisions concerning teaching and learning—that is, decisions that require expertise in the concepts of a discipline to make them competently. Included in this category are the selection and organization of the curriculum, the right to direct the process in the classroom in profitable directions, and the right to evaluate the intellectual competence of the student's work. When admission to an intellectual profession is at issue this, too, is the prerogative of experts.

The teacher also owes certain duties to the student. Included are the obligations to represent the field to the student honestly and fairly, to evaluate the student's work on relevant criteria, to give reasons, and to initiate the student into standards of the discipline.

The student likewise has a set of rights and duties. The student has the right freely to inquire, to ask for reasons, to open access to information, and to question and debate the conclusions reached by experts. These 'intellectual liberties' secure for the student the right to participate in the intellectual affairs of the classroom in a way that assists the student in internalizing the standards and procedures of a discipline. And they recognize the student's status as a moral agent who is ultimately responsible for his beliefs and actions.

I have argued that the teacher has certain kinds of authority over the student. However, the student also has a *prima facie* right to be a voluntary participant in the pedagogical relationship. The grounds for this are again both moral and pedagogical. That the student is a responsible moral agent is grounds for making his participation in an educational situation voluntary. From a pedagogical perspective, the point is that rational learning cannot but be voluntary. Students may be made to go to class and do homework. They cannot be made to internalize the standards and values of an intellectual enterprise. This kind of learning requires the willing involvement of the student in the enterprise.

Lest this emphasis on the voluntariness of the student's participation be misunderstood, let me note that this does not entail that there be no required courses, or required standards, or that academic decisions be made either democratically or in response to 'consumer demand.' There are academic decisions legitimately made by experts. The real issue is that students must accept the legitimacy of the education to which they are asked to submit. Education can take place when students believe that educational institutions are in possession of something worthwhile. Since the values and standards of intellectual enterprises are internal to these enterprises and cannot be fully appreciated by the novice, the student's submission to his education cannot be fully rational. It must be based, in part, on trust.

Education loses its legitimacy when students begin to believe that the values educators or educational institutions pursue are self-serving or perverse. They will then either drop out or come to see themselves as a captive audience. Genuine education ceases when students see themselves as held to their tasks by coercive factors, as, for example, when they see their economic future arbitrarily linked to some level of educational attainment. Students may go through the motions, pass the tests, and gain the certificates. A few may even be seduced into an appreciation of the forms of life intellectual enterprises represent. On the whole, however, when students lack a commitment to the value of what they learn, the consequences of learning on their values and their view of the world—the things that matter—will be minimal.

Demands for democracy or voluntariness in the detail of course selection, curriculum or instructor are signs that education is not seen as legitimate. The arguments I have given concerning the 'epistemic gap' between novice and expert indicate that yielding to such demands is not the cure for the disease of illegitimacy. Democracy in academic affairs is governance by the incompetent. An institution faced with such demands or with passive resistance to the education it provides needs, rather, to look to the values it pursues and how these values become viable to its students.

Some further caveats concerning the way in which education should be voluntary are required. I initially suggested that students have a *prima facie* right to be voluntary participants in the pedagogical relationship. That the right is *prima facie* suggests that there are considerations that may override it. There are two sorts of considerations. I shall note them here and take them up in more detail in later chapters.

The first is that a lack of maturity can override the right to voluntariness. General maturity must be distinguished from intellectual competence. The novice in physics lacks competence in the standards of physical argument. Such a person may, however, be mature. Maturity is the general capacity to discover or choose a stable and rational set of goals, needs and interests and make choices that further them. A student who does not know physics may, nevertheless, know himself well enough and know enough about what physics is like to make a competent (if tentative) commitment to study it. A student who lacks maturity cannot do even this. Some form of paternalism toward such a student's education may, therefore, be warranted.

Second, a student's choices may have an impact not only on himself, but on others. A student who fails to learn to read harms not only his own prospects, but those of others. In such cases, the society has some interest in the decision and may act coercively when a significant threat to its legitimate interest exists.

I assume that these restrictions on the voluntariness of student decisions apply primarily to younger children.

This view of the pedagogical relationship can best be summarized by calling it a master-apprentice relationship. *Its essential features are that the student is seen as a junior member of a community united by a shared commitment to some intellectual enterprise. Learning is a result of participation in the characteristic activities of the group under the guidance of an expert who sets educational tasks within the student's competence and evaluates performance. The relationship assumes the competence and the honesty of the master. Since the learner is not in a position to evaluate fully the competence of the master, the success of the relationship depends on trust. The learner in turn must willingly submit to the expertise of the master.*

When this master-apprentice relationship concerns some intellectual endeavour, I have suggested that the student has intellectual liberties that may appear quite similar to the intellectual liberties that are shared by members of intellectual communities and are exercised in the activity of inquiry. For the student, after all, learning is inquiry. The student thus has the right to relevant information and to question and debate the ideas he encounters.

It is, however, crucial to note that the student's intellectual liberty differs from that of the expert. Intellectual liberty for the expert is justified as an essential component of the institutional arrangements in which inquiry can be conducted and truth pursued. Intellectual liberty is the means whereby new ideas are subjected to the standards of the field and are accepted, rejected or modified. Intellectual liberty for the student, on the other hand, is a condition of the student exercising his responsibility as a moral agent and participating in an intellectual enterprise in a way likely to lead to the internalization of the concepts and standards of that enterprise.

Consider some features concerning these arguments. Note first that the appeal to moral agency is a non-consequentialist argument. It argues for granting intellectual liberty to students, not because doing so has beneficial consequences, but rather because doing so recognizes their status as moral agents. This moral argument for liberty does not, however, sharply distinguish the role of the expert from the role of the student, for the simple reason that the argument applies to any moral agent and therefore to novice and expert alike. Perhaps the only salient difference here is that there is more need to insist on the rights of students as moral agents since students are more likely to be in a subservient position than are experts.

The epistemological arguments for liberty distinguish more sharply between the expert and the novice. The student faces a task logically similar to that of an expert: new ideas must be assessed, and accepted, modified or rejected on the basis of relevant evidence. But the tasks are also different. For the expert the standards of the enterprise are known—the point of the inquiry is to add to human knowledge. The novice, however, has not internalized the standards of the enterprise— the point of inquiry is to do so. Moreover, while the student may be adding to his personal store of knowledge, he is not likely to add to the general store of human knowledge. That the student is a novice means that he is hardly in a position to do so. Arguments that justify liberty on grounds that it is a precondition of productive inquiry are not, therefore, likely to be successful when applied to students.

This difference in justification of intellectual liberty suggests that the nature of the particular liberties available to the expert and the student may differ as well. The major difference is that the intellectual liberties available to the novice are constrained by the requirements of effective pedagogy and may, therefore, be regulated by the teacher. The tenured professor or lecturer has earned the right to pursue his inquiries regardless of where the argument leads. Perhaps no one is required to publish his ideas or reward him for them, but neither is anyone empowered to stop his inquiry. The student, however, has not similarly earned the right to pursue his ideas or interests beyond the point where they contribute to his education or the education of his peers. The teacher thus has the right to curtail a line of inquiry when it becomes fruitless or disruptive. This does not mean that the teacher should cut short every line of thought that diverges from the truth—students learn from following a false trail. But it does mean that the teacher may cut short an unprofitable pursuit because he can see that it leads nowhere. The liberty of students has a different point from the liberty of the expert, functions according to a different set of rules, and can be regulated by the teacher. We shall need to give more detailed attention to precisely how the rules differ. That, however, is not a task for this chapter.

Academic Paternalism*
Joan C. Callahan

Though the campus unrest of the sixties is long over and a disquieting
quietism sometimes seems to be the distinguishing mark of contemporary American university students as a group, it is sometimes objected
by students in the university that a university, college, or department
policy or practice, or that a policy, practice, decision, or behavior of
an administrator or faculty member is paternalistic. The kinds of
policies, practices, and behaviors which students complain about as
being paternalistic fall into two major classes—academic and nonacademic. In the academic class are university and college distribution
requirements, departmental requirements for successful completion of
a major or minor, and the particular educational practices and decisions of individual faculty members (e.g., requirements in courses). In
the nonacademic class are policies governing dormitory life (e.g.,
curfews and rules concerning visitors), policies governing faculty/
student relationships, and hosts of decisions made by administrators
governing all areas of student life, as well as the personal interactions
of administrators and faculty with individual students.

I shall limit my remarks in this paper to the question of academic
paternalism. I do not pretend, then, to offer an adequate account of

From *International Journal of Applied Philosophy,* vol. 3, no. 1 (1986), 21–
31, reprinted here with the permission of the journal's editor.

* An earlier version of this paper was prepared for presentation to the North
American Society for Social Philosophy with support from the Louisiana State
University Council on Research. I am grateful to Tziporah Kasachkoff, Hugh
LaFollette, and the editors of this *Journal* for suggestions which have improved
the paper.

paternalism in the university. Nor do I pretend to offer even an adequate account of the purported problem of academic paternalism in the university. Rather, I simply want to begin to understand whether the university and its departments and faculty in general function in a way that is to be understood as paternalistic at all. I shall, then, be primarily concerned with the appropriate model of the university/student and faculty/student relationship.

I begin with the assumption that university students are no longer children, and therefore, that treating them as children in any way requires a special justification. But even this presupposes an understanding of paternalistic treatment that requires some clarification. Let me begin, then, with the paradigm case of paternalism in order to see what the problem-generating features of paternalism might be.[1]

The Paradigm Case

'Paternalism' is an analogical concept derived from the special relationship between parents and children.[2] As John Kleinig points out, central to the paradigm case of paternalism is the picture of a relationship where one party acts on the presumption that he knows what is best for the other party.[3] There are at least three things to notice about the paradigm case: (1) that in acting paternalistically, a parent need not interfere with his or her child's liberty—parents are benevolent providers as well as benevolent enforcers; (2) that despite this, paternalism in the paradigm case often involves the imposition of the parent's will on the child, which does involve an interference with the child's liberty; and (3) that we think of paternalistic actions or policies in the paradigm case as involving protection or promotion of the child's well-being as their rationale—that is, the policy adopted or action undertaken is chosen (a) out of concern for the child's best interest and (b) on the basis of the parent's presumption that he or she *knows best* (what is in the child's best interest).

This last sub-feature of the paradigm case of paternalism, however, points to certain policies governing adults and behaviors toward adults that commonly lead to their classification as paternalistic policies and behaviors. These are policies and behaviors not grounded in some good of the targets of the policies or behaviors, but which assume an offensive and non-benevolent superiority on the part of those who set the policy or who behave in these ways. The management of a plant, for example, which, for the sake of greater efficiency, requires that workers get the permission of the supervisors to go to the restroom, treats its workers non-benevolently, yet is said to treat them paternalistically. That is, it acts in a way which is not intended to protect or promote the interests of the workers and is degrading of adults because it treats them like children who cannot be expected to act responsibly.[4]

Given these clues from the paradigm case and from other cases which we have come to classify as cases of paternalistic treatment, I take the problem of paternalism in higher education as arising in two major ways: (1) when policies, decisions, or behaviors involve an interference with the liberty of students for their own good; and (2) when policies, decisions, or behaviors toward students involve treating students in patronizing or other ways which fail to recognize their adult status.[5] Paternalism of the first kind is morally problematic because it involves the violation of the adult's right to make self-regarding choices. There is a general presumption against such interference in a free society; and when the interference is for the sake of benefiting an adult interferee, that presumption is very strong indeed. I shall focus most of my remarks on this form of paternalism; and I shall argue that much of what appears to be and is sometimes criticized as being paternalism of this kind in the academic structure of the university and its departments and in the practices of its faculty need not be so, and should not, in any general way, be understood as falling under the paternalistic model.[6]

The Instructor/Student Relationship

Even though the paradigm case of the paternalistic relationship is appropriately described as involving a picture where one party acts on the presumption that he or she knows what is best for the other party, all policies adopted or actions undertaken on the basis of this presumption are not appropriately described as paternalistic actions or policies. In writing a brief, an attorney acts on the presumption that he knows what is best for his client; in bending the knees of her trainee in a certain way, the suburban golf pro acts on the presumption that she knows what is best for her pupil; in showing his apprentice how to use a lathe, the skilled cabinetmaker acts on the presumption that he knows what is best for his novice. Such actions fall under models other than that of the parent/child relationship. The attorney acts as a fiduciary in behalf of his principal; the golf instructor and cabinetmaker act as masters passing on skills. Parents, of course, can and do act in these ways; but central to the relationships in our examples is the fact that the trained professional uses his or her skills to provide a service *requested* by the client or trainee.[7] What is more, though the client or trainee must trust the professional's expertise, the client or trainee always retains the right to require a justification for professional decisions, a right (and the freedom) to ignore the professional's advice, and a right to withdraw from the relationship. At the same time, the professional retains the right to terminate the relationship if the client demands that he or she act in ways below acceptable professional standards; or, in the case of training, if the pupil simply refuses to cooperate in the learning process.

These features of professional/client and master/trainee-apprentice relationships serve to differentiate them from the relationship between parent and child. To be sure, within these relationships, the professional may impose his or her will on the client for the client's own good, or may treat the client in degrading (i.e., downgrading) ways; but the relationships themselves are not appropriately characterized as essentially paternalistic ones. They are, rather, relationships of contract, where a professional expertise is presumed, and where the client or trainee is justifiably assumed to have voluntarily entered into an arrangement for the purposes of benefiting from the professional's expertise, while retaining certain rights to accountability and rights of withdrawal.

The first suggestion I want to make, then, is that the relationship between university faculty and students more closely approximates the professional/client, specifically, the professional/trainee relationship, than the parent/child relationship. In part, this is to follow Kenneth Strike, who suggests that we understand the relationship between faculty and student as falling under the master/apprentice model.[8] We do need to distinguish in general, however, between graduate and undergraduate education and between undergraduate programs which complete professional training and those which do not. The master/apprentice model is most appropriate to the graduate student/faculty relationship. Although it may be true that the relationship between faculty and exceptionally gifted undergraduates or the relationship between faculty and undergraduates in certain undergraduate professional preparation programs often most closely approximates the master/apprentice relationship, the relationship between faculty and undergraduates, is in general, more like the suburban golf pro/trainee relationship than the cabinetmaker/apprentice relationship, insofar as the preparation being given is not assumed to be training for professional work in the faculty member's field, or is not late-stage training for work in that field. With this modification to Strike's analysis, my suggestion is that students should be understood as entering the university in much the same way that a client enters into a relationship with a trained and/or experienced professional, with the attending rights to professional accountability and rights to withdrawal of any professional/client relationship. In these relationships, the professional is presumed to have an expertise which, it is assumed by the client on contract, will be used to further the relevant interests of the client, but where pursuit of the client's relevant interests is also presumed to be constrained by some norms of professional practice.

The University/Student Relationship

But it must be acknowledged immediately that the university/student relationship is far more complex than relationships between clients and attorneys, and trainees and golf pros, and apprentices and master cabinetmakers. The university is not an individual; nor is the university expected to serve some single, relatively simple interest of its students. Rather, the university is an extremely complex institution which is expected to serve a variety of interests of its students, as well as interests of others, both within and outside the university community. Chief among the university's responsibilities toward its students and the wider community is the transmission of knowledge in particular fields which, in many cases, is part of preparation for a particular profession or occupation. Contemporary philosophers of education sometimes urge that we understand the main purpose of education to be to produce autonomous individuals. Kleinig, for example, argues that "the purpose of education, as a valuable enterprise, [is] to bring people with activated and developing capacities for autonomous agency" into being.[9] Other theorists urge that in addition to preparation for the professions, the university's main purposes include the formation of educated persons fit for citizenship in a free society, and the cultivation of individuals for their own purposes.[10] Let us assume for the sake of efficiency that such goals are proper to the university. But now it can be argued that goals like developing capacities for autonomous agency, preparation for citizenship, and cultivation of the person for his or her own purposes begin to make the university/student relationship more resemble the relationship between parent and child than the professional/client relationship. Thus, if we accept this variety of obligations towards its students, the university seems to share features of the professional/client relationship in general, and in particular the master/trainee relationship and the master/apprentice relationship, as well as the parent/child relationship. But even if it is the case that the university shares some responsibilities with parents, I want to suggest that the university/student relationship is more *unlike* the parent/child relationship than it is like these others. And this is essentially because (1) the student voluntarily enters into a relationship with another agent (in this case, a corporate agent), for the presumed purpose of forwarding certain interests or pursuing certain goods which the agent (or agency) has made clear it will pursue; (2) the student and the university are both free to terminate the contract for the variety of reasons already mentioned. Thus, these features of the student/university relationship seem to place it squarely in the class of contractual arrangements.

Academic Paternalism and Paternalistic Rationales

It might be suggested, however, that the student's so-called contract with the university is itself paternalistic, since, among other things, it is a contract which gives the university a right to forward certain (presumed) interests of the student. We could decide to describe the relationship this way; but to do so would obliterate any meaningful distinction between the contract model of relationships and the paternalistic model, since the description entails that any contract which involves serving some good of the client is to be classified as a paternalistic one. This muddies the conceptual waters in a way it seems preferable to avoid if we hope to retain any distinction between relationships between adults which, by their very nature, require a special justification and those which do not. Thus, for the purposes of conceptual clarity, it seems best to distinguish contracts for service from relationships which involve imposing benefits independent of considerations of the agreement of beneficiaries.

Despite this, it is important to emphasize that within a contractual relationship, a client may be treated paternalistically, either by having his wishes ignored for his own good, or by being otherwise treated (by agents or policies) as a child. Thus, even if we characterize faculty/student and university/student relationships as contractual, they may yet be quite unlike other professional/client contractual relationships where clients are assumed to have a veto power over actions (or policies) in service of the client's interest. When we think of academic requirements within the university, it is clear that students do not have such a veto power. Let me turn, then, to academic policies which are often thought to be paternalistically grounded; but which, I shall suggest, are not in reality grounded in paternalistic rationales (i.e., are not and should not be supposed by their proponents and enforcers to be justified primarily because they are assumed to be in the best interest of students) and are not policies which otherwise treat students as children, even though students are not free to decline completing these requirements as part of their coursework or degree programs.

Departmental Requirements

Consider, for example, typical departmental requirements for the successful completion of a major—for example, a philosophy major. If we were to ask philosophy faculty in standard departments why we have such requirements, the initial response is likely to be something like, "These are things any philosophy major should know." I shall return to this "argument" for requirements in a moment, because I think it is a crucial part of the most plausible justification for major requirements; but first let us consider a concrete case.

Suppose that a major comes to the philosophy faculty and says that he would prefer not to meet the distribution requirements—he wants, let us suppose, to skip logic and the histories. We can imagine that at least some faculty might initially respond with the argument that having the required background is in his best interest. That this *is* in his best interest might be the case if he hopes to go on to graduate school in preparation for teaching philosophy at the university level. But suppose that the student has no such aspirations—suppose that he is already a successful entrepreneur or is preparing for a career in medicine—he simply likes French existentialism, or American pragmatism, or eastern philosophy and wants to do all his work in that area. Is it the least bit likely in such a case that the faculty would take its justification for insisting that he complete the requirements to rest on his interests? When pressed, the argument is surely that there are certain standards to be met for the completion of a major, and that, we might say, is that, whether meeting those standards is in this young man's best interest or not. In fact, "forcing" such a student through departmental requirements for a major in philosophy may not be in his interest at all. Of course, the faculty might try to persuade him of the value of a rounded background in the discipline, or advise him to take another major; but the fact that his interests would not be best served by completing the distribution requirements in philosophy will not suffice as a justification for waiving the requirements if he wants to complete his university tenure with a degree in philosophy.

This argument from standards implicitly appeals to the somewhat vague concepts of what I shall call 'academic ideas' and 'educational ideas.' I mean for these terms to cover a wide variety of paradigms which count for universities, departments (and other academic units), and instructors as standards of perfection or excellence to be approximated in university education. By an 'academic ideal' I mean (roughly) a notion of what any educated person should know. The core commitment here is to the transferral of a certain subject matter and the development of certain skills. Understood in this way, universities, departments, and instructors may each be said to have academic ideals. For example, a university committed to the ideal of providing a liberal education will require that all students distribute their coursework in ways which help to expose them to the questions, methods, factual content, and major theories in a wide variety of disciples. Or a philosophy department concerned with providing its students with a broad substantive and methodological background may require that students show competence in (say) logic and complete courses which expose them to figures in the history of philosophy, various schools in contemporary philosophy, as well as various questions in metaphysics, epistemology, ethics, and so on. Some academic ideals may emphasize formal preparation in method over content, others may emphasize content over method. Thus, one philosophy program might require more training in, for example, logic, linguistic analysis, and/or phenomenology while another requires more in, e.g., the history of philosophy. Similar things might be said about various curricula in English, some of which might require more coursework in, for example, literary criticism, while others require more in literature proper. As regards instructors, they too can be expected to have academic ideals in the sense under discussion—general views regarding what any educated person should know, more specific views regarding what should be achieved in content and method in a given field, and quite particular views regarding what content and methods should be mastered in their own courses. In addition to all such views on content and methods, academic ideals may include certain standards of achievement, that is, criteria for judging incompetence, competence, and excellence in mastery of the content to be passed on and the skills to be developed.

I understand 'educational ideal' somewhat more broadly (and also roughly) to include academic ideals as well as the more general goals of university education as those goals are sought through academic requirements, and standards for *how* what is to be transmitted is to be transmitted, as well as standards for what kinds of personal characteristics an educator should manifest. Thus, a university's educational ideal may involve goals like those mentioned earlier (e.g., the preparation of qualified professionals, the development of persons with an activated and progressing capacity for autonomous agency, the preparation of persons capable of taking an intelligent part in a free society, etc.), a commitment to the academic ideal of liberal education, as well as to certain parameters governing characteristics educators should manifest. Departments and individual faculty may share the educational ideal of the university and may add to this as part of their educational ideal an academic ideal for education within a particular field of inquiry, and certain views on how content is to be passed on and skills developed. And an instructor's educational ideal may include special commitments—for example, to improving her students' abilities to argue orally, to conducting herself and her courses in ways which approximate certain standards which she takes to manifest excellence in teaching. Thus, an instructor might be committed to a lecture/discussion format, to providing class time for student debates or sustained discussion of concrete cases, etc., as well as to approximating certain standards governing how an educator should respond to various communications from students, including questions in class, responses to answers on examinations and student efforts in papers, and so on.

Although these remarks on academic and educational ideals still leave the boundaries of these concepts somewhat blurred and overlapping at points, they should be enough to make the point of my argument clear. And that point is just that universities, departments, and individual instructors may be said to have educational ideals which serve as the grounding of their academic requirements.

To return to our maverick philosophy major and departmental requirements—the example suggests that what might have the appearance of paternalism of the interfering kind is not paternalism of any kind at all. Requirements do limit student choices. But we begin to see that the most plausible fundamental justification of such requirements lies in a justifiable commitment to an academic ideal, which is believed to be captured in academic requirements, and which must be approximated if a department is to give its stamp of approval to someone's work in the form of a degree. This, of course, is not to suggest that *any* set of departmental distribution requirements will do. But it is to suggest that the real justification for departmental requirements does not lie in a paternalistic rationale, but in the attempt to approximate an academic ideal.

What is more, I do not mean to simply put forth an empirical prediction about how faculty would, when pressed, justify departmental requirements. My claim is stronger than that, and empirical predictions are meant to serve only as a bolstering consideration. Departments have an obligation to make public the meaning of having completed a course of study within them. And I mean to suggest that this obligation, coupled with an academic ideal believed to be captured in academic requirements, is *formally* sufficient to justify departmental requirements—that is, there is no need to make a direct appeal to the interests of students for a justification of such requirements. Again, any particular set of requirements must itself be justified, and what goes into that justification will involve the history and current status of a field of inquiry. The point is just that obligations of a university department other than the best interests of students (in general or in particular) play the crucial role in establishing the general right to impose certain program requirements on all its majors; and once we see this, it should be apparent that the charge of imposing departmental requirements on students for their own good is blunted.[11]

College and University Requirements

If we turn to typical college and university requirements, the same argument applies. The institution has duties not only to its students, but to the wider society as well. Part of the university's duty to the wider society consists in seeing that knowledge and skills are passed on from one generation to the next, and this involves making clear that certain standards in accord with an academic ideal will be met.[12] Thus, though a student may decide that he does not want to complete college or university requirements for a regular degree, the college or university may (and will) decide that he must complete them or forego the degree, and this without making any appeal whatever to the student's best interest. The university's commitments to certain academic requirements, as well as certain standards of excellence, is, then, prior to the contract with the student, and these commitments serve as the background conditions of that contract itself.

I have already suggested that the student enters the university freely. I do not want to underestimate parental pressures and the pressures of occupational preparation in modern life. But insofar as there are reasonable alternatives to entering the university in general, and any given university in particular, the assumption that the student enters the university voluntarily is justified (in the ordinary case).[13] When the student enters the university, she enters a system where, essentially, the agreement is that if she successfully fulfills the academic requirements, she will leave certified by the system as, minimally, having successfully completed a specified academic program.

Once in the system, there should be nothing to prevent the student's working for changes, including changes in the academic terms of the contract. For its part, the system (at all levels) needs to take well-considered requests for such changes seriously. This is merely a requirement of reasonableness, which binds any relationship between persons, and social systems generally. But if a system refuses to change the terms of a contract (e.g., by refusing to drop distribution requirements), it does not follow that it has acted outside of its just domain. It may refuse for good or bad reasons; but any complaint about refusal to change the academic terms must be based either on the claim that the initial terms were themselves unjust, or that the reasons for refusal to change the terms are themselves unreasonable.[14] It is not enough that one party to the academic contract (or even a majority of parties to the contract) want the terms changed—as an *academic* institution, the university is not and should not be a democratic community. If it were, the university could not fulfill its obligations to the wider society. If the original terms of the academic contract are fair and public, then the university does not act unjustly or paternalistically or otherwise immorally *simply* because it refuses to release students from established requirements.

In-Course Requirements

The same sorts of things can be said about the justification of teaching policies of individual faculty members. A faculty member need not act paternalistically in setting out requirements for a course. Though it may be true that Professor Writebedder assigns two papers instead of one in his lower level philosophy courses because he thinks this will be most helpful to the students both as regards writing and grades, his deepest justification for such a practice need not stop here.

Indeed its stopping here would be more strange than one might at first think; for why should *this* instructor be requiring anything at all of *these* persons for their own good? Imagine that we question Professor Writebedder on his paper policy, asking if the policy is firm—that is, if no exceptions will be made for either those students who do not care about improving their writing and/or grades or for those who write excellent first papers. How might he answer? If he says the policy is firm, and we ask for a justification, what might he say? As regards students who do not care about improving their writing and/or grades, he might appeal to some educational ideal which he is convinced his position as a professional educator binds him to aspire to; and this, he might argue, includes requiring certain exercises of students, whether or not they care about the gains to be made from those exercises. As regards students who have done well in a first exercise, he might say quite the same thing—that a large part of his idea of what it means to be a good educator is to arrange a course so that *he* has done all he might to have his students leave the course taking all that might be taken from it.

But, again, the question arises as to why *this* instructor is involved with *these* students in pursuing *his* educational ideal. Were we to ask Professor Writebedder why he believes he is justified in imposing his academic ideals on these people, the most plausible reply is that *these* students, by coming into his course, are to be understood as having contracted him to do his best to educate them. They might, of course, attempt to persuade him to alter his ideal. But the point is that the most plausible deep justification of what might seem to be paternalistic course requirements and teaching methodologies is again tied to contract and professional standards which form part of the background assumptions of contract in the professional/client relationship.

The instructor who provides his students with the best education he finds it feasible to provide because it is to be understood as part of the background that this is what he has been hired to do does not, then, act in a way best captured by the paternalistic model. Rather, he acts as an employed professional; and if he is asked to lower his standards he acts within his moral right to refuse, just as a doctor who refuses to prescribe laetrile for the treatment of malignancy acts within her moral rights in so refusing. This is *not* to suggest that any such refusal will itself be justified, or that any educational ideal is as desirable as any other. Nor is it to deny more generally that well-meaning professionals can ever violate a client's rights by adhering to some wrongheaded professional ideal. But it is to hold that a faculty member who sets firm course policies has a general entitlement to do so—that the setting of such policies is within his or her proper sphere of authority, in just the same way that setting public policy is within the proper sphere of government authority—and that setting such policies is not plausibly understood as being in need of justification because it involves interference with the self-regarding choices of adults for their own good, or because it otherwise necessarily treats adults as children. A government may set a bad or unjust public policy; but when it does, the problem is not with public policy setting itself, but with the injustice or undesirability or harmfulness of a particular policy. And it is quite the same with universities and their faculties.

Conclusion

I have suggested that the most plausible moral underpinning for academic requirements in the university is not a paternalistic one insofar as paternalism is understood to involve the imposition of will on another for that other's own good or an offensive superiority which treats adults like children. Like the golf trainee or the cabinetmaker's apprentice, the student who comes to the university is expected to be relatively inexperienced in the fields she undertakes to study. And the university is expected to provide her with instructors who do indeed know better than she does what is good for her as regards her learning in those fields. This arrangement, I have argued, is not to be understood as a paternalistic one.

But this is a highly general point, which does no more than clear the way for addressing more concrete questions. Not the least among these is the question of deciding when the pursuit of an educational ideal might become an unjustifiable imposition of an educator's values on students. There is no such thing as value-free educating, just as there is no such thing as a value-free practice of medicine. And in both cases, the hard questions involve deciding precisely what values and where a practitioner's values appropriately enter into the professional/client relationship. Sometimes, it might seem that worries like this are not as troublesome in higher education as they might be in a practice like medicine, since students can more easily drop a course and pick up another than patients can drop a physician and pick up another; and, particularly, since what will be expected of the student is easily learned in advance of entering the university and (if faculty members are, as they should be, concerned with informed consent) since what will be required in a given course will be clearly explained to students before they commit themselves to that course. But taking this question as it arises in education as less worrisome than when it arises in other areas of professional practice is mistaken and morally dangerous. Indeed, it may well be the case that the imposition of values in the educator's pursuit of some educational ideal is far more worrisome than (say) the physician's refusal to prescribe laetrile. And this is because the educator's values might be more deeply hidden, and thus, the imposition of will may be less recognizable. This, then, is just one of the many issues that need to be dealt with in detail in a full discussion of academic paternalism.

I have not discussed non-academic policies and decisions governing student life, or the worrisome (benevolent and non-benevolent) attitudes toward students which sometimes motivate policies and individual behaviors on the parts of administrators and faculty in the university. But it should go without saying that policies and behaviors which treat students in degrading ways will not bear moral scrutiny. The university has a right to maintain order in its community, and faculty have a right to maintain order in their courses. But policies, practices, or behaviors which fail to accord students the respect due to generally competent adults in the wider society have no more place in the university than they have elsewhere. Student life is not and should not be life with father (or mother). It is life in the free society, life among citizens; and the university must be a place where citizenship, with its attendant responsibilities and rights, is carefully practiced. Part of what this means in a free society is that matters pertaining to student life must be decided democratically within the bounds of the academic responsibilities of the university. In the past decade new democratic policies governing student life have emerged in many universities (e.g., those governing dormitory life). These are steps in the right direction. But student publications are still unduly influenced by administrators; and deans of students are still often too eager to be surrogate parents; and too many faculty still fail to realize that though many are young, university students are to be treated as adults and shown the same general respect for freedom of choice and freedom to dissent due any adults.

Adopting the contract model does not, then, do any more than establish the most general parameters for thinking about the relationship between the university and its personnel and students. The next, and most difficult, questions pertain to carefully specifying acceptable academic and non-academic terms of that contract.

Notes

1. Although there are obvious reasons for preferring 'parentalism' (and its cognates) to 'paternalism' (and its cognates), I shall use the standard terminology, partly because linguistic behavior dies hard, and partly because the technical notion of 'paternalism' has come to include degrading treatment not associated with being a good parent. (See the next section in the text.)

2. See N. Fotion, "Paternalism," *Ethics* 89:2 (1979): 191–98, for an interesting comparison between the paradigm case of paternalism and so-called paternalistic public policies.

3. John Kleinig, *Paternalism* (Totowa, NJ: Rowman and Allenheld, 1984), p. 4.

4. The example comes from Joel Feinberg, *The Moral Limits of the Criminal Law, Volume 3: Harm to Self* (New York: Oxford University Press, 1986). The governance of student life, which involves so much in the way of concern about order in the university, constantly involves the challenge to avoid paternalism of this sort.

5. It is common in the contemporary philosophical literature to characterize paternalism as the interference with an individual for his own good. See, e.g., Gerald Dworkin, "Paternalism," in R. A. Wasserstrom (ed.), *Morality and the Law* (Belmont, CA: Wadsworth, 1971): 107–26; Jeffrie G. Murphy, "Incompetence and Paternalism," *Archiv für Rechts-und Socialphilosophie* 60:4 (1974): 465–85; Rosemary Carter, "Justifying Paternalism," *Canadian Journal of Philosophy* 7:1 (1977): 133–45; Dennis Thompson, "Paternalism in Medicine, Law, and Public Policy," in Daniel Callahan and Sissela Bok (eds.), *Ethics Teaching in Higher Education* (New York: Plenum Press, 1980): 245–75; John D. Hodson, "The Principle of Paternalism," *American Philosophical Quarterly* 14:1 (1977): 61–69; C. L. Ten, "Paternalism and Morality," *Ratio* 13 (1971): 55–66; David A. J. Richards, *The Moral Criticism of Law* (Encino, CA: Dickenson, 1977): chap. 5; and Bernard Gert and Charles Culver, "Paternalistic Behavior," *Philosophy and Public Affairs* 6:1 (1976): 45–57, among others. Although I believe there are significant problems with this as a general characterization of paternalistic behavior or policy (see my "Liberty, Beneficence, and Involuntary Confinement," *Journal of Medicine and Philosophy* 9:3 [1984]: 261–93), I shall accept it as a working characterization of the kind of paternalism I focus on in this paper.

6. In searching for the appropriate model of the university/student and faculty/student relationship, I want to find a description which is both empirically plausible (i.e., one which does not make false empirical assumptions about the parties involved) and morally attractive (i.e., one which takes rights and interests seriously). On this, see, e.g., Michael D. Bayles, *Professional Ethics* (Belmont, CA: Wadsworth, 1981): chap. 4.

7. There are some cases, of course, where a professional/client relationship exists, but the client has not requested the professional's services—e.g., cases

128   *A Professor's Duties*

of involuntary psychiatric hospitalization and treatment. But in looking for a general model, one should not look to unusual cases, since these cases lack features of the normal case or have additional features. Again, see, e.g., Bayles, *supra.*

8. Kenneth Strike, *Liberty and Learning* (New York: St. Martin's Press, 1982).

9. John Kleinig, *Philosophical Issues in Education* (New York: St. Martin's Press, 1982): 146.

10. See, e.g., Robert S. Morison, "Some Aspects of Policy-Making in the American University," *Daedalus* (Summer 1970): *Rights and Responsibilities: The University's Dilemma:* 609–44.

11. I do not mean to ignore the fact that departments sometimes put in requirements for self-serving reasons. The moral status of some reasons for adding requirements, however, is unclear. For example, a department might add to its requirements in order to justify hiring a specialist in some area, and a hefty part of the motivation might be to elevate the department's status in the eyes of the profession. Such an addition may or may not serve the genuine educational interests of that department's students. Though assessing academic ideals is beyond the scope of this paper, it should go without saying that any such additions which do not clearly serve as an academic ideal conscientiously accepted by a department will not be justified.

12. Much of this assumes that we are discussing the typical university. But there is, of course, room in society for a variety of educational institutions with a variety of educational ideals. The traditional university functions according to the expert/trainee model—the experts are presumed to know their arts and presumed to have the capacity to make competent judgments about content and method in their areas of expertise; students are expected to be educated up to some level within those areas. But this need not be the only model of higher education. Some institutions elect to adopt a more Rogerian model, where the exclusive aim of education [. . .] is the development or revelation of natural capacities, and where it is held that the pressing of students through a preconceived process, designed by so-called experts is repressive and a genuine enemy of development. (See, e.g., A. S. Neill's *Summerhill* [New York: Hart Publishing Company, 1960] for an example of this view of the aims of education.) Traditional ways of educating can surely be (and certainly sometimes have been) repressive. But it is not necessary that education which guides and offers content be viciously restrictive, repressive, or otherwise growth inhibiting. See Strike, *supra,* for a thoughtful discussion of this point and the liberating function of traditional education.

13. I deal with the question of standards for presuming voluntariness in "Paternalism and Voluntariness," *Canadian Journal of Philosophy* 16:2 (1986): 199–220.

14. Unreasonable refusals to make a change might include refusals to alter methodologies or course offerings when such changes are needed to enhance understanding or keep a department current with widely accepted disciplinary standards.

SECTION TWO

Neutrality and Grading

The Philosopher as Teacher: Tolerance and Teaching Philosophy*
Hugh T. Wilder

For several years I have been including on assignment sheets passed out to my philosophy students a note expressing what I will call here the principle of liberal tolerance.[1] The principle is important, and seems to be shared by most teachers and students, in most disciplines. I usually express the principle to students in something like the following way: "In evaluating papers, I care more about the arguments you give than the conclusions you defend. Although I care about what you believe, my immediate concern is with *why* you believe what you believe. Papers will be graded more on cogency of argumentation than on the substantive claims made. And of course, students don't have to agree with me on substantive issues in order to get a good grade."

I recently helped team-teach an introductory philosophy of religion course, in which the principle of liberal tolerance assumed some importance. Most of the rest of this paper is taken up with a discussion of worries I have about the principle of liberal tolerance; an anecdote taken from the introductory philosophy of religion class should help to introduce some of these worries. The course was taught by five instructors, all atheists, to over 200 freshmen, mostly believers in God. It was mainly because of this difference in belief between instructors and students that I stressed the principle of liberal tolerance; because of the imbalance of power in such a large lecture class, I was sensitive

* From *Metaphilosophy,* vol. 9, Nos. 3 and 4 (July/October, 1978), 311–323, reprinted here with the permission of Blackwell Publishers.

129

to issues about fairness and prejudice in grading, and I wanted to assure students that believers as well as atheists could get A's in the course.

Because we spent some time in this course analyzing and evaluating the traditional proofs for the existence of God, I introduced some basic concepts in logic, such as truth, falsity, argument, validity, soundness, and inductive strength. I pointed out that although logicians are mainly concerned with techniques for determining the validity of arguments, the paradigm cases of what we intuitively take to be good, persuasive arguments are *sound* arguments, i.e., valid arguments with true premises.

Now, a perceptive student confronted me with a problem after class one day. She had put together this lesson in logic with my principle of liberal tolerance, and accused me of being disingenuous when I assured students that, thanks to my principle of tolerance, believers as well as atheists could get A's in the course. Her point was that my lesson in logic had revealed my principle of tolerance to be a sham: according to my principle, I was supposed to value good arguments above conclusions which I take to be true; but according to my logic, arguments which I think are good must have conclusions which I take to be true. The student, a believer in God, became quite angry in making her point: "You say you look for good arguments, not necessarily conclusions you agree with; but now we find out that 'good arguments' must have true conclusions, or at least what *you* take to be good arguments must have conclusions *you* take to be true. So your principle of tolerance is empty; you're an atheist, so no one will be able to give you a 'good argument' for the claim that God exists; so much for your kind of tolerance!"

This confrontation was very troubling to me. The student seemed to be pointing out a contradiction which is deeply rooted in my thinking and teaching. On the one hand, I do value reason and careful argumentation in philosophy, and I also think it incorrect to give students good grades simply because they agree with me. But on the other hand, I am an atheist; I believe that no good argument can show that God exists. It seems, therefore, that believers *would* have a hard time getting good grades in my class, because they would not be able to give the good arguments for their position which would earn them the good grades.

Considerations such as these helped me come to believe that the principle of liberal tolerance is untenable. This is an important issue, because the principle seems to be so widely accepted, by both teachers and students, especially in courses on controversial topics, such as normative ethics, political philosophy, and philosophy of religion. It is in precisely these controversial areas that the principle of liberal tolerance is usually thought to be most important; but, as I shall argue later, it is in these same areas that adherence to the principle can cause the most harm. In what follows, I first examine some reasons teachers and students have for accepting the principle of liberal tolerance. Second, I explain why I think the principle is untenable, and, in conclusion, I suggest an alternative approach to the issue of grading and tolerance, which seems to me to be a humane and honest alternative to adherence to the principle of liberal tolerance.

Let me say immediately that despite my reservations, the principle of liberal tolerance has much to recommend it; many of our reasons for endorsing it are laudable. For example, a teacher whose grading procedures are guided by this principle is surely preferable to an authoritarian teacher whose grading procedures are not based on reason, but on arbitrary personal prejudice and whim. And, the concept of liberal tolerance seems to provide one way for distinguishing between honest teaching—based on liberal tolerance—and indoctrination. Because indoctrination is to be avoided in philosophy classes, and liberal tolerance helps us avoid it, liberal tolerance seems to be a valuable principle. I will return to these apparent advantages of adherence to the principle of liberal tolerance later.

I have made it a practice to tell students during the first few days of classes that I endorse the principle of liberal tolerance; I try to explain the principle, and my reasons for accepting it. In doing so, I want to stress to students the importance of reason in doing and teaching philosophy. I want students to know that reason, rather than appeals to authority, prejudice, or unsupported opinion should be their guide in writing papers, and that I try to make it my guide in evaluating papers. I want students to know that agreement with me on substantive issues is much less important to me, as a teacher and grader, than is agreement with me on the standards of argumentation and other methodological concerns.

Another motive I have for explicitly endorsing the principle of liberal tolerance is to avoid the hubris involved in the usual alternative to liberal tolerance, namely, that sort of professional omniscience which results all too often in repressive intolerance in classrooms. Needless to say, I do not know all the answers to all the problems in philosophy and I do not pretend otherwise while I am teaching. Since I am not sure of many answers myself, I can hardly criticize and down-grade students for not agreeing with me. This professed ignorance of answers to philosophical problems supports my toleration of positions different from mine in class.

Adoption of this attitude of tolerance in class has several other salutary effects. It encourages creativity and independence in both class discussion and students' written work, by de-emphasizing the teacher's role as authority figure. And, the principle of liberal tolerance does something to help eliminate a form of epistemological relativism which seems to be endemic among students today. The sort of relativism I am talking about consists of the adoption of contradictory sets of beliefs for use in different contexts—specifically, different classrooms.[2] Students hear teachers lecture with great authority on different topics; often these teachers (e.g., a liberal political scientist, a conservative economist, and a Marxist political philosopher) don't agree with each other on basic assumptions, and all too often don't say anything that matters very immediately to the students. In such a situation, students are likely to come to believe that one set of beliefs is true for economics, a second set, perhaps contradicting the first, is true for philosophy, and so on. The principle of liberal tolerance, if adopted by teachers, can help to overcome this kind of relativism (although it can also support it, as I shall argue below). Liberal tolerance can help overcome this kind of relativism by eliminating one source of it, namely, the dogmatism in teachers who claim to know all the correct answers and are not willing to listen to (and give good grades for) alternatives. If students know their teachers will tolerate reasoned disagreement, then they do not have to unreasonably adopt their teachers' beliefs as true, at least "as true while in teacher X's class." Put very simply, the adoption of the principle of liberal tolerance encourages independent thinking in the classroom, insofar as it liberates students from the need to parrot back the teacher's beliefs in order to get good grades.

I suspect that most teachers of philosophy agree with my principle of liberal tolerance, and that they do so for reasons similar to mine. Most students also seem to agree with the principle. Again, let me say at the outset that some students' reasons for agreeing with the principle are laudable, even though, as I have already suggested, I believe adoption of the principle to be inimical to the students' best interests.

I think that students agree with the principle of liberal tolerance for two basic reasons: it helps to ensure fairness in grading practices, and it helps guard against professorial dogmatism, which so often allows teaching to degenerate into indoctrination. It is true that dogmatic teachers are often unfair graders, and adoption of the principle helps guard against both dogmatism and some kinds of unfair grading.

In addition, most students have learned, very early in their careers, several general political/epistemological principles which seem to support the principle of liberal tolerance. One of these general principles is that people have the right to believe whatever they want. This principle seems to be almost universally accepted among students today. I have heard vague appeals to the U.S. Bill of Rights in defense of the principle, and J. S. Mill explicitly argues for the principle in *On Liberty*: he says that the private sphere of action

> is the appropriate region of human liberty. It comprises, first, the inward domain of consciousness, demanding liberty of conscience in the most comprehensive sense, liberty of thought and feelings, absolute freedom of opinion and sentiment on all subjects, practical or speculative, scientific, moral, or theological.[3]

Translated into the context of schooling and grading, the principle claims that people should not be graded for what they believe on substantive issues, especially on moral, aesthetic, religious, and generally philosophical issues. Especially, people should not be downgraded for believing things which the teacher does not believe. This political/epistemological principle leads directly to the principle of liberal tolerance, and I believe acceptance of it accounts in large measure for students' acceptance of the principle of liberal tolerance.

This first political/epistemological principle is often used in conjunction with two other similar principles in defenses of liberal tolerance. The two other political/epistemological principles concern, first, the alleged distinction between facts and values, and, second, a particular conception of scientific and academic objectivity. With respect to the fact/value distinction, students may agree with Mill that we ought to be free to believe anything we please in "all subjects, practical or speculative, scientific, moral, or theological"; but they admit that teachers are justified in down-grading students for disagreement with them on questions of *fact*. And further, argue defenders of the fact/value distinction, since truth and falsity are applicable to beliefs about facts, but not to beliefs about values, students should not be downgraded for disagreement with the teacher on value issues. Since there are no truths about values, the argument goes, teachers cannot claim to know any truths about values; and, since teachers can't know any truths about values, they can't down-grade students for not knowing these truths either. On questions about values, all beliefs are mere opinions, and one opinion is as good as another. Since nearly all of my students lump philosophy into the pile of value-oriented subjects, much is made of the principle of liberal tolerance in philosophy classes. Students believe that here, where personal, value-laden beliefs are the stock in trade, it is most important that the worth of every opinion be recognized—i.e., be given a good grade, at least if it is stated clearly and some reasons are given in support of it.

Finally, what I must call a myth of scientific objectivity is also frequently used, often in conjunction with the two other political/ epistemological principles just described, to support the principle of liberal tolerance. According to this myth of scientific objectivity, there is a split between matters of personal human concern and matters untainted by such concern. The realm of personal human concern is the realm of value, now called the realm of the subjective; matters untainted by human concern are the objective facts of the hard sciences. The subjective/objective distinction is usually drawn slightly differently than the fact/value distinction, as the subjective subjects are usually said to include the human sciences as well as art, morals, and religion. Philosophy remains, however, the queen of the subjective sciences, where subjectivity runs rampant. Truth and falsity are concepts reserved for use in the objective sciences, and nothing can be known with any certainty in the realm of the subjective. As my students invariably wonder, pointedly, at midterm and finals time, "Since everything in philosophy is subjective, how can you grade our papers at all, let alone down-grade us for disagreeing with you?" According to such thinking as this, the principle of liberal tolerance is axiomatic; it would be as absurd to down-grade a philosophy student for believing that God exists as it would be not to down-grade a geography student for believing that the earth is flat.

II

I believe we may now safely stop amassing defenses of the principle of liberal tolerance, and begin to sort out the tolerable from the intolerable defenses already given. In what follows, I hope to convince the reader that the principle of liberal tolerance is itself intolerable.

First, we may dispense with the fact/value and subjective/objective distinctions, insofar as these distinctions are used to support the principle of liberal tolerance. Even if it is true (and I doubt it) that (*a*) "facts" are different from "values," (b) the "subjective" sciences are different from the "objective" sciences, and (c) philosophy is neither "objective" nor "factual," we need not fly to the conclusion that rationality and truth are out of place in philosophy. Philosophers argue about the truth of philosophical claims, and with good reason. Philosophy is a rational activity, which means that some ways of doing it are better—i.e., more rational—than other ways. And, conclusions reached by these better, more rational ways of thinking are better, more rational, than conclusions reached by other ways. I am not saying that conclusions reached by non-rational means cannot be true; occasionally they are. What I am saying is that philosophy is a rational enterprise, and that conclusions reached in a rational manner, supported by sound argumentation, are more worthy (of good grades, in classroom situations) than conclusions reached in other ways.

Therefore, neither the fact/value nor the subjective/objective distinctions support the argument that since one opinion is as good as another in a philosophy class, opinions on substantive issues, such as the existence or non-existence of God, should not be graded. I believe (although I cannot argue here) that philosophical knowledge is both "factual" and "objective," if these epithets are taken to mean (as I think they should) that correct and unambiguous answers, independent of individual taste and authoritarian dogma, can be given to philosophical questions.[4] Since correct and unambiguous answers can be given to philosophical questions, I believe students should be down-graded for not knowing answers they may be expected to know. Of course, I will admit that philosophers know comparatively few of the correct answers to important philosophical questions; therefore, we ought not down-grade students for not knowing them either. The issue of what questions we can say we know the answers to is crucial, but not for my purposes here; what I am arguing is that the fact/value and subjective/objective distinctions do nothing to bolster the principle of liberal tolerance. Since philosophy is a rational enterprise, whether it is fact-oriented or value-oriented, subjective or objective, we can and should give good grades to rational answers to philosophical problems and bad grades to non-rational answers.

Lest I be misunderstood, let me add that for me the concepts of truth and falsity are subsumed under the concepts of rationality. Truth-value is one ingredient in rationality, but is neither a sufficient nor a necessary ingredient. True beliefs are not necessarily rational; they must be supported by good arguments in order to be rational. Therefore, when I argue for intolerance of non-rational work in philosophy classes, I am not advising teachers to give good grades for true beliefs and bad grades for false beliefs; I am suggesting that we take truth-value into consideration in determining grades, and to give good grades to papers which give good arguments for true beliefs. Since false beliefs stand a worse chance of being given good supporting arguments, papers expressing false beliefs stand a worse chance of being given good grades. Of course, as we all know, not all the evidence is in on all the issues in philosophy; so a strong argument can be given for a belief which may turn out to be false. But this does not damage my argument that philosophy teachers ought to be intolerant of non-rational attempts at doing philosophy.

My argument so far simply amounts to an indictment of the distinction between cogent argumentation and true conclusion, which is implicit in the principle of liberal tolerance. According to this principle, teachers were to grade arguments given, not conclusions reached. I have been pointing out that arguments include conclusions; as the student in the anecdote in Part I quickly recognized, it is unlikely that cogent arguments will include false conclusions. I have been urging that teachers of philosophy recognize this fact, and be intolerant of false conclusions when contained in weak arguments. If this means down-grading students for believing in God, then so be it.[5]

It may be objected at this point that I am glossing over the crucial distinction between claims *we take* to be true or false and claims which *are* true or false. The skeptic may argue that liberal tolerance is required, because it is unfair to down-grade students for not knowing what we merely take to be true. The skeptic argues either that we can't know any truths, or that we can't know that we know any truths; in either case, we can't down-grade students when they disagree with us.

This is an important objection, and the distinction is often recognized by students, as it was by the woman in the anecdote in Part I ("now we find out that 'good arguments' must have true conclusions, or at least what *you* take to be good arguments must have conclusions *you* take to be true"). My reply to the objection is that it is actually defenders of liberal tolerance who tend to obfuscate the distinction between claims taken to be true and claims which are true; my own position is, in part, an attempt to restore this distinction to its important place. First, I admit that it is very difficult to determine when we know that a claim is true; nevertheless, I also take it as obvious that we do know that some philosophical claims are true. To deny this is to deceive one's self: we *act* as if some philosophical claims are true, and as if we know them to be true (e.g., that murder is wrong, that "affirming the consequent" is a fallacy, etc., etc.). Rather than glossing over the distinction between claims taken to be true and claims which are true, I am urging that we make it a main part of our tasks as teachers of philosophy to teach this distinction to students. I must assert with little argument here that the skeptic is simply wrong when he claims that we can't know any truths, or that we can't know that we know any truths. Professors of philosophy do know some truths, and we must make the hard distinctions ourselves between the truth and what we have taken to be the truth. Most importantly, as teachers we must help students learn to distinguish between the truth and what they have taken as the truth. The principle of liberal tolerance does nothing to encourage teachers and students to make this hard distinction.

Of course, the risks in abandoning liberal tolerance are high; teaching can easily degenerate into indoctrination in beliefs the teacher takes to be true, and liberal tolerance helps guard against this. Indoctrination in beliefs taken by the teacher to be true (whether in fact true or not) is wrong, and has no place in true education. In the concluding section of the paper I will attempt to show further how teachers may avoid the Scylla of liberal tolerance and the Charybdis of indoctrination.

There are several further problems with the principle of liberal tolerance. One was hinted at above, and needs to be spelled out here. It is that the principle of liberal tolerance can lead to a pernicious kind of epistemological relativism, according to which contradictory beliefs can be true for different individuals. As I said earlier, liberal tolerance *can* help guard against adoption of this view, but it can also foster it. When teachers are tolerant of all views on substantive matters, this is often taken to mean that all views could be true. And, the tolerant, non-dogmatic teacher often means just that: any *one* of these alternative views could be true, and we don't know which is true now. Unfortunately, many people conclude from the teacher's tolerance of contradictory beliefs that he or she means by this action that *all* of the beliefs could be true at one and the same time. We need not be tolerant of this chain of reasoning.

Thus, liberal tolerance can lead to epistemological relativism; and, epistemological relativism can lead to misology, or distrust and hatred of reason. For example, in my earlier spirit of liberalism I have often presented in class several different answers to a question, suggesting that they could all be true; I would present the case for each as strongly as possible, hoping that my students would buy only the truth in this marketplace of ideas which I had set up. However, my plan often backfired; rather than buying the truth, my students often rejected all answers. They appeared to reject them, and often to reject reasoning itself, because they had been seduced into believing each of the successive answers to the question which I had described. They accepted each answer in succession, and then realized that not all the answers could be true. Because each answer had been presented so seductively, they concluded that there must be something wrong with reason itself, that its apparently good use could lead to such contradictory results. I now believe that my liberal tolerance led students to adopt this form of misology.

This hypothesis about the source of my students' misology is supported by Plato's beautiful analysis of misology in the *Meno* (89c–91c). Plato there argues that people can become misologists when they uncritically accept arguments and subsequently find them to be fallacious. Plato's cure for misology is to encourage people to be more critical in their first examination of arguments; if one is careful about choosing one's friends in the first place, one will not often be disappointed later. My arguments here amount to much the same recommendation. Liberal tolerance encourages students to adopt an uncritical attitude toward their beliefs, and this uncritical attitude can lead to misology. The cure is to give up liberal tolerance, which means, concretely, to stop presenting all sides of an issue as persuasively as possible, and to stop encouraging students to think that all answers to questions can be correct. We now know the answers to some questions, and we will be fostering misology if we do not teach these as clearly and unequivocally as possible.

Another reason why a teacher's tolerance of contradictory beliefs can lead to epistemological relativism or even skepticism is that tolerance can signify to students that the teacher doesn't care what his or her students believe. This lack of care could stem from a belief in the teacher that the students' beliefs don't matter, because they are not beliefs about practical matters of immediate concern. Thus, tolerance can buttress the students' prevalent belief that philosophical knowledge is "purely academic" in a pejorative sense, that the truth-value of philosophical claims is a matter of no practical importance. Since the truth of philosophical claims is so unimportant, reason some students, one belief is as good as another; in fact, we might as well call them all true. I have heard many students argue this way, especially in introductory classes, and it makes me realize how I have failed as a teacher to teach students the importance of reason in philosophy.

Because the principle of liberal tolerance can foster this kind of relativism, I have come to believe it is a dangerous way to help achieve a few good ends, such as a fair grading system.

What I have been saying is that the principle of liberal tolerance can foster an alienation of students from themselves—from their beliefs, specifically. Teachers' tolerance of all beliefs can signify to students a lack of importance in their beliefs, and students can come to view their own philosophical ideas as insignificant, not worthy even of the teacher's intolerance. I believe that as teachers we must do all we can to help students believe in the importance and efficacy of their ideas. This is especially true in those "value-oriented," "subjective" areas—ethics, political philosophy, philosophy of religion, etc.—in which liberal tolerance is usually esteemed as a virtue. Especially in these areas of personal concern to students, we cannot give students an appreciation of the importance of their ideas if we refuse to criticize ideas we disagree with.

Thus, the principle of liberal tolerance can alienate students from teachers as well as students from their own beliefs. We ought to care about what students think, not just about how they get their thoughts and how they argue for them. In my statement of the principle of liberal tolerance I said that I cared more about the arguments students give than about conclusions reached. But if I am going to have an honest, unalienated relationship with the students in my classes, I must care very much about the conclusions they reach. This will mean being intolerant of conclusions I believe are false. "Intolerance" means, in this context, explicitly stating to the student that I believe his or her claim is false, explaining why I believe it is false, arguing with the student about its truth value, and finally giving a low grade if necessary. If this thesis is unpalatable, then, I would urge, think about reforming schools and grading, but do not give up the sort of intolerance which I think is necessary in any caring, humane relationship.

It should be clear that I believe the principle of liberal tolerance to be a cover for a kind of moral cowardice on the part of teachers. It is a cover for cowardice because it encourages teachers to not deal with students as whole people. As professional teachers, we are often urged to deal only with parts of our students—the parts learning philosophy. We are cautioned against entering into full human relationships with students, with the admonition that to do so would be unprofessional. Refusing to care about what my students believe—being tolerant of all substantive beliefs—is part of this attitude of alienated and cowardly professionalism.

Tolerance is also a mask for cowardice in a more straightforward way, insofar as tolerence often signifies a lack of confidence in our own beliefs, and a fear of engaging in honest debate. We often fail to criticize the beliefs of others because we are unsure of our own. Now, modesty in teaching is to be admired, and immodesty, in the form of dogmatism, is to be deplored. But we should not forget that we are *professors* of philosophy; we have something to profess, and we are shirking our duties if we fail to profess it. Failure to perform this primary professional duty is a form of cowardice, which we can mask with an attitude of tolerance. Professing philosophy entails a rejection of the attitude of liberal tolerance, and we should recognize this fact.

III

I want to conclude on a more positive note. If professing philosophy entails a rejection of the attitude of liberal tolerance, with what does it leave us?

I have said several times that it does not leave us only with authoritarian dogmatism to fall back on. One reason many teachers seem to have for adopting the principle of liberal tolerance is that the only alternative to such tolerance they know is the authoritarian dogmatism of all too many teachers. But, quite obviously, the teacher who pretends to know nothing, calling it tolerance, and the teacher who pretends to know everything, calling it professional expertise, are two ends of a continuum. What we are left with if we abandon both extremes is the entire mid-range of the continuum, containing, as always the golden mean.

What I take the golden mean to be in this case is simply the honest teacher who tries to engage his or her students in the doing of philosophy, caring enough to argue, modest enough to admit ignorance and error, and proud enough to recognize real knowledge and the concomitant natural authority. Teachers *do* know enough about their fields to profess their knowledge, to correct errors in others, and to refuse to tolerate obstinacy in others in recognizing those errors. At the same time, teachers do not know enough about their fields to demand agreement from students on all issues; honest tolerance— tolerance based on ignorance rather than cowardice—is a virtue. And finally, as teachers we must care about the students we teach; some beliefs are intolerable, and we are not caring about people when we tolerate their intolerable beliefs.

Notes

1. I would like to thank my colleagues in the Philosophy Department at Miami University—Michael Goldman, Stanley Kane, Rick Momeyer, Rama Rao Pappu, Tim Richardson, Peter Schuller, Asher Seidel, and Bill Smoot—for their help on this paper. Many of the ideas are theirs, and my interest in the topic has developed out of many heated discussions we have had about the issues. I know that they each believe my position to be incorrect in some way; but it remains true that they helped me to come to adopt it, for better or worse. Especially helpful were Michael Goldman's paper, "Institutional Obstacles to the Teaching of Philosophy," *Metaphilosophy* (July–October, 1975), Vol. 6, Nos. 3–4, pp. 338–346, and Peter Schuller's paper, "Antinomic Elements in Higher Education," presented at the 1972 meetings of the Society for Religion in Higher Education.

2. See the papers by Goldman and Schuller cited in fn. 1.

3. J. S. Mill, *On Liberty,* quoted by R. P. Wolff, "Beyond Tolerance," in Wolff, Moore, B., and Marcuse, H., *A Critique of Pure Tolerance* (Boston: Beacon Press, 1965), p. 24. In writing this paper I have benefitted greatly from all three essays in this book.

4. See Barrington Moore, Jr., "Tolerance and the Scientific Outlook," in Wolff, Moore, and Marcuse, p. 70.

5. Of course, I am not suggesting that students be graded merely on the strength of the arguments they give; many other factors ought to enter in, if students are to be graded at all.

The Teaching of Ethics and Moral Values in Teaching: Some Contemporary Confusions*
Larry R. Churchill

Ethics has become fashionable. The past decade has witnessed a proliferation of ethics courses and workshops in public and professional schools. Institutes and professional societies now regularly sponsor meetings, study groups, and journals in ethics. Two presidential commissions have labored over the ethics of research in biomedicine and the social sciences.

Despite this moral self-consciousness in America, some basic misunderstandings about ethics, moral values, and higher education are still current. Indeed, the fact that so many people are talking and writing about ethics may have contributed to and supported these misconceptions.

One of the most frequently voiced misconceptions concerns the relation (if any) of the teaching of ethics courses to the ways students actually make choices and conduct their lives. An interesting and typical example of this is an essay by Harvard President Derek Bok entitled "Can Ethics Be Taught?" [3]. The response Bok gives to this question forms the polemical setting for this article, so I will examine his reasoning and his assumptions in some detail. It is because his approach is both clearly stated and a part of the current moral orthodoxy that it merits this analysis.

---

* From the *Journal of Higher Education,* vol. 53, No. 3 (May/June 1982), 296–306, reprinted here with permission of the publisher. Copyright 1982 by Ohio State University Press. All rights reserved.

The response Bok gives to this question rests on a number of conventional assumptions. He argues that, in the strict sense, courses in ethics cannot realistically claim to make people morally better. Yet, he continues, the teaching of ethics does serve an important function. "Unless one is prepared to argue that ethical values have no intellectual basis whatsoever, it seems likely that this process of thought will play a useful role in helping students develop a clearer, more consistent set of ethical principles that takes more careful account of the needs and interests of others" [3, p. 29]. Near the end he concedes that the question he poses is unanswered, but asserts that it is "plausible to suppose that students in these courses will become more aware of the reasons underlying moral principles, and more equipped to reason carefully in applying these principles to concrete cases" [3, p. 30]. Bok concludes "surely the experiment is worth trying" [3, p. 30].

At first glance Bok's formulation of his problem is puzzling. After all, ethics is routinely taught in philosophy departments and theological schools. Does Bok think that philosophers and theologians who offer classes in ethics are not really teaching ethics, but something else—or perhaps does he think they are not teaching? What is amiss here is Bok's conflation of "morals" and "ethics." Ordinarily the term "morals" refers to human behavior, while "ethics" denotes systematic, rational reflection upon that behavior. Morality is the practical activity, ethics the theoretical and reflective one. Because Bok confuses these he misfires on his question. What he wants to ask is, "Does the teaching of ethics have any relation to the learning of moral values?", or possibly, "Do students learn moral values by being taught ethics?"

In addition, Bok labors under some conventional assumptions about both the nature of moral values and the activity of teaching that lead him to suppose that his misplaced question—"Can ethics be taught?"—is an experimental one. These assumptions form a protective corona that prevents Bok's discussion from penetrating to an examination of the more important questions of *what* moral values are transmitted in teaching, and how this occurs.

My first task in this article is to examine these conventional views about the nature of moral values. Second, I will assess a related set of biases about how such values are learned. Bok does not discuss these assumptions, since assumptions by definition *underlie* his discussion rather than being a part of it. By restricting his essay to orthodox notions of both "morals" and "teaching," he has forced the question he poses into a narrow framework and prejudiced the sort of answer that is possible. He has also neglected many of the subtleties of the educational process.

My chief aim is to make patent the inevitable presence of moral values in all teaching. Moreover, I will argue that not only are such values present in teaching, certain ethical norms are *constitutive* of teaching. The absence of these values in teaching constitute fundamental ethical problems in education.

The Nature of Moral Values: Two Conventional Views

Two views about the nature of moral values are: (1) values must be absolute if they are to be worthy of our esteem and (2) values are a strictly private and personal affair, and hold no greater validity than a purely aesthetic validation. These are, of course, mutually sustaining options. Moral absolutism and moral relativism feed from the same plate. One position holds values to be sacred decrees while the other position endorses a values "free for all" in which no particular values have privileged places because none have more depth of reference than the condition of one's palate. I find both assumptions present in the current college and professional student population.

In contemplating the issue of abortion, for example, many students feel that not only must others act as they do (to be morally correct), but others must also hold the same principles they do; that is, that there must be consensus in both doing and thinking. Such a student might contend that abortion is not only wrong, but wrong because of a specific duty grounded, say, in religious convictions about the sanctity of life. For such a student, morality is contingent upon agreement in every detail. Other students see no difficulty in radically individualizing values to the point that agreement between decision makers is not a relevant issue in ethics. Even consistency within decisions made by a single moral agent is an inappropriate standard for the thorough-going relativist, who may be pro-life today and pro-choice tomorrow, depending on how one "feels."

The difficulty is that neither position allows room for the operations of the intellect, for critical reflection and discussion. One posture encourages a dogmatic militancy in which values are thought to be chiseled in stone and delivered like the law to the unwashed multitudes. I find this position frequently leads to a vilification of those "others" who hold different opinions, combined with a pious assertion of one's own moral integrity. The alternative posture, held by more "enlightened'' students, is a relativism in which value judgments are a matter of taste (sometimes one prefers chocolate, sometimes vanilla). Yet, it really matters little which of these positions is espoused since they both amount to the same thing pedagogically. In either case our critical intelligence—what Hannah Arendt [1] calls the power to think—is disregarded. Neither position opens to reasoned argument and leaves the power to judge between competing values mystified and dysfunctional. On the terms of either view, there would be *no point* to a discussion of the teaching of ethics.

Assumptions about How Moral Values Are Learned

Two assumptions about how moral values are learned continue to influence the discussion of the teaching of ethics, in spite of the fact that there is no compelling evidence to support either of them. The alternatives tend to support each other, and they are mistaken, primarily, by being too simplistic. When examined, these assumptions appear unwarranted because neither is couched in a conceptual framework complex enough to account for the fact that it is *persons* who learn and hold moral values.

One position is a variation of psychological determinism, which holds that the values of any given individual are fixed at an early age. It asserts that education does nothing to permeate this value fortress. Teachers merely reinforce or develop more fully a predetermined value set. One either has a desirable value sensibility or one does not, and formal education is impotent to alter the powerful processes that preceded it.

Psychological determinism is at worst a way of abrogating responsibility for the values we hold, at best a thin reading of the capacity of intellect and will to assess and alter the values that define our persons and actions. In brief, this position holds that since values do not change, or change only in some established sequence, the examination of values in teaching can be no more than a purely descriptive inquiry, something like a sociological description of the values teachers and students hold. We would be prohibited from asking "Are these values the appropriate ones?"; critical inquiry would be disallowed. Though I grant there may be a few who hold this theory of how values are learned, college and professional school teachers frequently proceed in the practice of the craft *as if* this theory were in fact true. We do this when we assume that *how* we teach—tactics, methods, and the intellectual ethos of the class—makes no difference as to the learning process so long as knowledge is acquired in some quantifiable increment.

The other major assumption about how values are learned is perhaps best embodied in the desire of a senior surgeon, who once asked me, "Can't we just give these medical students a lecture and tell them what's right?" If knowledge can be cubed and ingested in discrete blocks, or modules, why can't we do the same with ethics? Despite the repugnancy we may feel for the application of Cartesian principles to the study of values, it is a widely held opinion that values can be learned in formal course work in ethics in the same manner in which one might study Romantic poets, or gross anatomy.

Psychological determinism pays too little respect to our power to alter our behavior and attitudes through intellectual effort. By contrast, the alternative position commits the "intellectual fallacy," viz, the assumption that high ideals, or important values, are self-actualizing, that cognitive change means behavioral change, and ultimately, that we hold inferior values because of our ignorance. It neglects the view— foundational for Western religious traditions—that what we value will be greatly influenced by egoistic and selfish considerations.

The Inevitable Presence of Moral Values in Teaching

It is frequently said that ethics cannot be taught. Upon examination this assertion usually means that moral values cannot be forced down a student's throat, that no coercive tactics seem to work. The assertion usually masks an explicit effort to "teach" some specific moral value to a student—an effort that invariably fails. I generally take encouragement from such accounts because they tend to confirm that students are not mindless and demand to be taken seriously.

In a deeper sense, however, values are taught constantly insofar as value dimensions are present in any significant human relationship—of which teaching and learning are examples. Inevitably, values are taught and learned. What is needed is a more accurate sense of how these processes occur. Sometimes we tend to identify values exclusively with either the cognitive or the affective domain, whereas values characterize persons as a whole. To isolate values as cognitive or affective is to commit what Alfred North Whitehead termed the fallacy of simple location. The tacit and attitudinal elements of values are more likely to be demonstrated than formally taught. This sort of demonstration is ubiquitous in medical education, where clerkship experiences and patient care responsibilities provide a workshop in values for apprentice physicians. Medical educators speak frequently about the importance of good role models for students, and the axiological impact of these models in the intense setting of clinical training is unarguable. And medical education is not unusual in this regard. Hannah Arendt puts the case well: "The fact that we usually treat matters of good and evil in courses in 'morals' or 'ethics' may indicate how little we know about them, for morals comes from mores and ethics from ethos, the Latin and Greek words for customs and habit" [1, p. 5]. Aristotle made the same point. In *The Nicomachean Ethics* he distinguished between intellectual and moral virtue, and insisted that while the former might be attained by formal study, the latter was characteristically acquired through custom, habit, and experience [2].

In addition, as Kant insisted—and Piaget and Kohlberg have shown—there is an important cognitive dimension to the learning of values. Though there are powerful affective forces in value formation, the more precise dimensions of values (perhaps the "higher" values) depend upon careful discussion and reflection in formal teaching situations.

Yet, my purpose here is not to map the domain of values for cognitive/affective designation (an overused and wooden typology), but to clarify how values are present in every teaching situation. Even when we are not teaching ethics (perhaps especially then), moral values are taught. Values are embedded in teaching styles and strategies and in the general environment of the classroom, laboratory, or hospital ward.

Let me underline my thesis about the inevitable presence of moral values in teaching by citing some examples. On the question of how to tell cancer patients their diagnosis, a senior physician remarked to a young medical student: "You'll have to work that one out for yourself." The encounter between medical students and patients, when a distressing or catastrophic diagnosis must be shared, is one of the most anxiety-provoking in medical education. What is objectionable about the above scenario is both what *is* said and what *is not* said. What is said implies two criteria for judging moral values: individualism and pragmatism. First, this medical student is left with the impression that how to relate a diagnosis is pretty much a private affair about which collaboration with others is of no use. Second, the implied norm is "If it works, it's okay"; there really isn't a question of intrinsic right or wrong involved.

The physician's silence on other aspects of this student's problem is equally troublesome. Isn't there a body of wisdom (not knowledge) that this professor could share with the student? Doesn't concern for the student (not to mention the patient) dictate a more responsive and supportive role for the professor? Aren't there, after all, ways in which the student can go wrong in this task; for example, if overcome by anxiety, he tries to withhold the diagnosis, or espousing a rigid dogma about truth-telling, he forces a list of grisly details of physical degeneration upon the patient? As a teacher, the physician must be prepared to say that these actions would be morally wrong, and furthermore, to indicate why. The refusal of a teacher to challenge and even critically evaluate the values of a student, however benevolently motivated, undermines appreciation of the moral life and handicaps the development of students into self-affirming and self-critical moral agents.

Several years ago I was doing research on the value dimensions in medical education. After explaining the purpose of my study to a third-year medical student, he replied: "There's no time to learn values here; what we learn is how to be competent physicians. The old family doc was great with his patients, but he simply didn't know any medicine." Such a response is, of course, a vivid commentary on one set of moral values that *was* learned in medical education.

Assertions of the absence of moral values in a teaching endeavor should not be taken as indications that the teaching is value-free, but are better understood as indices for judging precisely what values are being taught. A theory of education that fails to acknowledge value transmission in teaching is revelatory of the value system at work in that educational theory, even if unacknowledged. Yet, even when we allow a place for values in an educational process, we frequently tend to treat them as a finishing touch—icing on the cake, or a desirable frill. Actually, our thinking should be inverted if it is to reflect our practice. Moral values permeate the entire structure of education, even those educational endeavors that claim for themselves a value-free agenda of "training for competence." Value dimensions are not merely an additional component of our teaching, but are definitive of the intellectual and social ethos in which education takes place. It is in this sense that values are not only present, but central in teaching. Moral values are taught—like it or not—unless one artificially (and inaccurately) confines the term "teaching" to the transmission of formalized units of knowledge. There are values in teaching. The critical questions are, "Which values?" and, "Is their presence acknowledged or do they go unacknowledged, and hence unexamined?"

Another contributor to this volume, Professor Baumgarten, has argued eloquently that a neutral stance is to be preferred over one in which a professor advocates for his own views. Baumgarten is right to argue that narrow-mindedness and parochialism are great flaws in a teacher. I discuss this below in terms of the importance of a teacher's commitment to objectivity. Yet neutrality is not always desirable. Neutrality about some issues (like what to tell the cancer patient) would be devisive. For many other questions neutrality would have to be feigned for the teacher who has thought about the issues in any detail.

Yet at a more fundamental, methodological level, neutrality is, strictly speaking, impossible. Every act of teaching values some mode of presentation over others, from the opening question to the last exam. In this sense, the Socratic method (which Baumgarten favors as "neutral") is itself an item of advocacy in Baumgarten's pedagogy—a method of teaching with expectations, norms, and values. Hence, while I agree with Baumgarten's views and "advocate" their use, I think he is wrong in asserting their relative neutrality. Indeed, the Socratic method's embodiment of certain values is precisely why Baumgarten (and most effective teachers) literally could not teach without it. In what follows I indicate what some of those values are.

Some Values Definitive of Teaching

In what follows I will explore four characteristics. Others could be listed, but these are essential. In their absence, the activity ceases to be teaching and becomes some other mode of relating to students. Their absence, in other words, becomes an ethical problem for the profession.

Respect for the Otherness of Students

I mean here, quite simply, respect for the way in which students differ among themselves and from their teachers. This means more than appreciating the pluralism in American universities or acknowledging the wide variety of life-styles, ethnic groups, and cultural and religious traditions among students.

Students are "other than" teachers by virtue of the asymmetry of power between teacher and student grounded in differences in expertise, experience, and skills. This asymmetry is appropriate, and I do not suggest that it should be diminished. Yet this asymmetry may pose a barrier to teaching. The problem arises not so much because the teachers abuse their authority, though this sometimes occurs. The more frequent difficulty is that teachers—like priests, physicians, parents, and others in authority—forget what the dependency side of the learning relationship is like. We forget that things that we now perform routinely and with ease were initially learned with laborious effort and often in great anxiety. Options that appear obvious to the teacher may be unimagined possibilities to the student struggling to make sense of a problem.

The physician with the cryptic remark on how to relate a diagnosis failed as a teacher because his advice was disrespectful of the student's situation. Instead of engaging the student within the student's perception of his problem, the physician left the student to struggle within the confines of his own resources. This is not always a bad teaching strategy, but in this case it is an injustice—one based in lack of appreciation of and respect for the student's predicament and induced by a forgetfulness of the tension this problem poses for the student.

A Commitment to Objectivity

Here I mean to denote a scrupulousness about presenting accepted knowledge as knowledge, and opinion as opinion. One of the temptations of the asymmetrical teacher-student relationship is to present one's own opinions, hunches, or intuitions as if they were established facts, or inversely, to present established knowledge that runs contrary to one's own views as merely opinion. Another name for this prejudicial form of teaching in which one's own ideas are given a critical status is "indoctrination." Indoctrination in the classroom is manipulation of the methods of inquiry so that conclusions reached will simply confirm the teacher's opinions and foreclose on inquiry.

One of the ways that a teacher can fail to be objective is exemplified in the scenario between the senior physician and the medical student. The physician fails in objectivity because he fails to bring his own experience and skills to bear in assisting the student. In other words, the physician espoused a value relativism that supposes that it really doesn't matter how one breaks the news to a patient. That it does matter a great deal, that there is greater or lesser skill to be employed in this action toward the patient, and that one shouldn't expect to do it appropriately the first (or every) time, would be invaluable lessons to this student. The neutrality of the physician, his failure to indicate these things, constitutes a bias, a lack of objectivity about the student's problem.

It is sometimes thought that bias only arises in issues of adherence to proper methods of research. One can also be objective in teaching in terms of the acuteness of empathy and in the methods and strategies employed in teaching. Only the extreme moral relativist, or the disappointed moral absolutist, would be led to believe that in teaching we are left to guesswork, while in research we can be objective.

A Commitment to the Integrity of Inquiry

Universities are among the few places in which inquiry is valued for its own sake, that is, without pretense of political or economic utility and with accountability for social maintenance or improvement left unspecific. Teaching must include some sense of protection over the forms inquiry can take, some standards that disabuse the tendency on the part of both teachers and students to use the space reserved for inquiry for some other purpose.

In a recent faculty meeting it was suggested that a policy be adopted that would disallow the giving of both "failing" and "honors" evaluations in a first-year medical course. The entire class of 164 students was to be blanketed with a mark of "satisfactory." Three rationales for this proposal were offered: (1) since the course in question is not a "hard science" course, uniformity among faculty and objectivity in evaluation would be impossible; (2) those who might fail would only be required to do remedial work, which would be a distraction from other course work; and (3) the honors designation in medical school is relevant only to the attainment of a prestigious residency, and in these cases only the last two years of medical school are considered.

Several assumptions need to be challenged in this proposal: the hard science/soft science bifurcation; the parochial view of objectivity; the sense that only the extrinsic rewards for excellence are meaningful to students. Each of these underlying assumptions is an encroachment on the integrity of teaching. They devalue inquiry and usurp the space of learning. They preempt the line of accountability of teachers toward those they instruct for evaluation of the quality of their work. Finally, they encourage crude utilitarian standards for education and succumb to cynicism.

Enablement

In examining the knowledge of those around him, Socrates found that not only were people making false claims to knowledge, but that these claims prohibited them from thinking critically. His task was then to purge people of their opinions, that is, of unexamined prejudgments that would prevent them from conducting an inquiry. Thus, Socrates' task was to bring others to an acknowledgement of their ignorance. Yet, Socrates claimed only ignorance for himself in this endeavor. Merleau-Ponty articulates the point I wish to emphasize. "The story of Socrates is not to say less in order to win an advantage in showing great mental power, or in suggesting some esoteric knowledge. 'Whenever I convince anyone of his ignorance,' the Apology says with melancholy, 'my listener imagines that I know everything that he does not know.' Socrates does not know any more than they know. He knows only that there is no absolute knowledge, and that it is by this absence that we are open to the truth" [4, p. 22].

Teaching—as opposed to indoctrination, facilitation, being a "neutral" resource person, or whatever fashionable surrogates one might prefer—invariably involves a kind of Socratic dialogue in which the teacher, being knowledgeable in the range of his or her own knowledge and ignorance, *enables* the student to think, to critically examine, to resist premature closure or tenured ideas. In order for this to happen, the questions posed by the teacher cannot be counterfeit, or mere posture. Teachers must also be open to novel ideas in a fundamental way, else they cannot conduct an inquiry or initiate one in their students.

Socrates suggested that teachers are essentially midwives, seeking to help in the difficult process in which each student gives birth to the knowledge that gestates within. Educational philosophies since the Enlightenment have functioned out of another paradigm, with knowledge on the outside to be placed into the blank receptacle of the mind. The efforts to place this exterior knowledge within have frequently done violence, both to the student and the knowledge itself. It may be helpful to remember that, at least etymologically, the Socratic view is more accurate—*educate* means literally *educe*, to draw out.

Summary

If teaching occurs, moral values are present, though frequently these values go unacknowledged. "Can ethics be taught?" is a conceptually confused question. Ethics are taught. Moreover, moral values are taught and cannot fail to be taught in the sense that such values permeate teacher-student relationships and the ethos, methods, and objectives of the classroom.

The urgent questions are *what* moral values are taught, and what theory of education will be rich enough to reflect this practice. Until we are clear on these issues, questions about ethics in the academic profession will continue to repeat the old orthodoxy and flounder in trivialities.

References

1. Arendt, H. *The Life of the Mind*, Vol. 1. New York: Harcourt, Brace and Jovanovich, 1977.

2. Aristotle. *The Nicomachean Ethics*. Book II, Section I. Translated by W. D. Ross.

3. Bok, D. "Can Ethics Be Taught?" *Change*, 8 (October 1976), 26–30.

4. Merleau-Ponty, M. "In Praise of Philosophy." In *The Essential Writings of Merleau-Ponty*, edited by A. L. Fisher. New York: Harcourt, Brace and World, 1969.

Ethics in the Academic Profession:
A Socratic View*
Elias Baumgarten

University teachers have become increasingly concerned with professional ethics, particularly medical, legal, and business ethics. However, they have not given similar attention to the ethical issues associated with their own profession, though important moral issues do arise in university teaching. A major reason for this omission is that college teaching is not recognized as a distinct profession. Much has been written about the professional responsibilities of scientists, psychologists, and philosophers, but I would like to present a case for recognizing college teaching as a distinct professional activity, one with its own purposes and obligations. In this article I will focus on the humanities and the teaching of values, but much of what I say will have implications for other areas of university teaching as well. I will employ a Socratic view of professional responsibility and claim that university teachers have a social obligation to help other citizens, both inside and outside the classroom, formulate reasoned principles for themselves. And I will contend, more controversially perhaps, that to be an advocate for particular substantive positions is inconsistent with this responsibility.[1]

Before turning to academic ethics, let us look briefly at a principle that underlies professional ethics generally. In evaluating professional conduct, we still find useful the Socratic dictum that no craft or

---

* From the *Journal of Higher Education,* vol. 53, No. 3 (May/June 1982), 283–95, reprinted here with permission of the Publisher. Copyright 1982 by Ohio State University Press. All rights reserved.

profession should seek its own advantage but should benefit those who are subject to it [4, p. 23]. We employ this principle when we condemn a physician who uses an experimental technique without a patient's informed consent, when a more reliable treatment is available. Such a doctor's actions are unprofessional and immoral, and this is so regardless of the very real benefits that might accrue from the experiment, not only for the doctor's research but possibly for many more patients than just the one presently under treatment. Our condemnation does not imply that medical research is an inappropriate role for physicians. We might easily concede that research, including research that requires human experimentation, complements physicians' therapeutic work and enhances their value to their patients. We blame such doctors because, in their role as doctors, their primary responsibility is to their patients, not to the community of medical researchers or even to future victims of disease in general.

The ethical case against the freely experimenting doctor is persuasive because we recognize that "medicine" actually encompasses more than one profession: there is the activity of the researcher who is committed to scientific investigation, and there is also the work of the physician whose project is to use medical knowledge to treat particular patients who have particular diseases. Though one person may assume both roles, the clinical practice of medicine is a distinct profession with its own imperatives.

When we look at the academic profession, however, we do not find the same kind of recognized distinction between the responsibilities of scholars and those of teachers. When university professors select their courses and plan even their undergraduate lectures primarily in the service of their own research interests, they may appear to be fulfilling their professional obligations as scientists and scholars. They are rewarded by their colleagues, and they may begin to conceive of their relationship to students as one of master to apprentice, perhaps even believing that introductory students are best served by having a glimpse at the latest disputes raging in the scholarly journals. Unlike physicians, college teachers do not confront a recognized code of ethics directed specifically to their teaching function, and they are quite likely to conceive their profession in the specialized terms of their own discipline.

But my contention is that, in important respects, the role of university teachers does parallel that of physicians. Whereas medical researchers and scholars are engaged in inquiry that does not, in principle at least, require any other person, the work of physicians and teachers conceptually requires the presence, respectively, of patients and students. Moreover, the Socratic imperative addressed to professions in general, that they benefit those "subject to them," applies in both instances. I think a consideration of this principle will help to define the distinctive responsibilities of university teachers.

The Socratic precept emphasizes that professional activity exists in a social context and that professionals have obligations toward at least some segment of the community. Applying this maxim to our profession, we can say that our teaching should benefit our students. We encounter most of our students in our classrooms, but, in the broad sense I have in mind, we also act as teachers, communicating with students, when we participate in community forums or offer commentaries for the mass media. So I would include among the "students" whom our profession should benefit all those who do not share our professional training, and we are "teaching" when we communicate with this audience. By way of contrast, we may learn from our colleagues but are not, in a professional context, their students; and when we publish our own work for our peers to read, we are not acting in the role of teachers. On this view, then, university teaching necessarily relates to the larger public in a way that professional scholarship does not. I would like to discuss that public responsibility and then consider what implications this view of university teaching has for classroom practice.

University professors often wish to see their work exert a greater influence in the world but are uncertain how to bring this about. By including the general populace among the university teacher's potential students, I am accepting the Socratic notion that knowledge can improve ordinary citizens.[2] For scientists this presents relatively little difficulty: few people doubt that scientific information may affect their decisions and even alter their view of the world. But in the area of knowledge most important to Socrates, the humanities and the study of values in particular, communication between academicians and the public faces special obstacles. The public has no clear view of how it can be helped by academic philosophers, historians, or literary critics. Like Socrates, many of our contemporaries seek "the good life," but most believe either that how one conceives it is purely a matter of personal taste or that whatever authority there is on this matter rests with the clergy or with a sacred text that can provide definite answers. How, then, can that group of academicians who take seriously the *study of values* presume to communicate with, teach, and even "improve" those who lack their professional skills?

To teach values in a pluralistic society, academic humanists must help people develop that faculty that most other professions either ignore or consider tangential: the capacity for critical questioning. As teachers of values, we cannot simply inform—nor can we heal, inspire, or save—but we can affect people powerfully if we induce them actually to engage in the kind of examined life for which Socrates is rhetorically held up as a symbol. Our professional responsibility is a unique one: neither to be a provider of values nor merely a clarifier of them, but to struggle toward a synthesis of these two more familiar, but flawed, conceptions of our role. I will first discuss what I take to be the weaknesses of these two alternative views, then propose a conception of the teacher of values that, I will claim, promotes both individual improvement and political freedom. .

Some humanists, particularly those with strong religious or political convictions, are concerned about their weak impact on society but misconceive their professional responsibility. Today's philosophers are especially distressed about how far they have come from the time of Socrates, when the public listened to a philosopher enough to feel threatened by him. Some claim that philosophers have a special responsibility either to propose solutions to ethical and political problems or to offer answers that will provide some respite from the anguish that people suffer when they confront life's mysteries. Edward Regis, for example, regrets that "philosophy has all but abdicated its proper role of provider to man of objective values and a conceptual framework by which he can make some sense of existence" [6, p. 123].

There are, however, two problems with this view of the philosopher's role: philosophers are incapable of offering the public objective values, and philosophy *teachers* would not be teaching philosophy if they tried. Philosophers have reached no consensus on value questions, and their professional scholarly debates are not accessible to a public that lacks advanced philosophical training. When ethical theorists write as scholars rather than as teachers, we cannot reasonably expect their work to benefit the average person, just as we do not expect articles in medical journals to help the untrained patient. Moral philosophers could, of course, easily convey just their *conclusions*; but, deprived of the argumentation that supports them, the public would be left with only the conflicting personal convictions of a few scholars—and no guidance at all. And even if philosophers *could* provide people with "a conceptual framework by which [they] can make sense of existence," the teacher who transmitted it would not be teaching philosophy, only offering a creed or doctrine. Accordingly, philosopher Alison Jaggar objects to the idea that philosophy teachers can help people by assuming the role of moral authorities. To do so, she claims, would discourage people "from taking seriously their own ability to engage in what should be the central project of every human life, deciding how [to] live." Jagger claims, moreover, that "to accept one's philosophy on the authority of another is the ultimate form of alienation" [3, p. 112].

To overcome this alienation and to promote autonomous thinking are primary goals of the humanities teacher. But those who respect their students' individuality and stress that teaching is different from indoctrination often overcompensate by claiming that teaching values is nothing more than putting students in touch with their own desires. On this view, since no value is known to be more rational than any other, there are no moral truths toward which people can be encouraged to strive. How, then, can teachers help students make "better" decisions? According to a teacher's manual for a course in values clarification, "the result of a decision is only good or bad in terms of the decision maker's own personal preferences" [2, p. 68]. Values are purely subjective, and one's beliefs or choices are bad only if they fail to be a true expression of oneself. Somewhat paradoxically, this form of extreme subjectivism shares a fault with indoctrination: both fail to engage the full reasoning powers of students. In its praiseworthy concern to help students distinguish what is truly their own from what they have accepted purely on the authority of others, values clarification, at least as it is usually described, puts students in touch with their own unique *feelings*, which cannot be true or false; but it cuts them off from their faculty of rational *evaluation*, which can judge what feelings are most worthy of expression. Whereas indoctrination claims an objective truth that need not be scrutinized by individual reasoning, values clarification individualizes ethical assessment and implicitly denies that objective moral improvement is possible or worth seeking.

The Socratic tradition avoids the mistakes of these two extremes. According to Socrates, our central mission should be to seek wisdom about the human condition and to learn "the excellence which a man and citizen is capable of attaining" [5, p. 24]. To seek wisdom implies both that there is something real worth seeking and that it has not already been found. We value the activities of interpretation and reasoning as ways of approaching the sought-for-ideal, whether or not it can ever be reached.[3] People often disagree because they start from different assumptions, but those assumptions may be held for good or bad reasons. Merely to help students see what their assumptions are and how they differ from those of others is a healthy exercise in self-awareness, but it is not the teaching of values. To teach values, one must encourage students to become aware of, to question, and to evaluate even their most fundamental presuppositions. Philosophy stresses this activity, but other fields teach it as well. Acquaintance with different cultures and religions or the felt experience of literature and the arts can, like philosophical argument, provoke students to question what they had previously taken for granted, and this is a primary purpose not only of the humanities but of liberal education in general.

When it succeeds, liberal education not only benefits students by expanding their awareness of personal choices; it also benefits a free society by providing it with gadflies: persons who are familiar with their own cultural tradition and who are at the same time capable of criticizing what is merely habitual or current or faddish. So conceived, liberal educators benefit citizens in a way that is neither inherently liberal nor conservative: insofar as they transmit the great ideas of their cultural heritage undiminished, they promote respect for what is best in it; insofar as they teach critical thinking and an awareness of alternatives, they foster questioning of beliefs and practices that have been accepted merely because they are traditional.

Though liberal educators advocate no particular ethical or philosophical system, their procedural commitment to reasoned inquiry powerfully expresses a moral and political conviction: the rejection of both authoritarianism and nihilism. In this way liberal education is intimately linked to the values of a pluralistic democracy. Neither can exist in a dogmatic atmosphere that forbids questioning, but neither can flourish where no answer is considered any better than any other. Both need to cultivate two potentially conflicting human faculties, autonomy and objectivity. Autonomy encourages diverse forms of individual development, while objectivity stresses the value of universally acceptable standards and absolute knowledge. Autonomy without objectivity leads to a shallow respect for "doing your own thing," and a denial that any real learning is possible. Communication is viewed mainly as self-expression; it can change opinions but not improve them. Objectivity without autonomy denies the possibility of intelligent disagreement and debate, holding as it does that only one "correct" conclusion is admissible, or perhaps that some minority (or majority) has a corner on morality.

Both liberal education and democracy must oppose these extremes. Both regard the capacity to formulate and express one's own positions as an essential aspect of human dignity. And both are also committed to public discussion as a way not merely to express, but to test, privately held opinions that may contain obvious mistakes or be based on narrow assumptions. Liberal educators must be essentially respectors of both autonomy and objectivity and are therefore especially well suited to make an important contribution to free government.

The university teacher, as conceived here, is essentially a liberal educator with significant social responsibilities. Though we cannot offer others a creed to live by, we do have a unique role to play in helping people confront personal issues of the most fundamental kind. Everyone faces the choice of either developing the ability to interpret his or her own adult experience or of being enslaved to the interpretations of others. And there is no lack of ideologues vying for each person's acquiescence: politicians, advertisers, editorialists, popular psychologists, the clergy, and even musicians, painters, and architects all present partial or total world views for our acceptance—blatantly or subtly, manipulatively or sincerely, consciously or unconsciously. The proper role of the university teacher is not to join the competition but to help others reach a critical understanding of the history of human creative expression and thereby to escape some part of the human ignorance that is escapable. Critical intelligence, of course, cannot guarantee morality: evil can result not only from ignorance but from a failure of will—here we must part company with Socrates. But *some* evil is caused by ignorance, and Socrates' conviction that humanistic inquiry can improve people receives perhaps its most dramatic support from the testimony of a former Nazi, Albert Speer. When asked in an interview how he, a person with some formal education and not evidently mean-spirited, could have cooperated with Nazi atrocities, he answered, "We were taught never to question." If we, as teachers, can help to promote a spirit of reasoned inquiry and critical questioning, we may also, in some way large or small, be aiding the cause of social justice.

Through university teachers, as conceived here, are strongly committed to unrestricted inquiry, they are not advocates of *particular* ethical or political positions, and this has important implications for classroom practice. In addressing these issues, I have in mind the actual situation that we face in colleges today, where the relationship of teacher to student includes grading and other forms of evaluation that will affect students' prospects for success in a competitive society.

It may be that another kind of university in another kind of society would allow a more humane teacher-student relationship and a more desirable conception of academic ethics. But my defense of a nonadvocacy role for liberal arts teachers takes as a given the context within which we now work.

A strong criticism that is often made of this conception of teaching, particularly when it involves normative issues, is that neutrality on a teacher's part leads to relativism and cynicism. Students and ordinary citizens, it is argued, have a right to expect those trained in the study of values to come to some conclusions, but if all they do is interpret, question, and uncover hidden assumptions, then people will come to believe that all reasoning is rationalization and that no opinion is better than another.[4]

My answer is two-fold. First, the position of neutrality is recommended not in scholarship but in teaching, and this represents a significant distinction between the two activities. Scholars do take positions and argue for them, but this has not made works like Kant's *Critique of Practical Reason* instructive to the average person. My point is that there needs to be a profession specifically devoted to conveying the content and spirit of humanistic inquiry to nonprofessionals without any overt or hidden partisan agenda. Without such a profession, the ideas of humanists may get transmitted, by journalists and popular writers, for example, but often with gross distortions.[5]

Second, the solution to cynicism that is envisioned by the critic of neutrality, having people directly confront the opinions of their teachers, is workable only if those people are shielded from any opposing views. Students of ethics or political philosophy who venture beyond their first professor and are exposed to reasoned argument for opposing positions may be more likely than ever to conclude that any belief in the humanities can be equally well supported with reasons, especially if both professors claim to have knowledge of the correctness of their positions.

For a humanities teacher to present all available arguments but no definite conclusions is only to convey the disappointing truth, that we have no absolute certainty on most of the enduring questions that are worthy of discussion. Whether we teach history or ethics or literary criticism, we know that sound arguments are advanced to support opposing positions when each position starts from different premises. We may be doing well to unveil a previously hidden assumption, even if we are not yet able to demonstrate its truth or falsity. The most contrived and least honest position a teacher could take would be to attempt to counter students' skepticism of reason by claiming that rational argument can absolutely resolve a particular ethical or political issue. Normative inquiry is, of course, futile if reason has no efficacy, but it is also foreclosed if the truth has already been found and is not open to further question. The disappointment that is experienced by many students in the humanities may be traceable to the exaggerated claims often made on their behalf, and the teacher who feels compelled to assuage that disappointment with final solutions would do well to heed Bertrand Russell in his characterization of the value of philosophy: "Philosophy is to be studied, not for the sake of any definite answers to its questions, since no definite answers can, as a rule, be known to be true, but rather for the sake of the questions themselves" [7, p. 161].

In any case, the risk that is associated with not satisfying students' desires for definite answers must be weighed against the greater danger that comes with offering introductory students solutions to humanistic problems. Most college students are more accustomed to courses, such as chemistry or accounting, that convey basic information, and they are often uncomfortable with interpretive, analytical, or normative issues of the kind that arise in history, literature, or philosophy. Many such students claim that the only alternative to definite information is purely subjective and even arbitrary opinion, a matter of "taste" in which reasoning has no relevance. For an instructor to present one position as being the "strongest" shortcuts the process of questioning that is the essence of humanistic study; and it may deprive students of the creative anguish that comes with having to think through an issue and come to a conclusion purely by assessing opposing arguments, not knowing in advance what the "correct" position is supposed to be.[6]

The Socratic teacher is also criticized for adopting a contrived and even cowardly and inhumane attitude toward students. Philosophy teacher Hugh Wilder contrasts a neutral attitude of "liberal tolerance," which emphasizes the students' process of reasoning, with a "caring, humane relationship," wherein a teacher will be concerned that students reach particular conclusions, will consequently argue for the truth of particular positions, and will finally give a lower grade to the student paper that opposes those positions. Liberal tolerance, he writes,

> is a cover for cowardice because it encourages teachers to not deal with students as whole people. As professional teachers, we are often urged to deal only with parts of our students—the parts learning philosophy. We

are cautioned against entering into full human relationships with students, with the admonition that to do so would be unprofessional. Refusing to care about what my students believe—being tolerant of all substantive beliefs—is part of this attitude of alienated and cowardly professionalism. [8, p. 322]

This criticism, like that of Alison Jaggar, ties professionalism to alienation. But whereas Jaggar claims that the height of alienation occurs when we pose as moral authorities, Wilder implies that our relationship to students is most alienated when we conceal our presumably authoritative conclusions from them and when we do not care enough to try to persuade them to the beliefs we hold to be true.

Teaching is, I agree, an act of caring, but I am uncomfortable with the notion that I best express my concern for students by trying to secure their agreement with my own values. I would like to indicate two reasons for opposing this method of teaching values. The first reflects my conception of ethics; the second, my defense of a professional relationship between teachers and students.

First, the history of ethics is one of disagreement, and divergent views will be represented in any good ethics course. If an ethics teacher is an advocate of utilitarianism but nonetheless includes Kant on the reading list, primary attention will be devoted to exposing the weaknesses of formalist theory and showing the way in which its criticisms of utilitarianism can be successfully met. Now if a student, exposed to Kant's own arguments, finds them more persuasive than either the professor's or Mill's, then the student cannot be judged to have performed excellently in the course: according to Wilder's thinking, the student's arguments lead to a false conclusion and therefore cannot be as strong as a well-reasoned paper that defends utilitarianism. This must be true even if the student's work is judged to be on the same philosophical level as Kant's. Were he a member of the class, Kant himself could not earn an "A" (or be judged an excellent philosopher) unless he changed his mind. This position is absurd because it is rarely possible to trace what a professor judges to be a false conclusion in the work of a great moral philosopher to some obvious flaw in reasoning for which even an undergraduate student may be criticized.

What many find unsettling about teaching without advocacy is its implicit assertion of a class difference between teachers and students. The teacher is seen as saying, "Since I cannot expect you to understand ethical theory as fully as Kant or Mill or I do, it's okay for you to believe whomever you choose, as long as you have some good reasons. If I gave you my opinion and my reasons, you wouldn't fully understand them anyway.'' Implied here is a criticism of the idea that teachers must, as a result of their authoritative position, withhold some part of themselves from their students, must withhold what humanities teachers presumably regard as a most important part, their convictions on enduring issues. This refusal to be full persons in relation to students is, I take it, what threatens to make the relationship alienated. But the alternative of posing as an authority can, as Jaggar maintains, also cause alienation, now as a result of asserting rather than withholding one's superior degree of knowledge. On these terms, the only way of avoiding the dilemma would be for a teacher to deny being superior in *any* respect and to relate fully to students as peers.

The source of the dilemma is, I think, a confusion about the meaning of such concepts as professionalism, superiority, and alienation. To overcome it, I would like to offer several considerations in defense of a professional teacher-student relationship.

First, the entire conduct of teachers in relation to students should be guided by what will be most conducive to the students' learning. As a classroom method, to share one's own convictions may be to give more of oneself but is not, for that reason, more effective teaching. The superior knowledge that teachers have is part of what makes them professionals, and this status does affect—and even restrict—their relationship with students. In a professional relationship one does not give one's whole self; for example, one tries not to express impatience (even if one feels it) with a slow learner, or irritation with a student whose manner one finds displeasing, or condescension for a student's poor reasoning. Furthermore, a professional relationship is not fully reciprocal: teachers should try to frame their comments in a way that will best help students to learn; students need not be so concerned to enlighten their professors and may appropriately experiment with arguments for the sake of their own self-edification. Thus, in their professional activity teachers are, it is true, withholding a part of themselves, but this does not make their relationship with students uncaring or inhumane. Professional activity should "benefit those who are subject to it," and humanities teachers should offer those interpretations and arguments (as well as teach those works and assign those papers) that will be most helpful to students in the specific way that humanities teachers are trained to help them.

This leads to a second consideration in favor of professionalism. By a student's presence in my course, I may infer only that he or she has elected a professional relationship with me. I have no unilateral right to assume that students want a "full human relationship" or want even to know my opinions, let alone that they can benefit from hearing them. To avoid alienation, a relationship need not be equal in all respects, nor need it be "full"—very few if any human relationships meet these criteria—but it does, I think, need to be based on mutual consent with respect to its range and depth.

Finally, having a professional relationship with students does not preclude a wider human relationship as well. If the restrictions I have proposed in the name of professionalism implied that I could not simultaneously have other kinds of relationships when both the student and I freely chose them, then I would agree that we would be paying too heavy a price to be professional. The best teachers are probably those who genuinely like the company of many of their students and who enjoy discussion with them that is unrestrained by the conventions appropriate to a classroom. No doubt some of our warmest friendships may even develop from these associations. But this does not mean that the freedom that befits a friendship should be our model for classroom behavior; unlike our friends, our students are not obliged to indulge our intellectual prejudices or our personal idiosyncrasies.

Ethics in the academic profession has not received adequate attention. When it is considered at all, it is too often conceived only in negative terms, through prohibitions aimed at preventing the exploitation of students. Like physicians, university teachers should, of course, "first, do no harm." But our professional responsibility includes a distinctive positive dimension as well. Through university teaching, we express our conviction that thoughtful inquiry ennobles a human life and contributes to human excellence. Outside our professional work, as individuals, writers, and citizens, we may also advocate particular causes by joining organizations, making speeches, and writing articles. Such activities are evidence of our moral concerns. But our professional commitment to help others critically assess their experience, may, though it excludes advocacy, be our most powerful moral activity. In a world where the proverbial marketplace of ideas—and not infrequently even the university catalogue—is crowded with sophistry, propaganda, and hyperbole, there is special reason to value a profession that is solely committed to enlarging the power and influence of reasoned discourse and imaginative questioning.

Appendix

A Checklist for Essays

Please consult the following checklist before and during the preparation of your essay. Ideally, every question would be answered YES.

1. Does your essay respond to the topic precisely?
   Do you indicate which topic you are writing on?
   Do you see the topic as posing a *problem*? (If not, you should probably consider choosing another topic.)
2. Do you have a clear *central thesis*?
   Can you state it in one sentence?
   Does everything in your essay in some way relate to this central claim?
   Do you *show* exactly *how* it relates?
3. Do you *develop* ideas rather than simply state them?
   Did you consider and respond to the strongest arguments that might be used to oppose your own position?
   Does your essay offer a *reasoned discussion* that would have something challenging to say to someone opposing you?
   Do you recognize that this is different from just stating your unsupported "opinion"?
   Have you really had to *think through* the issues in order to write your essay?
4. Is your essay clearly and logically organized?
   Is it as short as it *can* be? (No excess verbiage, please.)
   Do you have an introduction and conclusion?
   Does your introduction get *right to* the central problem and indicate your central thesis? (No long lead-ins, please.)
   Does your conclusion really *follow from* what preceded it?
5. Does your essay show a solid understanding of the text(s) upon which it is based? Is your essay *rooted* in these texts?
   Do you quote or refer to passages to support your points (or use them to argue against)?
   Are you careful to avoid over-quoting?
   Are your quotes the best, most appropriate ones for your purposes?
   Do you cite page references for *all* sources you use?
6. Have you worked over your sentences to be sure that they are clear, precise, and grammatical? Have you used a dictionary?
   Have you proofread for errors?

7. Did you *learn* a substantial amount about the issues with which your essay was concerned?

Do you have more questions now than you had before you started?

Do you consider the topic more *complex* now than you did before writing your essay?

References

1. Dyer, W. *Your Erroneous Zones*. New York: Avon Books, 1976.

2. Eger, M. "The Conflict in Moral Education: An Informal Case Study." *The Public Interest*, (Spring 1981), 62–80.

3. Jaggar, A. "Philosophy as a Profession." *Metaphilosophy*, 6 (January 1975), 100–116.

4. Plato. *The Republic of Plato*. Translated by F. M. Cornford. London: Oxford University Press, 1941.

5. ———. *Euthyphro, Apology, Crito*. Indianapolis: Liberal Arts Press, 1956.

6. Regis, E., Jr. "The Layman and the Abdication of Philosophers." *Metaphilosophy*, 6 (January 1975), 117–26.

7. Russell, B. *The Problems of Philosophy*. New York: Oxford University Press, 1959.

8. Wilder, H. T. "Tolerance and Teaching Philosophy." *Metaphilosophy*, 9 (July–October 1978), 311–23.

Notes

1. My concern in this article is the teaching of introductory and other students who do not intend to become professional scholars. My remarks do not apply to graduate education.

2. Socrates, of course, went even further, claiming that anyone with moral knowledge would *necessarily* be a moral person.

3. In this respect the Socratic pursuit of wisdom parallels the religious quest for purity or moral perfection: both value the activity of striving, even though their ultimate goals are impossible to attain. In this respect both forms of spiritual life stand sharply opposed to a life that values only the practical and the achievable.

4. This argument is made by Wilder [8, pp. 320–21].

5. For example, in an article in the *Wall Street Journal* some years ago, Clare Booth Luce declared definitively that the actions of the radical SLA were an expression of existentialism. And in his 1976 bestseller, Wayne Dyer

appears to invoke the authority of John Stuart Mill in support of his claim, "Nothing is more important than anything else" [1, p. 156].

6. I apply this principle in my philosophy courses by having students write essays that require them to defend a definite position and to consider and respond to opposing arguments. See the appendix above for an indication of the criteria used in evaluating student essays.

Rethinking Examinations and Grades
Steven M. Cahn

It is astonishing to realize how little college teachers may know about the academic lives of their students, and conversely, how little students may know about the academic life of their teachers. I recall one professor who for several years taught a large lecture course without ever realizing he was addressing a captive audience, since unbeknownst to him, the course was required for graduation. On the other hand, I have spoken to students unaware that just as students can be required to take a course they would prefer not to take, so teachers can be required to teach a course they would prefer not to teach. How many teachers, even in a very small class, know whether their students are sophomores or seniors, a matter of some importance to the students? But again, how many students know whether their teacher is an assistant or full professor, a matter of some importance to the teacher? A teacher may never realize that the sleepy students in an 8 A.M. class are there only because all other sections of the course were already closed when they registered. Likewise, students in the 8 A.M. class may not understand that their teacher is standing wearily before them at such an hour because of lacking the seniority to claim any other time.

Such mutual ignorance extends over many aspects of academic life and is nowhere more apparent than in matters regarding examinations and grades. A basic source of the misunderstandings is that normally such evaluation has vital consequences for the one being evaluated, but not for the one who does the evaluating. The grades students receive not only determine whether they graduate with honors or fail out of school; grades may also help choose a specialization, affect plans for graduate study, and ultimately influence choice of career. On the other hand, the grades a teacher gives do not affect professional stature, commitment to a field of study, or future success as a scholar. Students may for a long time harbor a deep resentment against a teacher who grades harshly, but were they to confront that teacher years later, the teacher might not even remember the students and would almost surely not remember the grades. Indeed, the teacher would most probably be astounded to learn the students cared so deeply about the grades. I once heard a woman who had taught for over thirty years remark in a faculty meeting that she could not understand why students were so interested in grades. Apparently in moving from one side of the desk to the other she had developed amnesia.

Some students believe that teachers are fond of examinations and grades and employ these devices to retain power over students. Although undoubtedly a few teachers do possess such motives, most do not. A scholar enjoys reading and writing books, not making up questions to test the knowledge others may possess. And a great many activities are more fascinating than reading one hundred or so answers to the same question and deciding how many points each answer is worth. Whether Johnny understands the problem of induction is not crucial to Professor Smith's intellectual life, for Professor Smith finds the problem stimulating, even if Johnny neglects to study it.

The system of examinations and grades thus places important decisions affecting students' lives in the hands of those who are comparatively unaffected by these decisions and perhaps uninterested in making them. Such a situation is fraught with unpleasant possibilities, often compounded by the difficulty of constructing and applying suitable examination and grading procedures. But to refer to "suitable examination and grading procedures" implies that such procedures are intended to fulfill certain worthwhile purposes, and so we would do well to consider just what those purposes are. Why bother with examinations or grades at all?

Examinations ideally serve at least four significant purposes. First, they provide the opportunity for students to discover the scope and depth of their knowledge. Much like athletes who test themselves under game conditions or like musicians who test themselves under concert conditions, students test themselves under examination conditions and thereby determine whether they are in complete control of certain material or whether they possess merely a tenuous grasp of it. It is one thing to speak glibly about a subject; it is something else to answer specific questions about that subject, relying solely upon one's own knowledge and committing answers to paper so they can be scrutinized by experts in the field. A proper examination procedure makes clear to students what they know and what they do not know and thus can serve as a valuable guide to further study. By paying close attention to the results of examinations, students can become aware of their strengths and weaknesses. They can learn whether their methods of study are effective and can recognize the areas of a subject in which they need to concentrate future efforts. In short, an examination enables students to find out how well they are doing and assists in deciding how they can do better.

Students, however, are not the only ones tested by an examination, for the second purpose examinations should serve is to provide an opportunity for teachers to discover how effective their teaching has been. By carefully analyzing students' examination papers, teachers can learn in what ways they have succeeded or failed. Of course, many teachers would prefer to believe the reason three-quarters of their students missed a particular question is that the students are not bright or have not studied hard enough. But in this matter, college teachers have something to learn from those who teach in elementary school. When three-quarters of an ordinary third-grade class find multiplication confusing, the teachers do not assume the students are not bright or have not studied hard enough. They assume that their teaching methods are in need of improvement. A college teacher ought to arrive at the same conclusion when three-quarters of a class are confused by a fundamental point supposedly explained clearly. In one sense, then, teachers as well as students can pass or fail examinations, for by paying close attention to the results of their students' efforts, teachers can become aware of the strengths and weaknesses of instruction. They can learn whether certain methods are effective and recognize the areas of a subject which need concentration. In short, an examination enables teachers to find out how well they are doing and assists in deciding how they can do better.

We have thus far considered examinations only as tests of learning, but they can be more than a means of evaluating previous learning experiences: they can be themselves worthwhile learning experiences. During an examination most students are working with an extraordinarily high degree of concentration. If the questions place familiar material in a slightly unfamiliar light and thereby lead students to develop for themselves significant connections between various aspects of the subject matter, then the students will be working intensely on challenging, important problems and so gain intellectual perspective. Ironically, in this day of large lecture classes, examinations sometimes provide greater opportunity for active learning than any other part of the course. Yet too often students complain about uninspired, unrewarding examinations. Such complaints are entirely legitimate, for a boring, banal examination indicates pedagogic laziness and is a waste of a potentially valuable learning experience. Long after completing a course, students who have forgotten virtually everything else may still remember some of the examination questions. They should be worth remembering.

An examination, however, consists of more than the two or three hours spent sitting in the examination room. Most students prepare for examinations, and such preparation itself possesses significant educational value. The nature of an examination requires that one not know what questions will be asked or which aspects of the subject matter spotlighted. The only adequate preparation for an examination is a thorough study of all the subject matter and a careful consideration of as many as possible of its various interconnections. In trying to anticipate the examination questions, a student is led to analyze and synthesize the course material, thereby strengthening and solidifying a grasp of the subject matter.

In this connection it is important to note that the writing of a term paper, though potentially a beneficial educational experience, is not a suitable substitute for preparing for an examination. In writing a term paper, even one which is given a strict time limit and misleadingly dubbed "a take-home examination," students need master only those parts of the course material bearing directly on their topic. Rarely does a term paper require mastery of most or even very much of the course material. Furthermore, it is not difficult to copy ideas from a book, alter them slightly so as to avoid the charge of plagiarism, and use them in a term paper without ever thoroughly understanding them. Such a tactic is almost impossible in an examination, for few students have a strong enough memory to answer questions intelligently without understanding their answers. Thus, preparing for an examination is in some ways, though hardly all, more demanding and more rewarding than writing a term paper.

This fact was strikingly brought to my attention several years ago by a student who came to see me after I had returned her examination paper. She had received a C and was very disappointed, for, as she explained, she had always been an A student. I asked her whether she had studied as hard for this examination as for previous ones, and to my surprise she informed me that never before in her academic career had she taken an examination. As it turned out, she had gone to a "progressive" secondary school where examinations were considered outmoded, and she had then attended a college that prided itself on having replaced all examinations with term papers. I was fascinated by this woman's academic background and inquired whether she thought she had been helped or hindered by it. She replied that until she had taken this examination she had always assumed it was to her advantage to have avoided the pressure of examinations, but that now she believed her grasp of previous course material flimsy. She had learned how to write term papers but never had thoroughly mastered an entire body of material so that she could draw upon it at will and utilize it effectively wherever it was called for. In short, she had never received the benefits of preparing for an examination.

Of course, examinations serve yet another purpose, for they are in part the basis on which course grades are determined. However, since we have already seen that examinations provide an opportunity to discover the scope and depth of students' knowledge, we have little reason to doubt that if grades are to be given, they should be based, at least to some extent, on the results of examinations. The crucial question is: why should grades be given?

Ideally, a grade represents an expert's opinion of the quality of a student's work within a specified area of inquiry. Viewed in this perspective, a grade serves a variety of significant educational purposes. First, it is to students' advantage to be aware of their levels of achievement, for that information can be a valuable aid in assessing past efforts, evaluating present abilities, and formulating future plans. Knowing whether one's approach to a subject has been fruitful is a helpful guide toward further study; recognizing one's strengths and weaknesses is vital to intellectual growth as well as to decisions regarding how one's abilities might most effectively be utilized in and out of school. A college student is directly concerned with questions such as "Which courses should I take?"; "Which fields should I specialize in?"; "Which graduate schools, if any, should I apply to?"; and "Which career should I choose?" Intelligent answers to all these questions depend, among other factors, upon the individual's academic abilities and accomplishments, and grades indicate these reliably, though not infallibly. Granted a teacher's judgment may occasionally be mistaken. At least the judgment is based upon relevant expertise and experience and is not subject to the sort of delusions which so often distort self-evaluation. A student may not always be pleased by the knowledge grades afford, but the important point is that such knowledge is almost always useful.

Students, though, are not the only ones to whom such knowledge is valuable, for in order for a teacher to provide the detailed educational advice often so helpful to students, they need to have an exact record of their student's academic performance. How can a teacher intelligently advise a student in choosing a program of study and in planning for the years after graduation if an accurate measure of the student's level of achievement is unavailable? If, for example, a chemistry teacher does not know how well a student has done in science and mathematics courses, how can the teacher intelligently advise the student which level of chemistry to study, which areas in the student's background need strengthening, and whether it is reasonable for the student to continue work in graduate school? And if the student should decide to become a political science major, how can a teacher in that discipline intelligently advise the student what course of study to follow without knowing the level of achievement in history, economics, sociology, philosophy, and nowadays even in mathematics? In short, students' academic records are a great aid to those teachers who try to use their knowledge and experience to advise students wisely. But if a student's record is sketchy, vague, and inadequate, the advice will most likely also be sketchy, vague and inadequate.

We have already noted that grades can be a valuable guide to a student in planning for the years following graduation; we should note as well that grades are a valuable guide to those who must make critical decisions directly affecting a student's future plans. Graduate work usually presupposes a firm command of undergraduate work, and thus most graduate schools necessarily employ selective admission policies. Those who face the difficult task of deciding whether a particular student is to be admitted to graduate school can make that decision intelligently only if they are aware of the student's level of achievement in various college courses, and grades are a reliable, though not unerring, measure of such achievement.

On occasion, however, someone proposes that instead of receiving an applicant's grades a graduate admissions committee receive instead recommendations written by each of the teachers with whom the applicant has studied. But this proposal is impractical and, even if feasible, would nevertheless be inadvisable.

It is impractical for at least two reasons. First, the members of an admissions committee do not have the time to read twenty-five or thirty letters about each applicant. In the case of some of the larger graduate schools, an admissions committee with twenty-five letters for each applicant would be facing more than twenty-five thousand letters and could not possibly be expected to spend the time necessary to do justice to that amount of material. Second, the large size of so many college classes makes it virtually impossible for teachers to know each student personally. Thus they would be reduced to writing such conventional comments as "DeWitt is an excellent student who has mastered all of the course material" or "Davis is a fair student who has mastered some, though not much of the course material." But what do these comments mean except that DeWitt did A work in the course and Davis did C work?

However, even if it were feasible for every one of a student's teachers to write a personalized comment and for an admissions committee to read all of these comments, still they would not be an adequate replacement for grades. Recommendations sometimes contain valuable information, but taken by themselves they are often difficult to evaluate. A remark one teacher considers high praise may be used indiscriminately by another, and a comment employed by one teacher to express mild commendation may be used by another teacher to express mild criticism.[1] Furthermore, many recommendations are hopelessly vague and tell more about the teacher's literary style than about the academic accomplishment of the student. Thus although letters of recommendation may be helpful in conjunction with grades, alone they are no substitute for the relatively standardized measure of achievement grades effectively provide.

Such a standardized measure of achievement also affords a reasonable basis upon which to decide whether students ought to be permitted to continue in school, whether they ought to be granted a college degree, and whether they ought to be awarded academic honors. These decisions, however, have all been the subject of controversy, and so we would do well to consider each of them separately.

A student who consistently does unsatisfactory work is squandering the resources of the college, wasting the time and energy of teachers, and failing to contribute to, perhaps even interfering with the education of classmates. Such a student does not belong in that school, and, for the benefit of all concerned, should be asked to leave. But which students are doing unsatisfactory work? In answering this question it is clearly most sensible to rely upon the expert judgment of the faculty, and their judgement, as noted previously, is reliably reflected by a student's grades.

The faculty's expertise ought also to be relied upon in deciding whether the quality of a student's work justifies a college degree. Because most students are charged tuition fees, it is tempting to conceive of a college as an educational store in which the student customers pay their money, then are entitled to a degree. But a college degree is not purchased; it is earned. It represents to the community the college's certification of a student's academic achievement, certification respected because it is backed by the expertise of the faculty. If every student who paid tuition automatically received a degree, or if degrees were awarded by the vote of the student body, then they would become educationally meaningless and functionally worthless. For a college degree to retain value, and for a college education to retain its significance, the granting of degrees must be based solely upon substantial academic achievement as evaluated by recognized experts. The experts are the faculty, and their evaluations are indicated by the grades they give.

Grades also provide an effective means of determining which students are deserving of academic honors. Such honors are both an added incentive for students to pursue their work diligently and a symbol of a college's commitment to academic excellence. In order for honors to possess such significance, they must not be granted indiscriminately or on the basis of a student's popularity. Rather, they must be awarded only to those who have attained a high level of scholarly achievement. Grades provide a standardized measure of such achievement.

Grades serve one final purpose: to motivate students to study. In the classroom, as in most areas of life, those who expect their work to be evaluated tend to do that work more assiduously. Without grades, many students might possess sufficient interest to casually peruse the course material, but few would be strongly enough concerned to devote themselves to the mastery of that material. So grades have helped many students who otherwise would have neglected their work, and have led some to discover for themselves the intrinsic joys of scholarship.

We must recognize, however, that notwithstanding the many worthwhile purposes examinations and grades are intended to fulfill, much criticism has been directed against these educational tools. It has been claimed that examinations fail to provide a sound basis for evaluating a student's achievement but, instead, have the effect of inhibiting independence and stifling creativity. It has also been claimed that grades are inherently inaccurate devices which, in attempting to measure people, succeed only in traumatizing and dehumanizing them. These charges are serious, and each ought to be analyzed in detail.

Consider first the claim that examinations do not provide a sound basis for evaluating a student's achievement. Those who defend this claim argue that examinations require a student to demonstrate knowledge under adverse conditions: answering a restricted set of questions within a limited amount of time supposedly creates implicit pressure that prevents many from doing their best work. Thus the results of examinations are said to be invalid.

This line of argument overlooks the vital consideration that although examinations put pressure on students, such pressure exists whenever an individual attempts to prove competence. An athlete feels pressure when trying out for a professional team; so does a violinist when auditioning for an orchestral position. Pressure is inherent in such situations, for experts have high standards difficult to meet, and one must be able to meet those standards at an appointed time. The ballplayer who appears skillful in practice but plays poorly in league games lacks effective control of requisite skills. Similarly, the student who sounds knowledgeable in conversation but performs poorly under examination conditions lacks effective control of requisite knowledge. Thus the pressure of examinations does not invalidate the results of examinations; quite to the contrary, if there were no such pressure, the examination process would be amiss.

A second criticism of examinations is that they inhibit a student's independence, that they discourage the pursuit of topics of interest to the student and instead force the study of topics of interest to the teacher. Thus, it is said, examinations impede rather than promote the learning process.

The criticism, however, rests upon the mistaken assumption that learning a particular subject matter involves nothing more than learning those aspects of the subject matter one happens to find interesting. For example, to attain a thorough knowledge of American history, it is not sufficient to learn the history of the Civil War, no matter how interested one may be in that conflict, for American history, like any significant area of inquiry, has many important aspects, all of which must be mastered in order to attain a thorough knowledge of the field. Who is to decide which aspects of a subject matter are most important? The teacher is the recognized expert, and, therefore, is in a position to make intelligent curricular decisions. Furthermore, the teacher's responsibility is to use expertise to further a student's education, to guide the study of important aspects of the subject matter that might otherwise be neglected. Such guidance, in one sense, interferes with students' independence, but in another, more significant, sense, eliminates narrow preoccupations and leads to less restricted, more independent thinking. And that freedom, after all, is one of the essential purposes of a liberal education.

Another criticism of examinations is that they stifle creativity, that they emphasize the mindless reiteration of facts and techniques instead of encouraging original, imaginative thinking about significant issues. Thus, again it is said, examinations impede rather than promote the learning process.

This criticism is mistaken for at least two reasons. First, not all examinations emphasize learning by rote, only poor examinations do. Good examinations, as pointed out previously, place familiar material in a slightly unfamiliar light, so that in preparing for and taking examinations, students are led to develop for themselves significant connections between various aspects of the subject matter. Of course, an examination does not normally require the same degree of original, imaginative thinking required by a demanding term paper topic. But then a term paper does not require mastery of most or even very much of the course material; only examinations do. In other words, the two tasks serve different purposes, and there is no point in criticizing one for not fulfilling the purposes of the other.

The second reason why the criticism in question is mistaken is that it overlooks that in order to master any significant field of inquiry, one must acquire secure control of certain fundamental information and skills. As Whitehead wrote, "There is no getting away from the fact that things have been found out, and that to be effective in the modern world you must have a core of definite acquirement of the best practice. To write poetry you must study metre: and to build bridges you must be learned in the strength of material. Even the Hebrew prophets had learned to write, probably in those days requiring no mean effort. The untutored art of genius is—in the words of the Prayer Book—a vain thing, fondly invented."[2] It is simply unrealistic to suppose that original, imaginative thinking of a sustained and productive sort flows from the minds of those ignorant of the fundamental information and skills related to their field of inquiry. Of course, it has been said that the mark of knowledgeable people is not what they know, but whether they are adept at looking up what they need to know. But, then the most knowledgeable people in the world would be librarians. A person who lacks fundamental information and skills is not in a position to understand and intelligently evaluate material and so is unable to connect ideas in the ways necessary for sustained, productive thinking. And even if, as is highly doubtful, such individuals had the time to do extensive research, they would not know what to research, for they would not be aware of all they needed to know. How can it be determined whether an individual possesses the fundamental information and skills related to a field of inquiry? Examinations enable both teacher and student to make such determinations effectively, and thus, rather than stifling creativity, help to provide the framework within which original, imaginative thinking can be most productive.

Turning now from criticisms of examinations to criticisms of grades, consider first the claim that grades are inherently inaccurate. Those who defend this position argue that the same paper would be graded differently by different instructors, and therefore a student's grade is not a reliable measure of his achievement but merely indicates the particular bias of his instructor.

However, a student's work is generally not judged with significant difference by different instructors. In fact, teachers in the same discipline usually agree as to which students are doing outstanding work, which are doing good work, which are doing fair work, which are doing poor work, and which are doing unsatisfactory work (or no work at all).[3] Of course, two competent instructors may offer divergent evaluations of the same piece of work. But that experts sometimes disagree is not reason to assume there is no such thing as expertise. Two competent doctors may offer divergent diagnoses of the same condition, but their disagreement does not imply that doctors' diagnoses are in general biased and unreliable. Similarly, two competent art critics may offer divergent evaluations of the same work of art, but such a disagreement does not imply that a critic's evaluations are usually biased and unreliable. Inevitably, experts, like all human beings, sometimes disagree about complex judgments, but we would be foolish to allow such disagreements to obscure the obvious fact that in any established field of inquiry some individuals are knowledgeable and others are not. Clearly the opinions of those who are knowledgeable are the most reliable measure of an individual's achievement in that field. Thus, although teachers sometimes disagree, they are knowledgeable individuals whose grades represent a reliable measure of a student's level of achievement.

A second criticism of grades is that they traumatize students. Those who support this criticism argue that grades foster competition, arousing a bitterness and hostility which transform an otherwise tranquil academic atmosphere into a pressure-filled, nerve-wracking situation unsuited for genuine learning. In such a situation, it is said, students are worried more about obtaining good grades than a good education.

This criticism emphasizes only the possibly harmful effects of competition while overlooking beneficial effects. Often only by competing with others do we bring out the best in ourselves. As Gilbert Highet once noted, "It is sad, sometimes, to see a potentially brilliant pupil slouching through his work, sulky and willful, wasting his time and thought on trifles, because he has no real equals in his own class; and it is heartening to see how quickly, when a rival is transferred from another section or enters from another school, the first boy will find a fierce joy in learning and a real purpose in life."[4] In short, competition fosters excellence, and without that challenge most of us would be satisfied with accomplishing far less than we are capable of.

However, even if competition did not have beneficial effects, it would still be an inherent part of academic life, for it is an inherent part of virtually every aspect of life. Many people have the same goals, but only a comparatively few can achieve them. For example, not everyone who so desires can be a surgeon, a lawyer, an engineer, or a professional football player, and, indeed, marked success in any field of endeavor is necessarily quite rare. Thus competition arises. Since academic success is desired not only for its own sake but also because it relates to success in many other competitive fields, competition will always exist in academic life.

The question, then, is not whether competition should be eliminated from the academic sphere, but how it can be channelled so as to maximize beneficial effects and minimize potentially harmful effects. The key to this difficult task lies in encouraging all students to strive as vigorously as possible to fulfill potential, in praising efforts when students try hard and in appealing to pride when energies flag. Treating them so does not lead to emphasizing good grades rather than a good education, for they cannot achieve a good education without striving for mastery of subject matter. If grades are awarded as they should be, on the basis of accurate measures of a student's level of achievement, they will indicate mastery of subject matter. Thus a student concerned with grades is concerned with a prime component of a good education.

A third criticism of grades is that in attempting to measure people, they succeed only in dehumanizing and categorizing them, depriving them of uniqueness, and reducing them to a letter of the alphabet.

Thus, it is said, grades defeat one of the essential purposes of an education: to aid each individual in developing individuality.

A grade, however, is not and is not intended to be a measure of a person. It is, rather, a measure of a person's level of achievement in a particular course of study. To give a student a C in an introductory physics course is not saying that the student is a C person with a C personality or C moral character, only that the student has a C level of achievement in introductory physics.

Grades no more reduce students to letters than batting averages reduce baseball players to numbers. That Ted Williams had a lifetime batting average of .344 and Joe Garagiola an average of .257 does not mean Williams is a better person than Garagiola, but only that Williams was a better hitter. Why does it dehumanize either man to recognize that one was a better hitter than the other?

Indeed, to recognize an individual's strengths and weaknesses, to know areas of expertise, areas of competence, and areas of ignorance is not to deny but to emphasize individuality. If Delaney and Delancey are known to their teachers only as two faces in the classroom, then their comparative anonymity is apt to lead to individual differences being overlooked. But if Delaney has a reputation as an excellent history student with a weakness in mathematics, while Delancey is known as a generally poor student who has a gift for creative writing, then these two students are no longer anonymous cogs in a machine, and their education can be tailored to suit their needs. Thus grades do not dehumanize an individual; on the contrary, they contribute to a recognition of uniqueness and to the possible development of individual interests and abilities.

Yet there is one further challenge to the entire system of examinations and grades, for as was pointed out earlier, this system places important decisions affecting students' lives in the hands of those comparatively unaffected by these decisions and perhaps uninterested in making them. Such a situation is indeed hazardous, and the potential problems are, of course, compounded by the difficulty of constructing and applying suitable examination and grading procedures. Of course, suitable procedures are the ones most likely to fulfill the worthwhile purposes examinations and grades are intended to serve, and we have already seen those. But what specific procedures are most likely to fulfill those purposes? How can we ensure that teachers will be cognizant of the proper procedures and apply them conscientiously? These questions are important and deserve careful consideration.

Constructing a good examination is a creative endeavor, and, as in the case of all creative endeavors, there are no surefire formulas for success; the most one can reasonably hope for are broad guidelines to provide a sound basis for at least partial success. The first such guideline is that an examination should be representative of the course material. Consider, for instance, a course in the history of modern philosophy that devotes two or three weeks to the study of each of five philosophers: Descartes, Leibniz, Berkeley, Hume, and Kant. If the final examination is to serve its proper function as a test of the scope and depth of a student's knowledge of the course material, then the examination should be structured so that a student is called upon to demonstrate considerable knowledge about all five of the authors studied. The examination would be unsatisfactory if it tested only a student's general philosophical ability, not knowledge of the five authors studied, or if it tested a student's knowledge of only one or two authors studied and permitted neglect of the others. Whatever such unsatisfactory examinations might be intended to test, they would fail to test adequately the scope and depth of a student's knowledge of the history of modern philosophy.

An examination representative of the course material need not deny students a choice as to which examination questions they wish to answer. Such a choice is an attractive feature of an examination, since it allows students an opportunity to demonstrate special interests and abilities. The crucial point is that such choices should be so arranged that a student's answers will adequately reflect knowledge of the entire course material. Furthermore, if certain course material is so essential that all students should be familiar with it, then no choice should be given. For contrary to common practice, students need not always be offered a choice of examination questions. What they should be offered is an examination representative of the course material.

A second guideline for constructing good examinations is posing questions that require detailed answers. Perhaps the most serious fault of college examinations is that they allow a student to talk around the subject matter without ever having to demonstrate more than a superficial knowledge of course material. Again in contrast to common practice, much can be said in favor of questions that have answers, answers to be found in or at least closely related to the course readings. An examination lacking such questions is not merely a poor test of students' knowledge but leads them to suppose that thorough knowledge of the course material amounts to no more than knowing stray bits of information strung together by vague generalizations about even vaguer concepts. Such an examination is worse than no examination at all; it is an educational travesty that leads students to suppose they have mastered material about which they know virtually nothing.

That examination questions ought to require detailed answers is no reason why students should be overwhelmed with true-false or multiple-choice questions. Though these can sometimes be of educational value, unless they are well-constructed and appropriate to the aims of the course, they turn the examination into a guessing-game that stresses knowledge of minutiae rather than the understanding of fundamental concepts and principles. For instance, only a foolish examination in the history of modern philosophy would be filled with questions such as "The title of Section IX of Hume's *An Inquiry Concerning Human Understanding* is (a) Of Liberty and Necessity, (b) Of the Reason of Animals, (c) Of Miracles, (d) All of the above, (e) None of the above." On the other hand it would be equally foolish for such an examination to be filled with questions such as "Does it seem to you that anything in the work of Kant helps us to understand ourselves?" What is needed is neither a trivial nor vague question but a sharply defined, significant, challenging question: "Both Descartes and Berkeley raise doubts about the existence of the material world. Compare and contrast (1) the arguments they use to raise these doubts, and (2) their conclusions concerning the possible resolution of these doubts." An examination with such questions not only provides a rigorous test of a student's knowledge but also clearly indicates to the student that mastery of the subject matter is a demanding enterprise, requiring far more intellectual effort than the memorization of trivia or the improvisation of hazy, high-flown vacuities.

If an examination adheres to the two important guidelines just discussed, then there is reason to suppose it will fulfill the worthwhile purposes it should serve. However, several other pitfalls must be avoided for an examination to be as effective as possible. First, the examination should not be so long that most students are more worried about finishing than about providing the best possible answers. Of course, if students take too long to answer a question, they clearly do not have secure enough control of the required material. But basically an examination should not be a race against time; it should be constructed so a student working at a normal pace has sufficient time to read questions carefully, compose thoughts, write answers legibly, and reread work to make corrections. No matter how well constructed examination questions may be, if there is not sufficient time to answer them thoughtfully, the examination will turn into a shambles and be of little use to anyone.

A second pitfall to be avoided is the omission of clear directions at the top of the examination paper. Imagine sitting down to begin work and reading the following directions: "Answer three questions from Part I and two questions from Part II, but do not answer questions 2, 3, and 6 unless you also answer question 9. Question 1 is required, unless you answer questions 3 and 5." By the time a student has fully understood these directions and decided which questions to answer, time will already be short.

When students sit down to take an examination, they are understandably tense and liable to misread the directions, answer the wrong questions, and bungle the examination. If they do so, the fault is probably not theirs, for the teacher has the responsibility to make the directions so clear that the student will find them virtually impossible to misunderstand. A teacher has sufficient time to work out clear directions, and owes it to students to provide such directions. The examination should be a test of a student's knowledge of the course material, not a test of ability to solve verbal puzzles.

A third pitfall is the failure to inform students of the relative importance of each answer in the grading of the examination. Suppose students begin work on an examination in which they are required to answer three questions, but are not told the teacher considers the answer to the third question more important than the combined answers to the first two. Students will probably spend an equal amount of time on each, not realizing they should concentrate time and effort on the third. But the mistake indicates no lack of knowledge on their part. It is simply a result of the teacher's keeping intentions a secret, serving no function other than to distort the results of the examination. It is only fair that students be informed as to how many points each question is worth, so that they can plan work accordingly.

One final pitfall must be avoided for an examination to fulfill its proper purposes, and this pitfall relates not to the construction of the examination, but to its grading. A teacher is responsible for grading examinations as carefully and fairly as possible. To do otherwise is to waste much of the effort put into constructing and taking the examination, for one graded carelessly or unfairly does not provide an accurate measure of a student's knowledge. The most essential element in the proper grading of examination papers is the teacher's serious effort to carry out responsibility conscientiously, but many teachers have found a few simple suggestions about grading techniques helpful. First, a teacher should grade papers without knowing the author of each. An answer from a student who does generally good work is apt to seem more impressive than the same answer from a student who does generally poor work. Next, it is best not to grade a paper by reading it from start to finish but to read and grade all students' answers to one question at a time. This procedure ensures that a teacher will pay attention to each answer a student gives and not skim the paper after reading only the first one or two answers carefully. Furthermore, correcting papers in this way makes much less likely the possibility a teacher will alter standards while moving from one paper to another, for it is far easier to stablize standards for answers to the same question than for entire examination papers. Finally, before grading a question, a teacher should list the major points students should mention in their answers. The teacher can then check each essay against this list, providing yet another safeguard against altering standards from one paper to another. Such a list also provides teachers with the means to justify their grades, since they are in a position to indicate to students what a good answer should be. Such information makes clear that grades have not been meted out arbitrarily and also aids students in achieving both a better understanding of the material tested and an increased awareness of their own strengths and weaknesses. Of course, for such information to be most useful, examinations should be graded, returned to students, and discussed in class as soon as possible.

Examinations that adhere to these guidelines and avoid these pitfalls are almost sure to be reasonably successful. It should be kept in mind, however, that good examinations reinforce one another, since each one students take guides future study. Thus if they take a number of good examinations in a single course, as that course proceeds students learn how to derive the greatest possible benefit from their study time. Multiple examinations in a single course also serve to discourage students from the popular but disastrous policy of wasting almost the entire term and then cramming for one final examination. The more frequent the examinations, the less need for cramming. Thus it is not, as some have said, that examinations encourage cramming. Infrequent examinations encourage cramming. Frequent examinations encourage studying. And good examinations encourage useful studying.

Having now discussed suitable examination procedures, we should next consider suitable grading procedures. Much discussion has taken place about alternative grading systems, but the basic principle for constructing an effective grading system remains simple: it should contain the maximum number of grade levels teachers can use consistently. A grading system should be as specific as possible because grades serve as a guide for the educational decisions of both students and faculty: up to a reasonable point the more detailed the guide, the more helpful it is. Students with an academic record that is sketchy and vague will likely have a sketchy, vague idea of their own abilities and accomplishments and will be hindered in their attempts to assess past efforts, evaluate present capabilities, and formulate future plans. And not only will they themselves be hindered, but those who try to advise them or evaluate their accomplishments will be at a serious disadvantage. It is just not sufficient to know that Kubersky passed a course. Was he an A student, a strong B student, a weak C student, or a D student? Without an answer to this question, neither Kubersky nor anyone else knows much about his level of achievement.

But there is a limit to how specific a grading system should be. Ultimately we reach a point where no reasonable basis exists for deciding whether a student's work is at one level or another. There is little sense, for example, in trying to decide whether an English composition should receive a grade of 86.32 or 86.31, for no teacher can consistently differentiate between work on these two levels.

The question is then, using the principle that a grading system should contain the maximum number of grade levels teachers can use consistently, how many such grade levels should there be? My own experience has led me to believe that in college the most effective grading system is the traditional one, consisting of ten symbols: A, A−, B+, B, B−, C+, C, C−, D, F. This ten-level system is specific enough to provide the needed information about a student's level of achievement while enabling teachers to differentiate consistently between work on any two of the ten levels. Of course, borderline cases will sometimes arise, but the distinction between work on any two levels is clear, despite the possibility of borderline cases, just as the distinction between bald and hirsute persons is clear, despite the possibility of borderline cases.

Perhaps the most controversial aspect of the traditional ten-level system is its grade of F, for many have claimed that if students know they will have a failure permanently on their records, they may become so discouraged they will give up on education altogether. To preclude such a possibility it has been proposed that the grade of F be replaced by a grade of NC (No Credit), which would indicate to the registrar both that the student should receive no credit for the course and that the transcript should show no record of the student having taken the course.

Such a grade, however, would obviously be pure deception, for the student *did* take the course and failed to master any significant part of it. If the same course is taken again and passed, the transcript should indicate as much. Otherwise, those who are trying to evaluate the work will be misled, since, for example, it is likely a student who had to take introductory chemistry two, three, or four times before passing lacks the scientific or study skills of someone who passed the course on a first try. It is not a tragedy to fail a course, but it is a failure, and we must learn from failures, not give them another name and pretend they did not occur. Indeed, one mark of a mature individual is facing up to and taking responsibility for failures. As a colleague of mine once remarked during a faculty meeting in which the NC grade was being discussed: "When I die and stand before the Heavenly Judge in order to have my life evaluated, it may be that I shall receive a grade of F. But let it not be said that my life was a 'No Credit.' "

A suitable grading system, however, does not ensure suitable grading, for unless the system is used properly, grades will not achieve the worthwhile purposes they are intended to serve. Unfortunately, improper uses of the system are all too common.

One such misuse is to award grades on bases other than a student's level of achievement in the course work. Irrelevant bases for grades include a student's sex, race, religion, nationality, physical appearance, dress, personality, attitudes, innate capacities, and previous academic record. None of these factors should even be considered in awarding grades. To repeat what was said earlier, a grade ought not to be a measure of a person; it ought to be a measure of a person's level of achievement in a particular course of study, and the only reasonable basis for measuring this is the quality of work in that course.

The most effective way for a teacher to assure students that no extraneous factors will enter into the awarding of grades is to state clearly at the outset of the term exactly how final grades will be determined. How much will the final examination count? How much will short quizzes count? How about the term paper and other shorter papers? Will laboratory work count? Will a student's participation in class discussion be a factor? By answering these questions at the very beginning of the course, a teacher sets a student's mind at ease and, in addition, guides concentration of time and effort on the most important aspects of the course. Of course, some teachers assume that if they do not discuss their grading policy, students will not worry about grades. But quite to the contrary, a teacher's failure to discuss grading policy increases uncertainty and worry and furthermore provides no guidance as to how the students should work to do their best and get the most out of the course. After all, such guidance is precisely what the teacher is expected to provide.

A second obvious misuse of the grading system, exceedingly rare nowadays, results from the reluctance of some teachers to award high grades. Such teachers pride themselves on how rarely they give an A or B, and how frequently they give C's, D's, or F's. But low grading is a foolish source of pride, for such grading suggests the teacher is unable to recognize good work. That a student's work does not deserve immortal fame is no reason it does not deserve an A. Just as a third-grade student who receives an A in writing need not be the literary equal of a college student who receives an A in English composition, so a college student who receives an A in English composition need not be the literary equal of Jonathan Swift or Bertrand Russell. Giving an A in a course does not mean the student has learned everything about course material or is as knowledgeable as the teacher; giving a student an A simply means that, considering what could reasonably be expected, the student has done excellent work. If a third-grade teacher rarely gives an A or a B, the principal does not assume this teacher always has poor students. The assumption is, rather, that this teacher has a distorted sense of academic values. A similar conclusion should be reached about a college teacher who rarely gives an A or a B. Such a teacher is misapplying the grading symbols and preventing grades from fulfilling their educational functions.

A third misuse of the grading system, one especially prevalent today, results from the reluctance of many teachers to award low grades. These instructors pride themselves on never giving students a hard time or underestimating the value of a student's efforts. But high grading, like low grading, is a foolish source of pride; it suggests that the teacher is unable to recognize poor work. Not to differentiate between two students, one doing poor or unsatisfactory work and one doing fair work, is a subtle form of discrimination against the better student. Giving a student a D or an F in a course does not mean that the student is foolish or evil; the low grade simply means that, considering what could reasonably be expected, the student has done poor or unsatisfactory work. If a third-grade teacher rarely gives low grades, the principal does not assume that this teacher has the school's most brilliant students. The principal assumes, rather, that this teacher is giving the seal of approval to incompetent work. A similar conclusion should be reached about an excessively generous college teacher. Such a teacher, like the teacher who rarely gives high grades, is misapplying the grading symbols and preventing grades from fulfilling their functions.

A fourth and final misuse of the grading system is the practice commonly referred to as "grading on a curve." The essence of this widely adopted practice is deciding what percentage of students in a class will receive a particular grade, without considering the level of work actually done by any of the students. For example, a teacher may decide before a course ever begins that 10 percent of the students will receive an A, 20 percent a B, 40 percent a C, 20 percent a D, and 10 percent an F. Distributing grades in this way produces an aesthetically pleasing curve on a graph, but the procedure is invalid, for how well a student has learned a particular subject matter does not depend upon how well fellow students have learned the same subject matter. Perhaps in many large classes approximately 10 percent of the students actually do A work and a similar percentage F work, but this fact is no reason at all why in any specific class exactly 10 percent of the students must receive an A and another 10 percent must receive an F. Suppose 25 percent of the students in a class do excellent work and 5 percent unsatisfactory work; then the 25 percent should receive an A and the 5 percent an F. Or suppose 5 percent of the students in a class do excellent work and 25 percent do unsatisfactory work; then the 5 percent should receive an A and the 25 percent should receive an F. The grade a student receives is not to be a measure of rank in class; it is to be a measure of level of achievement in a course of study. Though judging a student's level of achievement does depend upon considering what can reasonably be expected, such a judgment does not and should not depend upon the level of achievement of other students who happen to be taking the same course simultaneously. Since the Procrustean practice of grading on a curve rests upon such irrelevant considerations, the practice ought to be abandoned.

Having now provided an answer to the question, "what specifically are suitable examination and grading procedures?", only one question remains for consideration: how can it be ensured that teachers will be cognizant of suitable examination and grading procedures and apply them conscientiously? The answer to the first part of this question is for those who administer graduate school programs to provide courses in methods of teaching for students intending to enter the teaching profession. These courses should be required of all students to be recommended for teaching positions and should include a detailed discussion of suitable examination and grading procedures. The persons chosen to teach such a course ought to be productive scholars and outstanding teachers, for they are in the best possible position to make clear to graduate students that good scholarship and good teaching are not incompatible, that publishing develops a teacher's ability to think critically by submitting ideas to the judgment of peers, while teaching encourages a scholar to express views clearly enough to communicate them effectively to those not as knowledgeable.

Even if teachers are cognizant of appropriate procedures, how can it be ensured they will apply them conscientiously? There is, of course, no practical way to ensure that anyone whether doctor, journalist, or taxi driver, will do a job conscientiously. The department head has the responsibility to make certain no member is guilty of gross negligence. But, ultimately, teachers must decide for themselves whether to be conscientious. If they are deeply committed to maintaining high academic standards, they will be willing to spend the time and effort required to make the most effective possible use of examinations and grades. But if they are unconcerned about promoting excellence and are satisfied with exalting mediocrity, they will be unwilling to give of themselves to provide students with effective examinations and accurate grades. What no teachers must be allowed to forget, however, is that if they choose to ignore proper examination and grading procedures, both students and society will be the losers.

Notes

1. Grade designations, however, are few in number and have a relatively standardized meaning. Therefore, teachers who use them idiosyncratically are not the victims of linguistic ambiguity but of pedagogic inadequacy.

2. Alfred North Whitehead, *The Aims of Education and Other Essays* (1929; reprint ed., New York: Free Press, 1967), p. 34.

3. These five levels of work are commonly symbolized by the letters: A, B, C, D, F. Teachers who misuse these symbols are an educational menace; their sins are discussed later in the essay.

4. Gilbert Highet, *The Art of Teaching* (1950; reprint ed., New York: Random House, 1954), p. 132.

SECTION THREE

Scholarship and Teaching

The Research Demands of Teaching in Modern Higher Education*
Theodore M. Benditt

In the past few decades institutions of higher education have demanded greater research efforts from their faculties. Actually, this has been a phenomenon of higher education for most of this century, but there is probably a perception among college teachers that the pace has quickened in recent years. Some have applauded the strengthened emphasis on research, while others have thought it a regrettable departure from the proper mission of higher education, which, as they see it, is teaching. Many professors think that research is appropriate for certain universities, but do not think it an appropriate emphasis for their own, middle-level institutions. This article will argue, to the contrary, that research is a proper and necessary adjunct to responsible teaching in higher education. The first half of the article will sketch the history of the American college and university, characterizing the kind of institution the American university has become, and will provide a context for the argument that follows.

I. The History of the American University

The early American college both before and after the Revolution was structured on the model of Oxford and Cambridge. It was, for the

---

** This selection is chapter five of *Morality, Responsibility, and the University,* edited by Steven M. Cahn (Philadelphia: Temple University Press, 1990), reprinted here by permission of the publisher.*

most part, set in the countryside, away from population centers (of which there were few). Such siting required living accommodations and naturally encouraged the paternalism (*in loco parentis*) that still lingers, although sharply diminished, as a feature of many American colleges. The colleges ministered to students' moral and religious lives through required daily morning and evening prayers and frequent revivals.

If the early American college encouraged moral discipline among students in keeping with its parental role, it also strove to instill its peculiar notion of intellectual discipline. In its earliest days the American college was under the influence of scholasticism, which penetrated college study in the form of the disputation, the use of deductive techniques to establish the validity of universal truths. Yet the colonial curriculum also reflected the Renaissance interest in literature and belles lettres and in the humanistic ideal of classical scholarship. Latin and Greek were central in the curriculum; indeed, until 1745, when arithmetic was added at Yale, Latin and Greek were the only subjects in which there were college entrance requirements. All other studies— logic, rhetoric, ethics, metaphysics, science, mathematics, and moral philosophy—were conducted in Greek and Latin.

The disputation was not designed, however, to encourage free thinking, and neither was either the curriculum or the mode of instruction in the early American college. Through all of the nineteenth century, even at institutions where sectarian ties were weak, professors were hired not for their scholarly ability or achievement but for their religious commitment. Scholarly achievement was not a high priority, either for professors or students. Colleges were concerned with supposedly inspired teaching aimed at molding young men of good character, young men who would become clergymen and statesmen. To this end, order and discipline, not inquiry, were considered essential. Students were tracked according to when they entered college—each class of freshmen, sophomores, juniors, and seniors was taught as a bloc, with no differentiation made on the basis of either ability or interest. Instruction consisted of daily classroom recitations of memorized portions of textbooks to ensure that students had read their assignments. It was assumed that the information content of the curriculum was adequate and appropriate—simple, indubitable truths purveyed by kindly, righteous professors and absorbed by dutiful and disciplined students. There was certainly no idea that students should use libraries or consult original sources rather than textbooks. Colleges had virtually no libraries at all, and those they had were limited mostly to religious books. And anyway, exposure to conflicting ideas would only undermine the inculcation of superficial truths students were meant to learn.

Sectarian interests very much informed the orientation of the early American college. Indeed, most early colleges, particularly after 1800, were founded by religious denominations eager to provide higher education for their adherents rather than see them attend the colleges of rival sects. But higher education was also religiously oriented in a general, not simply a sectarian, sense. College professors were often clergymen or at least had some theological training, and until the end of the nineteenth century college presidents were almost invariably clergymen. Piety, rather than scholarship, was one of the primary goals of higher education, holding a higher place in the scale of values than intellect. Indeed, some denominations did not believe in an educated clergy, and others, though believing in an educated clergy, thought that the purpose of education was to instill appropriate Christian virtues, if not to train young men for the clergy.

In addition to being pious, the early college was aristocratic, though these orientations were not unrelated. First, the early college was aristocratic in its focus and rationale. It took its justification to be the serving of social ends. President Joseph McKeen of Bowdoin College expressed it thus in 1802:

> It ought always to be remembered that literary institutions are founded and endowed for the common good, and not for the private advantage of those who resort to them for education. It is not that they may be able to pass through life in an easy or reputable manner, but that their mental powers may be cultivated and impressed for the benefit of society. . . . [W]e may safely assert that every man who has been aided by a public institution to acquire an education and to qualify himself for usefulness, is under peculiar obligations to exert his talents for the public good. (58)

Second, the early college was aristocratic in its clientele: it served the aristocratic elements of society, and sometimes even of English society. To be sure, being American, it was expected to be more democratic, but for a variety of reasons, financial and otherwise, it was not. For one thing, few could afford a college education. And finances aside, there was not much interest in being college educated. There were few positions for which a college education was a prerequisite. More important, the colleges were not interested in offering the practical sort of education that many Americans wanted. The colleges thus had a real problem. Although they had their own ideas of what education should be, they needed students in order to stay in business.

Challenges

A number of forces were producing pressure for changes in higher education. First, there was, consistently throughout the colonial period and into the nineteenth century, a desire on the part of many for more practical education, meaning business, agriculture, technology, and more modern science. These were not compatible with the classical approach for a number of reasons. First, they were not part of the Renaissance idea of an educated person. Second, to the extent that higher education was focused on social purposes, it was meant to train for leadership, which was thought to require cultivated, well-rounded individuals having "large and liberal views" that would give them greater distinction than the mere possession of property. Third, the primary orientation of colleges was not this-worldly; they really cared more about success in the next world than in this one.

The second force at work against the American college was dissatisfaction with the methods of teaching, spurred in part by doubt about the faculty psychology on which such methods were held to be based. The mind consists, in this view, of a number of mental faculties—the senses, the memory, reasoning, the mathematical, the poetical, and others—all of which need to be cultivated, and the right way to cultivate them is by rigorous and disciplined training of the mind. Furthermore, since everyone is the same, the same discipline, including the same course of study, is appropriate for all. By the middle to late nineteenth century this view of the mind and its powers, with its implications for education, was under attack from the new experimental approach to psychology.

Finally, the German model of education was beginning to have a significant impact on American thinking. Universities in Germany were faculty oriented, not student oriented. They offered specialized branches of instruction and graduate studies. They prized intellect and scholarship, promoting free inquiry rather than received truths. And they had *standards*. They sought excellence, not mediocrity. This orientation stood in sharp contrast to the lowest-common-denominator type of superficiality practiced in American colleges, which rested on classroom recitation of lessons from simplistic textbooks.

Early Efforts at Reform

At a number of institutions in the 1820s and 1830s there were attempts to change the character of college education in two ways, namely, to make it serve more people and to make it more intellectual. Harvard, Vermont, Amherst, the University of Nashville, and Thomas Jefferson's Virginia instituted such reforms as sectioning students according to ability; offering elective courses; offering education in manufacturing, agriculture, and finance; introducing more advanced courses; and teaching modern foreign languages and United States history. Actually, quite a number of institutions were willing to offer new subjects in order to appease demand and attract students, but the purity of the curriculum was preserved by not allowing such studies to count toward the degree.

In the end, these reform efforts were not widely accepted, withering even at the institutions that experimented with them, and the American orientation toward education was effectively set for at least another generation by the publication of a report in 1828 by the president of Yale on behalf of its faculty. In this extremely influential document the Yale faculty rejected the suggestion it had been hearing "from different quarters . . . that our colleges must be *new-modelled;* that they are not adapted to the spirit and wants of the age; that they will soon be deserted, unless they are better accommodated to the business character of the nation" (132). A superior education, it held, must rest on a proper understanding of the human mind, by which it meant faculty psychology and its accompanying psychology of learning. The study of modern foreign languages it regarded "as an accomplishment rather than as a necessary acquisition" (133). Those interested in careers in trade or manufacturing or agriculture would, it argued, be best served by the classical curriculum. The Yale Report even found that education by textbook and recitation was to be preferred to the use of original (and conflicting) sources, for "the diversity of statement in these, will furnish the student with an apology for want of exactness in his answers" (134). Frederick Rudolph sums up the report and its impact thusly:

> The Yale Report was a magnificent assertion of the humanist tradition and therefore eventually of unquestionable importance in liberating the American college from an excessive religious orientation. In the meantime, however, the report gave a convincing defensive weapon to people who wanted the colleges to stay as they were. The inertia of social institutions, the simple ordinary laziness of men, would of course support

the Yale professors and their disciples. They were joined by men of profound religious conviction who were disturbed by the suggestions of the reformers that colleges should prepare men to meet the needs of this world, rather than the needs of the next world. They received encouragement from the pious, for whom the excessive concerns with matters of intellect had always seemed a threat to the true faith. The privileged orders were pleased that Yale chose to withstand the demands for a more popular and practical education, demands that threatened to unleash the multitudes. And these—the religious, the very pious, the privileged— were the people who ran the colleges, people who also knew that the American college was running on a shoestring and that the old course of study, while the best, was also the cheapest. (134–35)

The Rise of the University

It was not until after the Civil War that significant changes in education occurred, driven by the rise of science and the land-grant movement. Among other things, the rise of science increased pressure for scientific and technological education, including agriculture and engineering. A number of private institutions were founded to serve these ends, and the new land-grant colleges also provided an outlet for public demand for a more practical type of education.

But while new institutions were being created that would teach new subjects, the character of virtually all American colleges was also about to change with the development of a university movement and its orientation toward intellectual excellence. Daniel Gilman, president of the University of California in 1872 and soon to become president of the new Johns Hopkins University, held that "the university is the most comprehensive term that can be employed to indicate a foundation for the promotion and diffusion of knowledge—a group of agencies organized to advance the arts and sciences of every sort, and train young men as scholars for all the intellectual callings of life" (333). Higher education was beginning to be interested not only in vocationalism and practical education but in knowledge, scientific truth, research and scholarship, free inquiry, and an understanding of the world—this world, not the next one. Critical to the new conception was the idea that an institution of higher education should be concerned with finding new truths and that it should adopt the attitude that knowledge (or, rather, what we think we know) is speculative, contingent, and subject to revision in the light of new evidence. This attitude toward knowledge was implicit in the new evolutionary ideas of the period, ideas that were fairly readily accepted in the colleges.

"The conflict over Darwinism in the colleges was less a matter of whether evolution was true than a matter of whether the old regime or the new regime would prevail, whether piety or intellect, whether authority resting on received truth or on scientific evidence" (347).

Within society at large there was an interest in new knowledge fueled by the rise of science. More to the point, this interest found a natural home in institutions of higher education. Institutions that at one time thought their role was to instill received wisdom and turn out classically trained leaders were now beginning to connect education with the acquisition of knowledge. Students were not only to be taught what was known, they were to be taught that it was known based on evidence and subject to alteration in the light of new evidence. That is, they were to be taught in a context of inquiry and scholarship, in a context of conflict of ideas, in a context in which they might be encouraged to participate in the development of new knowledge.

Within the colleges the mechanism of reform was the elective course. The elective was a significant break with the old curriculum. It allowed students and professors to pursue what most interested them. In so doing it bespoke both a new psychology and a new philosophy of education—that, on the one hand, people are different in their interests, their abilities, and the ways they learn and, on the other hand, that the ancients did not know everything worth knowing and that people who know different things can equally count as educated. The elective principle led to a number of ideas and institutions that ushered in a new concept of higher education. It encouraged depth of knowledge, as opposed to superficiality, and with this the notion that intellect, inquiry, and scholarship are important. In the classroom the effect was that standards of performance were no longer set by the slow students. The elective principle encouraged the accumulation of knowledge and, following upon this, specialization and the understanding that no one can know everything worth knowing. Finally, the elective led to the departmentalization of knowledge and its institutional manifestation, the academic department, "a symbolic statement of the disunity of knowledge" (399), and to faculty control over appointments. Close behind came the development of traditions of academic freedom and their institutional embodiment in the tenure system, made necessary because the orientation toward inquiry and knowledge often brought academicians into conflict with important interests in the community propped up by ideas no longer held sacrosanct.

II. Research and the Modern University

Higher education now takes place in institutions that have become the main focus of the acquisition of new knowledge. Corporations are involved in research and development, as are private and publicly supported research foundations and agencies of the federal government, but much if not most of the research in the United States is carried out in universities, and many of the significant research findings and breakthroughs have occurred in the universities.

Colleges and universities serve many functions. Even with respect to teaching there is not simply one purpose. Almost every college and university offers both general education and specialization and requires of its students that they fulfill requirements in each. As the foregoing historical sketch has shown, specialization is now an integral part of higher education, and it is hard to imagine modern academics arguing with the idea of specialization or with the psychological, epistemological, and social values that underlie it, although many might take issue with certain kinds of specialization or with the current balance between general education and specialization. The training of all academics involves a higher degree of specialization culminating in the doctoral dissertation, and most academics want to teach specialized courses to students. Their competence to teach such courses rests on their training as graduate students and, to a lesser degree, on specialized knowledge acquired since then.

These remarks should not be taken to minimize some of the problems associated with specialization and the compartmentalization of knowledge that goes along with it. At some point one wants to see a synthesis of some sort, a bringing together of the knowledge acquired in the disciplines. The recent push toward interdisciplinary instruction and research, waning now to some extent but still important, is the outcome of this desire. Nevertheless, it is widely conceded that interdisciplinary work cannot simply replace disciplinary work and that good interdisciplinary work must be based on good disciplinary work. Furthermore, it is unlikely that many professors would want to give up teaching their specializations altogether.

Teaching advanced subjects to upper-level students imposes on a professor certain obligations that everyone will easily recognize. It requires at a minimum that one keep current with the field; obviously, one may not simply teach, twenty years later, which is mid-career for most academics, what was learned in graduate school. Although important, however, keeping up with one's field is hardly adequate.

Advanced, upper-level courses, even at the undergraduate level, inevitably demand a research effort in support of such teaching.

What exactly is it that a professor teaches? A professor can either teach material developed by others and found in the literature or his or her own material or, of course, some combination of these. Obviously if a professor teaches his or her own material, not only thought but also research and scholarship will be required. For in the nature of any academic pursuit ideas do not arise in a vacuum. They have a context provided by the history of thought about a subject and by prevalent ideas about it. The professor must not only present his or her own ideas, but show how they respond to problems not answered by older or competing ideas or how they in some other way constitute an advance. One does not invent ideas simply to hear oneself talk. There is a context that gives ideas their point and their significance; one can advance new ideas only by showing how they function in that context. Doing this is, of course, engaging in research and scholarship. Thus, teaching his or her own ideas commits the professor to a program of scholarly activity.

Typically, however, a professor will primarily teach ideas developed by others. He or she reads the literature, attends lectures, learns the leading current ideas in the field, and presents them in class. This is a perfectly legitimate professorial activity, but it does not absolve the professor of the obligation to conduct his or her own research and scholarship. For one thing, there are invariably a variety of ideas available in a field, so that inevitably one must select among them. We select the material we present to undergraduates either on the ground that a particular set of ideas is more nearly correct than another or on the ground that it is more interesting or important to study than another. When it is the former, the professor is again committed to a research activity, for it is necessary to evaluate the ideas in question. Evaluation entails reading additional literature in order to see what the problems and objections might be and how they might be answered, but of course, *simply* reading what others have said *is* insufficient; one must at some point come to one's *own* conclusions.[1] One might, however, choose certain material to teach not because one judges it more nearly correct but because it is interesting or important to study or widely hailed in the field. Still, a professor who is doing a worthwhile job in the classroom cannot escape the research task. For one must understand *why* it is worth paying attention to or at least why *others* think it worth paying attention to. One must also understand what is wrong with the ideas being taught, since our hypothesis is that the professor thinks the ideas interesting or important but *not* the most nearly correct ideas in the area. And in any event the professor must understand the ideas well enough to deal with problems and objections that might be raised, even if only by students.

The brunt of the foregoing line of argument is that teaching cannot be dissociated from claims to truth; that is, a professor cannot stand in front of a class, present a lot of material, and then step away from representing any views of his or her own as to what is true and what is not. Thus, a professor cannot teach conscientiously while escaping the need to conduct what amounts to a research program. Let me clarify by means of an example, not necessarily involving upper-level teaching. In many ethics courses contemporary moral and social issues are discussed. Some professors teach by taking stands on the moral issues, letting their students know which positions they think correct and why. Others simply make critical presentations of the arguments on both sides but refrain from taking stands on the moral issues in question. Does this practice constitute stepping away from representing the professor's views as to what is true and what is not? No, because, while not taking a stand on the moral issue, the professor does take a stand on the main thrust of his or her teaching, which is whether the arguments that are used on either side of the issue are good arguments or not.

It is sometimes maintained that one of the important goals of undergraduate teaching is the passing on of an intellectual tradition. One has only to be reminded of the great medieval European universities to be aware of the important role universities play in perpetuating an intellectual tradition. This role continues in the modern university, where it is our responsibility to perpetuate the tradition in what we teach to our students in each generation. Though it may not be articulated, it is my impression that in some disciplines professors think that this is a particularly important, even dominant, goal of teaching, and it may be what many have in mind when they decry what they believe is the modern preference among academicians for research over teaching. This approach, if used to drive a wedge between teaching and research, is, I believe, mistaken, for the perpetuation of an intellectual tradition itself makes scholarly demands. The concept of "a tradition" or "the canon" or "past culture" or whatever it is we seek to instill in the next generation is not very precise; indeed, it changes over time. At one time there is a prevailing idea of, say, the literary canon, the body of literature that is most important in defining a culture or a period, which we and our students must study if we are to understand that culture or period. But then comes a group of scholars arguing that we do not properly understand that culture or period because this or that has been omitted, and the canon must be redefined to set things right (and, frequently, to allow us to come to terms with the biases of our own time that have been responsible for misidentifying the canon). Since the tradition or the canon is subject to change, a professor must inevitably exercise some judgment about what bits of the past to project into the future. As before, a professor's commitment must ultimately be to his or her idea of the most nearly correct set of ideas, and not to a prevailing set of ideas or a set of ideas either left by others or developed by one's contemporaries. In the case of the literary canon a professor does not, in teaching Melville or Dickens, have to represent their ideas as correct. What he or she must represent is, first, that the analysis of them is correct and, second, that they are indeed important and worth studying.

The idea of teaching as passing on a tradition, and of being a good teacher by doing a good job of it without engaging in scholarship, is tantalizing but unworthy. The only way to divorce it from any scholarly demands is to believe either that the tradition is unchanging and that we are sure we have the proper perspective on it or else that it does not really matter what we teach our students so long as it somehow makes contact with our past, is interesting, and gives our students the patina of education. Without putting too fine a point on it, this is similar to the approach of the early American college and suffers from many of its defects. In the modern university, however, passing on a tradition does not absolve one from the responsibility for taking a critical, scholarly attitude toward it.

Thus far I have maintained that a professor has an obligation to engage in research and scholarship because these are integral to conscientious teaching. A professor at the very least must make choices about what set of ideas is most nearly correct and therefore worth teaching, and research and scholarship are required in making such choices. There is yet another reason, of a different sort, for connecting research and teaching. Part of the educational enterprise is to promote the growth and development of students. The role of colleges and universities, as we have seen, has come to include the advancement of knowledge, and accordingly, the colleges and universities are in an especially good position to show students how knowledge advances. In the contemporary world, gaining some understanding of how knowledge advances is an important part of students' growth and development. Therefore, students should be shown, as part of their education, how knowledge advances, and the best way for professors to do so is to demonstrate it, to show themselves to students as engaged, in small and appropriate ways, in the advancement of knowledge. It is one thing to recite historical examples of the development of new ideas, but even though the ideas are likely to be considerably less influential, it is in its own way more impressive, and certainly more educational, to show the development being done by one's own example. Historical figures, however important their discoveries, will hardly seem to most students to be people they can expect to emulate, but a student's own (dare I say?) nonimportant professor can serve for some as a powerful role model. We always teach in our courses the big, important discoveries and innovations, but a student can probably gain much by being shown firsthand examples of how ideas come about and are examined and tested. Students should be shown where and how ideas really come from and that they can be developed not only by the giants but by people not unlike themselves. In order to do this kind of teaching, professors must be engaged in research projects.[2]

The aim of teaching in the early American college was to groom students to take their places in the world adequately fortified with received wisdom. There was, to be sure, the sense that students so educated would be appropriately alert to social needs and adept at leadership. Contemporary colleges and universities in fact function in some measure to develop leaders, and part of this function may well involve inculcating an updated set of received truths. But few people, and virtually no educators, would hold that this is the primary proper function of higher education. Educators and the public at large believe that one of the main roles of higher education is to develop critical abilities, including the capacity to deal with the constant barrage of new information and, generally, the pressures of a changing social and physical environment not only on a national but on a global scale. In fulfilling this role educators and others have to cope with an uneasiness about how to foster such abilities without capitulating to relativisms of knowledge and values. Yet even so, there are few who would opt for the teaching program of the early college. The life of the modern college and university is tied to the acquisition of new knowledge in a changing world, and the professor cannot escape by pretending that teaching can be done without research. Even if there are eternal verities, the main business of higher education lies elsewhere.

Having said this, however, I must acknowledge that not all teaching is going to have a research component. There are subjects, frequently technical in nature, that are noncontroversial, universally accepted as central to a discipline, and in which there is no room for the infusion of one's own ideas. Obviously, good teaching of such a subject does not require a research orientation. Nevertheless, the case for the scholarly obligations of professors is not affected, for such courses are not the main or even a significant focus of college and university teaching. For one thing, they tend to be lower-division courses. For another, few professors can devote all or most of their teaching careers to such courses, and no professor *should* be teaching such courses exclusively. Certainly it cannot be the existence of courses such as these that supports the case for augmenting the teaching focus and diminishing the research emphasis in higher education. Indeed, if such courses were the main focus of education, we would not need colleges and universities. Higher education is "higher" because it involves a level of complexity and subtlety that goes beyond mere information; it reveals the thinking, the theoretical framework, and the discarded alternatives that lie behind the facts presented. As Kenneth Minogue notes, "Technical subjects, as such, are not academic and only become so as they are seen to invoke a higher degree of abstraction than is technically useful."[3] The college curriculum needs such courses, but they are only the beginning of a college education.

If the role of professor as teacher inevitably carries with it a commitment to research, what is the case for *publishing* the results of that research? The research effort is a search for truth. In speculative matters truth is not easy to come at. Operationally, we try to get at it by testing our ideas—putting them forward for consideration and examination. We know, or should know, that we often fail to see deficiencies in our own ideas. Most of us depend on others to help with the critical task; we find that our ideas are often best worked out in the course of dialogue with others. Sometimes a professor will rely on students to provide criticism, and sometimes, particularly in graduate education, presenting our ideas to students is a good way to test them. Even in undergraduate settings students can provide valuable insights or at least provoke the professor to further thinking and revision. Nevertheless, undergraduates are not usually up to the critical task, and even the input of graduate students is usually of limited value. Interaction with colleagues and peers is almost certainly going to be needed. Informal interchange with one's local colleagues is good, but frequently, their insight is not as searching as that provided by other specialists in one's field. Thus, professional, public interchanges at conferences and in the journals is best.

This testing before our peers is something that we owe our students if we are going, as we inevitably must, to put our ideas before them. There is something most unseemly about professors who will parade before their students their wisdom and the (as it may seem to them and their students) overpowering persuasiveness of their ideas and arguments, but will not present these ideas for their peers' consideration, let alone defend the ideas before them. The classroom is a safe place and the professor has a lot of power there. Asking professors to advance their ideas to the profession at large will not prevent the abuse of power that consists of using the classroom as a platform for demagoguery, but it will help prevent the damage done by carelessness and incompetence.

Inasmuch as incompetence and carelessness can do damage of a sort, it might be worth commenting on a phenomenon common in many other fields but unknown in higher education. Secondary education and a great many professions, such as law, medicine, engineering, architecture, and others, not to mention welding and cosmetology, require some kind of professional certification and frequently demand continual upgrading of one's skills and knowledge. I would guess that professors escape this kind of regulation because there is no sense of risk to public welfare in higher education as there is in many other fields, including secondary education. And in any event there is probably a general feeling that completion of a terminal degree is a sort of certification, and also a general expectation that people at that high a level of a field will be motivated to keep up without the need of public regulation. Finally, the idea of upgrading one's skills and knowledge cannot be as clearly defined in higher education as it can in other professions. Keeping up as a practitioner in engineering or law means learning the latest developments that have become part of the corpus of knowledge expected of any competent practitioner. In an academic discipline, however, there is little new knowledge that is as widely accepted as that. Most new developments are speculative and much debated, requiring discernment and judgment about what to accept and leaving room for differences of opinion. What this means is that incompetence in higher education is harder to detect and that keeping current in a discipline is mostly left to the professor's integrity. We demonstrate this integrity by continuing to do that which we were educated to do and which convinced our various institutions of higher education that they could responsibly entrust us with the education of undergraduates.

There are other reasons, in addition to the testing of ideas, for the professor to publish his or her ideas. New ideas should be shared, even if they are only small accretions to knowledge. Few of us are going to make significant breakthroughs or write monumental treatises. Most of us do "normal science" or its equivalent, normal social science or normal humanities. Why should our findings not be shared with others? They constitute advances; someone may benefit from them. If they are worth making available to our students and our local colleagues, why should they not also be shared with others?

There is a related point. Everyone would agree, I believe, that scholars have a responsibility to preserve and perpetuate knowledge left by others. Historically this has been one of the most important things that universities have done; our understanding of our traditions and the antecedents of our culture have depended on it. But the responsibility of scholars is not only to preserve knowledge left by others but to preserve the knowledge they themselves possess. A tradition is not just the past; it grows and changes. For future generations tradition includes *us*, includes who we were and what we did and thought. Therefore these things must become part of the record. Future generations can decide what is worth preserving and what is not. For us, the task is to preserve the ideas that constitute part of the ongoing tradition, by presentation or publication or other forms of reproduction that will be available to others.

Notes

Acknowledgments: The first part of this article is based largely on Frederick Rudolph, *The American College and University* (New York: Knopf, 1962), and to a lesser extent on Burton R. Clark, *The Academic Life* (a Carnegie Foundation special report) (Princeton: Princeton University Press, 1987), chaps. 1 and 2. Parenthetical page references in the text are to Rudolph.

1. "The duty of giving lectures is a pressure upon the academic to rethink what he takes to be the fundamentals of his subject. . . . This fact is a clue to the nature of universities, a clue which is worth following because many people have been seduced by such metaphors as that of 'the frontiers of knowledge' into believing that universities are pre-eminently places where 'advanced' studies are pursued. This manner of thinking suggests that way back in the 'centre' of knowledge there is something secure and fixed. This is a superficial and popular view. The real distinction of universities is that they are unusual combinations of 'advanced' work, on the one hand, with the continuous rethinking and restatement of many things which, for all practical purposes, we take for granted. They deal as much with simplicities as with complexities.

The ordinary lectures for the undergraduates . . . force scholars to re-examine their subject as a whole. . . . [I]n academic terms, to teach a subject is to rethink it." Kenneth R. Monogue, *The Concept of a University* (Berkeley: University of California Press, 1973), pp. 57–58.

2. In an interview conducted by the Carnegie Foundation "a biologist in a leading liberal arts college explained that: If you are not doing research you really are only masquerading as a scientist, I think. That is my own prejudice: Technically, you won't keep up; and I have seen plenty of horror stories of people who haven't kept up as soon as they stop doing research. . . . [And] part of your teaching is directing student research and really serving as an example to students who ultimately want to become biologists. If you aren't doing anything, you don't provide that example. You are just somebody who lectures to them and stuffs their heads with information, but you don't serve as a model. I think [that] in the humanities it is more the model thing that is important." Quoted in Clark, *The Academic Life*, pp. 82–83.

3. Minogue, *Concept of a University*, p. 72.

Conflicts between Scholarship
and Teaching*
Kenneth Eble

Scholarship in many departments of a college or university exists in a somewhat uneasy relationship to teaching. Though ideally the two are harmoniously and necessarily related, in practice they are as wide apart as the phrase "publish or perish" claims them to be. The fit is better for those in the sciences, just as the range of teaching there is narrower. But all professors talk about scholarship quite apart from their teaching and commonly speak of getting rid of students in order to get back to their own work.

Scholarly Productivity

Studies of scholarly productivity, generalized across all fields, reveal clearly identifiable kinds of professors. The majority, fairly early in their careers, fashioned an article or two but have not written a book, have received some kind of grant or another, have received or will receive tenure. Most of these spend most of their working hours teaching, preparing for teaching, or meeting with students and faculty in matters related to teaching. This same majority, early and late in their careers, will both work and play at scholarship. When they fill out those vexing workload forms that some university systems require,

---

* This selection is chapter five of Eble's *The Aims of College Teaching* (San Francisco, Jossey-Bass, Inc., 1983), reprinted here by permission of the publishers.

they will check off twenty to thirty hours a week spent in research, swelling their working hours to sixty or seventy, impressive evidence of professional commitment. Examining these figures more closely and differentiating between beginning professors and the securely established, one guesses that a good deal of fudging goes on in the numbers submitted. Some part of even honestly recorded hours are more ritualistic than productive: the return to the laboratory at night on a regular basis, for example. Is this escape from domestic tedium or a true absorption in scholarly pursuits? Among humanists, who do not need laboratories, the fashion is to work at home. Certainly in my own department, few offices are ever occupied at night or on weekends; increasingly, many are occupied but little during the working day. Circumstantial evidence indicates that the show of work at home is more for claiming a tax deduction than for producing estimable scholarship. I would go further and say the after-hours work of professors is more likely to be the grading of papers and preparing for classes than the producing of articles. Such honorable if routine work lacks the market value of scholarship; so does the kind of discursive reading or study that cannot be entered in a bibliography.

Scholarly productivity can be fairly perceived as a great pyramid, the work of a very few appearing conspicuously in the upper air, the work of a larger but still small minority apparent in the upper blocks, the work of most down at the base. The king is buried within; few have seen him, most have a superstitious respect that has kept them at it, driving or being driven to do their part. The monument stands, as do the pyramids, as some testament to what human beings can collectively accomplish, some embodiment of the power of worship, social coercion, and economic necessity.

But even this basic building-block analogy is faulty. In theory, much menial work at the base supports crowning achievements at the top. In practice, few great achievements in any discipline are put together quite that way. A more accurate analogy would be a scattering of odd and small-scale assemblages over a great plain, from which now and again some more clever mason will fashion something of beauty or use. To test this hypothesis just a little, simply pull down from the shelves in any university library the bound copies of theses and dissertations. What a vast piling up for so little use! To pose a more strenuous test, apply to all disciplines the careful study (Cole and Cole, 1972) made of the use of research articles in the field of physics. In actuality, these researchers found that the work used by the producers of outstanding research is itself produced by a small minority of scientists. They estimate that 50 percent of all papers produced are the work of 10 percent of the scientists. As to the work of the other 50 percent, it apparently gets very little notice. "About one-half of all the papers published," Cole and Cole write, "in the more than 2,100 source journals abstracted in the SCI (Science Citation Index) do not receive a single citation during the year after [they are] published" (p. 372). Of the articles appearing in 1963 in the *Physical Review*, the leading journal in physics, about half were cited once or never in the SCI for 1966. This is not to deny that any discoverer stands, as Newton said of himself, on the shoulders of giants. But it is to say that few of the great number of living professors are or will be such giants.

What scholarship is produced in bulk will come from young scholars, not merely because of youthful vigor and quickness of mind, but because of the necessity to publish not only in order to achieve tenure but also to come up to the expectations placed upon them by their profession. At best, most of such work is provincial, the amplification of a dissertation for a highly specialized journal to which conscience may or may not lead contributors to subscribe. Considering the few hundred subscribers for a majority of journals, even conscience of this kind is not very active. Scholarly productivity varies across disciplines as it does from university to university. Nevertheless, one careful study of data (Blackburn, 1982) generalizes that scholarly productivity among a cross section of producing faculty peaks at the assistant professor level, declines during the associate professorship, rises again at the beginning of the full professorship, and declines thereafter. The pattern is not surprising. Sufficient work must be done at the lower level to meet the minimal requirements of scholarly productivity, just as another measure of scholarly work is required to attain a full professorship. For many, I suspect, meeting these minimum requirements is a way of earning the freedom to teach or to use one's mind more engagingly or to pursue more ambitious and far-ranging scholarship, or to expand one's social life. Boredom probably also turns the academic person who has achieved some security away from building-block productivity. Scholarly writing lacks style, individuality, and general interest. Academic scholars who have a facility for publishing master quickly the formula required and, if they persist, doom themselves to an essentially repetitive, hence boring, task of writing and thinking to a pattern and within the secure but often dull bounds of an exhaustively explored area. My picture is distorted; zest and excitement are to be found in scholarship as are utility and, less commonly, beauty. Pearls are found in oysters. But again, I suggest an empirical test for the validity of my basic claim. Read the contents of a handful of specialized journals in any area over a year's time. The enlightenment will be small, the excitement and beauty sparsely distributed, and the wearisomeness marked.

Teaching and Scholarly Productivity

Teaching itself, for all the lamenting about its being valued less than scholarship, exerts a claim upon the majority of professors that helps explain the decline in scholarly productivity that accompanies rising in rank. The necessity of carrying out mandatory scheduled activities, the social aspects of teaching, and the clear superiority one enjoys over students as contrasted with editors of scholarly journals argue for giving teaching the in-fact priority. A day's work done, the strength to turn to the typewriter or return to the laboratory is simply not there for the majority. There is no mystery in this, nor should there be much guilt. Few lawyers function as legal scholars after hours, though they may work long hours wrestling with the difficulties of a case. Doctors, like other professionals, must keep up with advancements in their profession, but they escape to those pursuits they enjoy on days off and during free hours rather than to obligatory research.

As for professors, many are constrained to think they should be producing outside hours, should be engaged in scholarly research, however it may be little related to their teaching or even to keeping broadly abreast of their field. Few can be found who will not speak of work in progress, perpetually and incompletely for most. And few, too, who do not compromise their actual teaching by this burden of being or appearing to be productive. Such compromises include shifting one's teaching hours away from the prime time for doing one's scholarly work (and most likely away from the prime time for students' doing their scholarly best). Or the curriculum can be altered to accommodate a professor's specialized interest, the aims of an established course bent to serve the professor's current research. Scholarship can settle for the easier task of doing a paper for a conference, or wangling an invitation to be a panelist without having to do a paper, or setting up a conference of one's own—all documentable evidence of scholarly productivity that makes legitimate claims on travel funds and bonafide reasons for absence from the classroom. The most baneful result of indulging in such compromises is the self-delusion that one could really be a great scholar if he or she were not burdened with students.

Among a minority—the stars on any faculty—are those who produce much, early and late in their careers. What they produce may include some of those stunning accomplishments of enlightened inquiry; in the main, their productivity will have substance and will justify their position as professors apart from their work as teachers. And yet, many of these are not the movers and shakers within a discipline, and their scholarly work is likely to be as little read now or in the future as the dissertations they sponsor. Teaching remains an important part of their professing, but for professors who achieve the highest degree of success by these measures, teaching loads shrink, students become largely those directed toward replicating their professors' accomplishments, and much of what is taught becomes vocational even though the vocation may bear a professional label. Again, there are exceptions—professors who continue to function in part as charismatic teachers whose teaching aims at some direct contribution to the broad education of large numbers of students, as well as journeyman professors whose teaching is animated by continuing scholarship albeit of a modest kind. Nevertheless, two generalizations hold. The first is that at the upper end of the profession, which embraces those most fruitfully and productively engaged in scholarship, a comparatively small portion of that intelligence and imagination affects the teaching program of a college or university. The second is that though college and university teaching does rest upon continuing scholarship, the kind of scholarship many professors are conditioned to do contributes little to teaching.

At the opposite extreme from the very productive professors, and constituting a much larger group, are those who have never produced much, will not produce much, and thus probably pay the penalties reserved for functioning at a conspicuously low level. One penalty is that they probably have to teach more. If we grant that there may be some connection between scholarship and aptness of mind and fertility of imagination, then we are forced to conclude that, as regards this group, a substantial amount of teaching is being done by faculty of modest or partial competence. If we distrust altogether the connection between productive scholarship and excellent teaching, we are still faced with speculating about the adverse psychological impact upon those who teach a great deal but who have not measured up to one of the central demands placed upon a professor. Given the number and kinds of courses that more successful professors have escaped from teaching, the chances of having too much to do and of a routine but necessary kind are great. Further, such low-level work is not rewarded;

promotion is slow and budgets are held down by equating productivity with salaries. Add the absence of opportunities for recognition, change, travel—the small perquisites successful academics enjoy—and you increase the chances of large numbers of chronically overworked and disaffected undergraduate teachers.

The members of this group are easily identified. Many are women; many have come into college teaching from lower schools; many are forced to accept an associate professorship as their highest achieved rank; many have come from undistinguished graduate schools or have undistinguished records in major ones; most have little voice in the shaping of the curriculum or the educational goals or the philosophy of the institution in which they teach, despite the large number of students who are their responsibility. Like those stellar performers from whom they are most distant, individuals in this group may teach well or poorly. But the conditions under which they work, like those different conditions that draw professors at the top away from teaching, are not conspicuously favorable to the overall quality of teaching within a college or university.

Such, in brief, is how I think it actually may be between much of university scholarship and teaching, a description at least as accurate as one that sees no conflicts between the two. Approached from the perspectives of what is necessary to scholarship, academic teaching positions may chiefly provide the freedom and leisure that seem necessary to great achievements of the mind. One of the greatest distinctions of American universities is the number of eminent researchers who have been sheltered there and without being placed under heavy teaching demands. The "joys of research" are eloquently documented in a book by that title that came out of the Smithsonian's celebration in 1979 of the centennial of Einstein's birth (Shropshire, 1981). The essays, however, all speak to a necessary disconnection between the routine demands of teaching and the highest levels of research. "Science," Einstein wrote, "is a wonderful thing if one does not have to earn one's living at it. . . . Only when we do not have to be accountable to anybody can we find joy in scientific endeavour" (Shropshire, p. 22).

Quality and Quantity in Scholarship

From 1969 to 1971, I directed a project to improve college teaching, which enabled me to visit dozens of campuses and question hundreds of faculty and students. The most consistent response of faculty to the question of how best to improve college teaching was "Improve the reward system." That meant make the system of retention, promotion, and tenure more favorable to teaching, which probably meant—take some of the heat off faculty to be producing, publishing scholars. I have some sympathy with that view, not because I am confident that teaching will be improved thereby, but because of deep suspicions about the quality and uses of academic scholarship. Setting medical research aside, where university-based research may have succeeded most is in developing an increasing capacity for blowing ourselves and our world to smithereens. Even as regards medicine, such an acute observer as Hardison (1981, p. 97) writes: "The history of medicine in the last century is anything but a history of continuous progress. Each major advance has caused problems and crises that have required the abandonment of old values and the creation of new ones; and as medicine has progressed, the process of destruction has begun to outpace the process of creation."

Where academic scholarship has succeeded least—that is, as measured by impact on the larger world—is, say, in the humanities, where the lofty and difficult task of civilizing ourselves has been passed over in favor of glutting libraries with unread works which must be catalogued, kept, and used to feed the workings of an organism chiefly engaged in feeding on its own innards.

If that seems extreme, let me draw some supporting data from my own disciplinary association, the Modern Language Association, and its efforts to keep abreast of the facts of academic publishing. Pell's (1973, p. 639) summary account of the situation from 1954 to 1973 made this point: "Lavelle's study accurately reflected the situation in 1965. Journals were increasing at a rate soon to be considered alarming; costs were continuing to rise, even more drastically than before; the quantity of material was, in the opinion of some, too great for even the increased number of journals to handle; and, most important, worried grumblings were being heard from many quarters about the quality of or indeed the need for much of the material. The problems Lavelle's article points out are those that the profession faces today, eight years later. They are even more urgent now, and there is no real sense of where solutions lie. The responses of many of the editors to the questionnaire for this survey seem to indicate the profession is facing the problems with much gloom and not a little despair."

Ten years after this article, the situation had worsened, though the signs of gloom or despair were chiefly among new Ph.D.s struggling to get something into print that might get them any kind of job. Academics with jobs still felt the larger satisfactions of placing an obscure article in an obscure journal that just happened to come into being in time to provide another step up the promotions ladder. With the depressed market for Ph.D.s and a rising disregard for the humanities, the proliferation of articles and journals may even be viewed by some as a sign of vitality.

In Pell's 1973 survey, the number of journals stood at 216. In 1971, a grand total of 43,932 submissions came in to these journals. About 33,000 of these went to the 127 journals established by 1965; the rest, some 11,000, went to the 89 that had been established within five years. Half of the subscriptions to these journals are library subscriptions, and librarians faced with cuts in budgets and this glut in every discipline are justifiably gloomy. As to quality, one might argue that with a rejection rate of about eight to one, a high degree of quality was being maintained. Having asked editors about quality and having been on the editorial board of a number of journals, I must conclude that much of the material published is marginal, even within the peculiar requirements of a specific journal, and the bulk of what is submitted does not deserve publication anywhere.

Pell's (1973, p. 643) concluding remarks support the argument I have been making here: "Money and subsidies notwithstanding, the editors' and press directors' concerned responses indicate that perhaps the profession should reconsider the publish or perish philosophy. To some, publish and perish are poisoned, wicked words; but, the survey reveals, they are very much a part of academic life in English and foreign-language departments at the present time. In the view of a significant number of editors and press directors, the philosophy is in large measure responsible for the proliferation of second-rate material on topics that interest few."

In surveying the state of scholarly publishing in 1982, Winkler (1982, pp. 21–22) gathered together a good sampling of responsible scholarly opinion. The report of a National Enquiry into Scholarly Communication, sponsored by the American Council of Learned Societies in 1979, had as one of its recommendations that "further net growth in the number of scholarly journals be discouraged" (Winkler, p. 21). Despite such a sensible recommendation and others like it in the last thirty years, *Ulrich's International Periodical Directory* charts a continuing growth from 28,000 titles in 1965, to 57,000 in 1975, to 63,000 in 1981. "There don't seem to be any penalties for publishing a bad journal"

(p. 21), wrote Michael West, professor of English at the University of Pittsburgh. The last word on bringing a rule of reason into this aspect of scholarship was probably said by Elliott Berry, a professor of medicine writing about the "journal explosion" in the sciences. The hope of limiting journals, he wrote "will probably turn out like any kind of birth control" (p. 22).

Some additional light on the actual nature of academic publishing comes from the field of psychology. Two psychologists (Ceci and Peters, 1982) conducted a study of peer review of articles submitted to scholarly journals. The method was diabolical but consistent with practices in the behavioral sciences and scrupulously carried out. Thirteen recently published articles that had already appeared in top psychology journals were stripped of their authors' names and university affiliations—all from the most prestigious universities—and resubmitted with changed titles, authors, and university affiliations. All then carried names of unknown authors from low-status institutions. All presumably went through routine editorial reviewing processes. Of the thirteen, only three were detected as being resubmissions. Of the remaining ten, nine were "recommended for rejection resoundingly," and by twenty peer reviewers. The authors' careful conclusions are available to any scholar taking an interest in this aspect of scholarly productivity, though they faced approximately two years of "an intense and negative reaction from many powerful individuals in our profession for having conducted the study."

My point in citing this study here is to emphasize both how touchy professors are about examining the particulars of academic scholarship and how suspect the relationships are between the quantity, quality, and ultimate purpose of much that is published. "Publishing in peer-reviewed journals," these authors wrote (p. 47), "seems to be at the heart of the tenure process, especially for university-level academics in the social and physical sciences, but also in business, humanities, education, and allied fields. Teaching, outside research support (which itself is highly correlated with publications), departmental service, and national professional service (e.g., site visitor, committee membership) are, for the most part, secondary in importance to the impact of one's peer-reviewed publications."

Research and Scholarship

I do not intend to disassociate scholarship from teaching, but rather to ask that academicians ponder the nature of both and to question many of the assumptions about both that underlie academic values and practices. I accept scholarship as a necessary part of teaching but plead for *scholarship* broadly interpreted to be maintained as the word rather than *research*. Research is surely a subcategory of the many ways a human mind seeks understanding of the world it occupies. Because of the practical success of science, however, research long ago fastened itself upon the university as that which every faculty member should—must—do. It is both an inappropriate term and, often, a lower-order mental activity. Let me illustrate again from my own field, English. Research is inappropriate to most of what we do, though the discipline is as occupied with it as if it were a laboratory science. Inappropriate, in the first place, because few institutions in this country have the resources for significant primary research into fresh and important literary documents. Second, major philological investigations, which were the beginnings of research in language and literature, have been done, and they cannot be done again in that same sense of original research. Third, few first-rate literary minds give first priority to literary research, though a good novelist may have to find out about many things, and some very good research scholars are also writers of distinction. English, one might say, is a peculiar example: clearly, its highest values are attached to writers and their creative works—Shakespeare, Chaucer, Homer, Aeschylus; its next highest values are probably toward critics, though a Dryden is not a Shakespeare nor is a Henry James, critic, a Henry James, novelist; somewhere below that are the philologists and bibliographers and linguists and of late semioticians and structuralists. Fourth, despite, in major research universities, universal pressure to publish, the great majority of published work comes out of a minority of scholars. Moreover, in one responsible survey, though faculty members in English said their major satisfaction came out of teaching, they also said their major professional responsibility was research. Finally, within dwindling graduate programs, institutions like my own have maintained their health because of the large numbers of graduate students opting for a Ph.D. in one form or another of creative writing. If that is not enough evidence for the unreal place research occupies in the real world of teaching English, or even professing it, consider that English is once again in the public eye, as it has been in the past, not because of some one or another stunning research accomplishment but because the public is concerned with its—and the university's—inability to teach students to write.

This last observation brings out the narrowness with which research is defined in English as in other disciplines. Following a Germanic, scientific model, American universities have always had a fondness for theoretical research, "pure" as against "applied." Research into how human beings learn to write and the application of such findings to teaching is still a marginally respectable activity for graduate work in English departments. Similarly, the teaching of writing is a responsibility thrown upon graduate assistants and lower-rank faculty. Graduate assistants who might be usefully assisting graduate professors in their research, if that research included how students learn to write, are instead employed as laborers whose daily work is far removed from the kind of research either they or their professors are doing. Somewhat similarly, the writing of poems and stories and plays was until recently rigorously excluded from graduate work in English largely because of the emphasis on research. Only shrinking enrollments in conventional Ph.D. programs, a large number of undergraduate students turned on to creative writing, and an increasing demand for teachers of such courses have forced creative writing to become a legitimate pursuit in a significant number of graduate schools. Academic departments cling tenaciously to narrowly conceived models of what should distinguish graduate study. Even within the so-called hard sciences, the narrowness is somewhat suspect, and where there are practical ends—bioengineering or computer applications—the marketplace breaks down academic conservatism.

If the term *research* is inappropriate for much of what English professors do, it is even more inappropriate for other human activities brought within the university system. The university, as a major patron of the arts, has had to modify its reward system with phrases like "research and creative activities" or "in lieu of publication, artistic works may . . ." Even performances have been made acceptable. A music department that has secured the services of, say, Yehudi Menuhin, tolerates his concertizing, does not tick off the articles he has placed in the American String Research Journal nor count the grants he has obtained to investigate the comparative vibratory properties of stub-tailed or long-tailed cats' guts.

If a distinction could be made even between research and scholarship, and if expectations placed upon faculty members could be defined both more generously and precisely, large numbers of professors might have a better fit between what they profess to do and the work they actually perform. I am not opposed to scholarship, only to the narrow definitions placed upon it. A teacher should know or be able to do something very well in order to assume the role of professor. Let us loosely call this "knowing" and "doing" scholarship and speculate about what might be sought after if scholarship is to be linked more tightly with teaching.

Linking Scholarship and Teaching

Appropriateness, which I have discussed with respect to English, is a vital consideration in all the disciplines. While it is vital for some—not all—physicists, chemists, and engineers to have laboratories, equipment, and perhaps teams of workers, it does not follow that clinics, laboratories, or even equipment are appropriate for education or history or philosophy departments. We must establish within the university, among our colleagues, a recognition of the various scholarly activities in which our many and varied departments engage and respect for the particular services they perform. A first order of business, then, is to widen the ordinary opportunities for faculty to become acquainted with the variety within their university. Interdisciplinary teaching and learning is no less a necessity for faculty than it is for students. Moreover, interdisciplinary scholarship—not formal research—is a similar necessity. Yet, the impediments to both are large. I have heard few strenuous arguments against interdisciplinary work and many affirmations of its desirability and attractiveness, but interdisciplinary work has had hard going from the time that the various disciplinary associations were formed. Similarly, I have never heard any arguments against the usefulness of professors in one field getting together with professors in another. Yet, the separateness in which professors live their lives, closeted within departments and even within subspecialties of departments, in small colleges as well as large universities, is one of the most disturbing aspects of places that call themselves either colleges or universities. Until faculty are willing to find out about what goes on elsewhere in the university, to educate themselves in this way, many will continue to suffer under a reward system that imposes upon them narrow views about both scholarship and teaching.

Not only must the faculty become acquainted with the diversity that characterizes a modern university but they must also shift their values to be consistent with this wider perspective. The closest example that comes to mind is the importance attached to writing and mathematics skills. In the abstract, such skills are highly valued by an entire university faculty. Graduate professors are as quick to lament the deteriorating ability of students to write as are beginning instructors who must actually deal with such supposed deterioration. Faced with such evidence as falling Scholastic Aptitude Test scores, even the faculty in the sciences come forward to lament the decline in literacy. In the current wave of anguish (only the most recent of periodic spasms), some headway is being made to make writing a university-wide responsibility. Still, even where this movement has had some success, the majority of professors take no active part in it. A more conventional and comfortable response to deficiencies in writing skills has been to blame the secondary schools. It follows that raising college entrance requirements is the way of "getting *them* to do their jobs." Such reflex gestures give cursory attention to the complexity of causes and largely ignore what is known about the acquiring of writing skills. Disclaiming any personal responsibility, the professors turn back to their own protected domains. In the avowedly scientific disciplines, writing in any demanding sense is neither practiced by the professors themselves nor exemplified in the journals in which they publish, nor fostered in their classrooms.

Of the many causes for students who cannot write as well as professors think they should, surely two are that the professors themselves practice poorly what they preach and that they play only a small part in the actual instruction of writing. It is a university faculty, supposedly acting with collective wisdom and knowledge, that assigns writing to a limited number of entry-level courses within a single department and then condones that department's relegating of instruction to teaching assistants and low-level faculty. It is a university faculty that looks with suspicion on any faculty members who by choice or assignment has made the teaching of writing a central professional concern. It is a university faculty, acting through its graduate research preoccupations, that casts doubt upon the value of practical research in the learning or teaching of writing. It is the separate departments and colleges of a university faculty that will not surrender hours in their vital subject matters to increase composition requirements and that do not value writing enough to teach it as a part of any department's major responsibilities. And it is the university faculty members who countenance writing within their disciplines that is bad by any standard of literacy that has existed in the long history of English prose as public discourse.

Necessary changes being made, much of what has been said about writing could be said about mathematical literacy. Clearly, teaching basic mathematics earns as little reward and recognition as the teaching of composition. Clearly, there is very little in-fact reinforcement of the need for mathematical literacy across the university. Clearly, the teaching and learning of mathematics is no respectable interest for mathematics professors wanting advancement and recognition. If there is any major difference, it is probably the general ruthlessness with which mathematics departments flunk out large numbers of students and then lament, along with their colleagues in the sciences, student aversion to science and the general low level of scientific literacy. The curious myopia reveals itself in a discussion of "the decline in mathematics skills" at the 1982 meeting of the American Association for the Advancement of Science, as reported in the *Chronicle of Higher Education* (Trotter, 1982). The university professors cited identified the problem with teachers, students, and attitudes in the public schools. No attention was given to the teaching of mathematics in the university or to the development of public school mathematics teachers, despite statistics that 22 percent of high school teaching posts in mathematics in 1981 were vacant and 26 percent filled by teachers who were uncertified or only temporarily certified in mathematics. Until faculty members are willing to modify the singular value attached to their most pretentious and hypocritical claim—that they are all and, of a right, should be working at the frontiers of knowledge—and acknowledge the value of much other university work, the universities will continue to turn out great numbers of technically trained graduates basically illiterate in one or more fundamental ways.

Though I will not charge mathematics or science with responsibility for the preoccupation with quantitative measures that exists in the university, I will argue that scholarship must, to some degree, be broken away from the mere doing of, piling up of, research. As regards the teaching faculty, the mere counting of articles and citations deserves the hostility it has aroused. What I would ask for is more vigorous and specific examining of the intellectual activities of a faculty member as they have outcomes in teaching. *Breadth* would surely be a measure here, as against the besetting narrowness that describes most of our scholarship. *Connectedness* would surely be important, particularly at that point where scholarship must connect with the students, as contrasted with the usual measure of connection with colleagues. *Valuing* is a third necessary criterion. That is, scholarship must ask value questions, including "How much is what I am doing worth doing?" Promotions committees have not begun to establish criteria of this kind, nor to seek ways of examining them. Failing to examine scholarship in these, rather than the received ways, faculty will continue the present uneasy and unsatisfactory relationship between scholarship and teaching.

Finally, *cooperation* need gain a larger place, as against the present competitive, free enterprise model. Departments must function as part of the common enterprise of educating students who are human beings before and after they are engineers, English majors, or physicists. And faculty members within departments must be engaged in this common enterprise rather than being purely the twelfth-century English history specialist or the turtle zoologist or the social stratification expert. There are strong social attractions in the linking of scholarship and pedagogy that might help offset the fact that much scholarship is a solitary activity. And there is also scholarship in pedagogy itself, the curious and probing mind finding out more about teaching and learning just as it investigates a subject matter, but with this difference: such scholarship would necessarily involve the cooperation of the human beings it seeks to understand as well as affect.

Changing Perspectives toward Teaching and Scholarship

Despite the strong liberal arts collegiate tradition, present-day colleges and universities are so influenced by the size and prominence of research universities that little can be expected in arriving at a better balance between teaching and scholarship. Nor is a faculty, pressed as it has seldom been before by an unfavorable academic market, capable of doing much to reverse the tendency of that very market to increase the necessity to publish. If we but had administrators who were informed by other than parochial views and who were willing to exercise the powers they have and the leadership they might exercise. If we but had institutions that represented more than the diffuse self-interests of the faculty and expedient responses to immediate public pressures. If we but had a culture less susceptible to values based on higher and larger. If we but had students more resistant to a faculty's tendency to replicate themselves and to carry out an institution's pressure for productivity. Even then, we would still not be free of the scholar-teacher's individual and collective self-interest.

For there is a great personal attraction to heaping up and getting higher, quite apart from any specific pursuit and as applicable to scholarship as to making money. Knowing more is easier when followed along a congenial line and within manageable dimensions. Specialization not only pays off—virtually all professional athletes are specialists, not only in one sport but within that sport—it can be gained early and leave time for other pursuits later. Working with the mind has a higher social value among the totality of jobs, probably a higher monetary value, than working with things or people. As the future according to Andy Warhol would give everyone an instant of fame, so it promises everyone professional status of a sort. All this goes against being just a teacher and particularly being a teacher possessed of both a broad learning and a broad competence in affecting students. The individual's urge to be a professional, which implies being a specialist—physicist, historian, cosmetologist—is overpoweringly strong.

At a practical level, the forces against teaching's being informed by a wider view of scholarship and practiced within a milieu awarding full value for teaching in itself are just as great. Hawkins (1979, p. 285) has well described the earlier struggle of research to win a place beside teaching in "the new and newly shaped institutions that revolutionized American higher education in the last third of the nineteenth century." The scholarly disciplinary associations founded during this period rest on traditions going back to the classical past. Present American collegiate institutions reflect a century of expanding and building upon a European model that has achieved tremendous success of a kind. Within these structures, a bureaucracy is in place that operates on machine-tooled replaceable parts distributed across the nation. No vice-president or dean is likely to be put in place who does not look remarkably like his predecessor. Chairpersons and division heads reflect the faculties from which they come. Presidents, whose selections are not as tightly controlled by the inner bureaucracy or faculty, still must fit the pattern of trustees overwhelmingly accepting of the university as it is rather than as it might be. Looking ahead toward the end of the century, demographic patterns promise no vast increase in student population that might affect some change in perspectives toward teaching and learning.

The issues behind the functioning of scholarship and teaching are larger than their manifestations in academic attitudes and practices. The furthest reach of these implications is survival itself.

Bibliography

Blackburn, R. T. "Career Phases and Their Influence on Faculty Motivation." In J. L. Bess (Ed.), *New Directions for Teaching and Learning: Motivating Professors to Teach Effectively,* no. 10. San Francisco: Jossey-Bass, 1982.

Ceci, S. J., and Peters, D. P. "Peer Review: A Study of Reliability." *Change,* 1982, *14* (6), 44–48.

Cole, J. R., and Cole, S. "The Ortega Hypothesis: Citation Analysis Suggests That Only a Few Scientists Contribute to Scientific Progress." *Science,* 1972, *178* (4059), 368–375.

Hardison, O. B., Jr. *Entering the Maze: Identity and Change in Modern Culture.* New York: Oxford University Press, 1981.

Hawkins, H. "University Identity: The Teaching and Research Functions." In A. Oleson and J. Vozz (Eds.), *The Organization of Knowledge in Modern America, 1860–1920.* Baltimore: Johns Hopkins University Press, 1979.

Pell, W. "Facts of Scholarly Publishing." *PMLA,* 1973, *88* (4), 639–644.

Trotter, R. J. "Decline in Mathematics Skills Worries Scientists." *Chronicle of Higher Education,* Jan. 13, 1982, p. 10.

Winkler, K. J. "When It Comes to Journals Is More Really Better?" *Chronicle of Higher Education,* Apr. 14, 1982, pp. 21–22.

Enlarging the Perspective*
Ernest Boyer

Since colonial times, the American professoriate has responded to mandates both from within the academy and beyond. First came teaching, then service, and finally, the challenge of research. In more recent years, faculty have been asked to blend these three traditions, but despite this idealized expectation, a wide gap now exists between the myth and the reality of academic life. Almost all colleges pay lip service to the trilogy of teaching, research, and service, but when it comes to making judgments about professional performance, the three rarely are assigned equal merit.

Today, when we speak of being "scholarly," it usually means having academic rank in a college or university and being engaged in research and publication. But we should remind ourselves just how recently the word "research" actually entered the vocabulary of higher education. The term was first used in England in the 1870s by reformers who wished to make Cambridge and Oxford "not only a place of teaching, but a place of learning," and it was later introduced to American higher education in 1906 by Daniel Coit Gilman.[1] But scholarship in earlier times referred to a variety of creative work carried on in a variety of places, and its integrity was measured by the ability to think, communicate, and learn.

What we now have is a more restricted view of scholarship, one that limits it to a hierarchy of functions. Basic research has come to be

* This selection is chapter two of *Boyer's Scholarship Reconsidered: Priorities of the Professorate* (Princeton: Princeton University Press, 1990). © 1990, The Carnegie Foundation for the Advancement of Teaching. Reprinted with permission.

viewed as the first and most essential form of scholarly activity, with other functions flowing from it. Scholars are academics who conduct research, publish, and then perhaps convey their knowledge to students or apply what they have learned. The latter functions grow *out of* scholarship; they are not to be considered a part of it. But knowledge is not necessarily developed in such a linear manner. The arrow of causality can, and frequently does, point in *both* directions. Theory surely leads to practice. But practice also leads to theory. And teaching, at its best, shapes both research and practice. Viewed from this perspective, a more comprehensive, more dynamic understanding of scholarship can be considered, one in which the rigid categories of teaching, research, and service are broadened and more flexibly defined.

There is a readiness, we believe, to rethink what it means to be a scholar. Richard I. Miller, professor of higher education at Ohio University, surveyed academic vice presidents and deans at more than eight hundred colleges and universities to get their opinion about faculty functions. These administrators were asked if they thought it would be a good idea to view scholarship as more than research. The responses were overwhelmingly supportive of this proposition.[2] The need to reconsider scholarship surely goes beyond opinion polls, but campus debates, news stories, and the themes of national conventions suggest that administrative leaders are rethinking the definitions of academic life. Moreover, faculty, themselves, appear to be increasingly dissatisfied with conflicting priorities on the campus.

How then should we proceed? Is it possible to define the work of faculty in ways that reflect more realistically the full range of academic and civic mandates? We believe the time has come to move beyond the tired old "teaching versus research" debate and give the familiar and honorable term "scholarship" a broader, more capacious meaning, one that brings legitimacy to the full scope of academic work. Surely, scholarship means engaging in original research. But the work of the scholar also means stepping back from one's investigation, looking for connections, building bridges between theory and practice, and communicating one's knowledge effectively to students. Specifically, we conclude that the work of the professoriate might be thought of as having four separate, yet overlapping, functions. These are: the scholarship of *discovery;* the scholarship of *integration;* the scholarship of *application;* and the scholarship of *teaching*.

The Scholarship of Discovery

The first and most familiar element in our model, the *scholarship of discovery,* comes closest to what is meant when academics speak of "research." No tenets in the academy are held in higher regard than the commitment to knowledge for its own sake, to freedom of inquiry and to following, in a disciplined fashion, an investigation wherever it may lead. Research is central to the work of higher learning, but our study here, which inquires into the meaning of scholarship, is rooted in the conviction that disciplined, investigative efforts within the academy should be strengthened, not diminished.

The *scholarship of discovery,* at its best, contributes not only to the stock of human knowledge but also to the intellectual climate of a college or university. Not just the outcomes, but the process, and especially the passion, give meaning to the effort. The advancement of knowledge can generate an almost palpable excitement in the life of an educational institution. As William Bowen, former president of Princeton University, said, scholarly research "reflects our pressing, irrepressible need as human beings to confront the unknown and to seek understanding for its own sake. It is tied inextricably to the freedom to think freshly, to see propositions of every kind in ever-changing light. And it celebrates the special exhilaration that comes from a new idea."[3]

The list of distinguished researchers who have added luster to the nation's intellectual life would surely include heroic figures of earlier days—Yale chemist Benjamin Silliman; Harvard naturalist Louis Agassiz; astronomer William Cranch Bond; and Columbia anthropologist Franz Boas. It would also include giants of our time—James Watson, who helped unlock the genetic code; political philosopher Hannah Arendt; anthropologist Ruth Benedict; historian John Hope Franklin; geneticist Barbara McClintock; and Noam Chomsky, who transformed the field of linguistics; among others.

When the research records of higher learning are compared, the United States is the pacesetter. If we take as our measure of accomplishment the number of Nobel Prizes awarded since 1945, United States scientists received 56 percent of the awards in physics, 42 percent in chemistry, and 60 percent in medicine. Prior to the outbreak of the Second World War, American scientists, including those who fled Hitler's Europe, had received only 18 of the 129 prizes in these three areas.[4] With regard to physics, for example, a recent report by the National Research Council states: "Before World War II, physics was essentially a European activity, but by the war's end, the center of physics had moved to the United States."[5] The council goes on to review the advances in fields ranging from elementary particle physics to cosmology.

The research contribution of universities is particularly evident in medicine. Investigations in the late nineteenth century on bacteria and viruses paid off in the 1930s with the development of immunizations for diphtheria, tetanus, lobar pneumonia, and other bacterial infections. On the basis of painstaking research, a taxonomy of infectious diseases has emerged, making possible streptomycin and other antibiotics. In commenting on these breakthroughs, physician and medical writer Lewis Thomas observes: "It was basic science of a very high order, storing up a great mass of interesting knowledge for its own sake, creating, so to speak, a bank of information, ready for drawing on when the time for intelligent use arrived."[6]

Thus, the probing mind of the researcher is an incalculably vital asset to the academy and the world. Scholarly investigation, in all the disciplines, is at the very heart of academic life, and the pursuit of knowledge must be assiduously cultivated and defended. The intellectual excitement fueled by this quest enlivens faculty and invigorates higher learning institutions, and in our complicated, vulnerable world, the discovery of new knowledge is absolutely crucial.

The Scholarship of Integration

In proposing the *scholarship of integration,* we underscore the need for scholars who give meaning to isolated facts, putting them in perspective. By integration, we mean making connections across the disciplines, placing the specialties in larger context, illuminating data in a revealing way, often educating nonspecialists, too. In calling for a scholarship of integration, we do not suggest returning to the "gentleman scholar" of an earlier time, nor do we have in mind the dilettante. Rather, what we mean is serious, disciplined work that seeks to interpret, draw together, and bring new insight to bear on original research.

This more integrated view of knowledge was expressed eloquently by Mark Van Doren nearly thirty years ago when he wrote: "The connectedness of things is what the educator contemplates to the limit of his capacity. No human capacity is great enough to permit a vision of the world as simple, but if the educator does not aim at the vision

no one else will, and the consequences are dire when no one does.''[7]
It is through "connectedness" that research ultimately is made authentic.

The scholarship of integration is, of course, closely related to discovery. It involves, first, doing research at the boundaries where fields converge, and it reveals itself in what philosopher-physicist Michael Polanyi calls "overlapping [academic] neighborhoods."[8] Such work is, in fact, increasingly important as traditional disciplinary categories prove confining, forcing new topologies of knowledge. Many of today's professors understand this. When we asked faculty to respond to the statement, "Multidisciplinary work is soft and should not be considered scholarship," only 8 percent agreed, 17 percent were neutral, while a striking 75 percent disagreed (Table 1). This pattern of opinion, with only slight variation, was true for professors in all disciplines and across all types of institutions.

The scholarship of integration also means interpretation, fitting one's own research—or the research of others—into larger intellectual patterns. Such efforts are increasingly essential since specialization, without broader perspective, risks pedantry. The distinction we are drawing here between "discovery" and "integration" can be best understood, perhaps, by the questions posed. Those engaged in discovery ask, "What is to be known, what is yet to be found?" Those engaged in integration ask, "What do the findings *mean?* Is it possible to interpret what's been discovered in ways that provide a larger, more comprehensive understanding?" Questions such as these call for the power of critical analysis and interpretation. They have a legitimacy of

Table 1

Multidisciplinary Work Is Soft and Should Not Be
Considered Scholarship

	AGREE	NEUTRAL	DISAGREE
All Respondents	8%	17%	75%
Research	7	9	84
Doctorate-granting	6	13	80
Comprehensive	8	14	78
Liberal Arts	8	16	77
Two-Year	9	27	63

SOURCE: The Carnegie Foundation for the Advancement of Teaching, 1989 National Survey of Faculty.

their own and if carefully pursued can lead the scholar from information to knowledge and even, perhaps, to wisdom.

Today, more than at any time in recent memory, researchers feel the need to move beyond traditional disciplinary boundaries, communicate with colleagues in other fields, and discover patterns that connect. Anthropologist Clifford Geertz, of the Institute for Advanced Study in Princeton, has gone so far as to describe these shifts as a fundamental "refiguration, . . . a phenomenon general enough and distinctive enough to suggest that what we are seeing is not just another redrawing of the cultural map—the moving of a few disputed borders, the marking of some more picturesque mountain lakes—but an alteration of the principles of mapping. Something is happening," Geertz says, "to the way we think about the way we think."[9]

This is reflected, he observes, in:

> . . . philosophical inquiries looking like literary criticism (think of Stanley Cavell on Beckett or Thoreau, Sartre on Flaubert), scientific discussions looking like belles lettres *morceaux* (Lewis Thomas, Loren Eiseley), baroque fantasies presented as deadpan empirical observations (Borges, Barthelme), histories that consist of equations and tables or law court testimony (Fogel and Engerman, Le Roi Ladurie), documentaries that read like true confessions (Mailer), parables posing as ethnographies (Castañeda), theoretical treatises set out as travelogues (Lévi-Strauss), ideological arguments cast as historiographical inquiries (Edward Said), epistemological studies constructed like political tracts (Paul Feyerabend), methodological polemics got up as personal memoirs (James Watson).[10]

These examples illustrate a variety of scholarly trends—*interdisciplinary, interpretive, integrative*. But we present them here as evidence that an intellectual sea change may be occurring, one that is perhaps as momentous as the nineteenth-century shift in the hierarchy of knowledge, when philosophy gave way more firmly to science. Today, interdisciplinary *and* integrative studies, long on the edges of academic life, are moving toward the center, responding both to new intellectual questions and to pressing human problems. As the boundaries of human knowledge are being dramatically reshaped, the academy surely must give increased attention to the *scholarship of integration*.

The Scholarship of Application

The first two kinds of scholarship—discovery and integration of knowledge—reflect the investigative and synthesizing traditions of academic life. The third element, the *application* of knowledge, moves toward engagement as the scholar asks, "How can knowledge be responsibly applied to consequential problems? How can it be helpful to individuals as well as institutions?" And further, "Can social problems *themselves* define an agenda for scholarly investigation?"

Reflecting the *Zeitgeist* of the nineteenth and early twentieth centuries, not only the land-grant colleges, but also institutions such as Rensselaer Polytechnic Institute and the University of Chicago were founded on the principle that higher education must serve the interests of the larger community. In 1906, an editor celebrating the leadership of William Rainey Harper at the new University of Chicago defined what he believed to be the essential character of the American scholar. Scholarship, he observed, was regarded by the British as "a means and measure of self-development," by the Germans as "an end in itself," but by Americans as "equipment for service."[11] Self-serving though it may have been, this analysis had more than a grain of truth.

Given this tradition, one is struck by the gap between values in the academy and the needs of the larger world. Service is routinely praised, but accorded little attention—even in programs where it is most appropriate. Christopher Jencks and David Riesman, for example, have pointed out that when free-standing professional schools affiliated with universities, they lessened their commitment to applied work even though the original purpose of such schools was to connect theory and practice. Professional schools, they concluded, have oddly enough fostered "a more academic and less practical view of what their students need to know."[12]

Colleges and universities have recently rejected service as serious scholarship, partly because its meaning is so vague and often disconnected from serious intellectual work. As used today, service in the academy covers an almost endless number of campus activities—sitting on committees, advising student clubs, or performing departmental chores. The definition blurs still more as activities beyond the campus are included—participation in town councils, youth clubs, and the like. It is not unusual for almost any worthy project to be dumped into the amorphous category called "service."

Clearly, a sharp distinction must be drawn between *citizenship* activities and projects that relate to scholarship itself. To be sure, there are meritorious social and civic functions to be performed, and faculty should be appropriately recognized for such work. But all too frequently, service means not doing scholarship but doing good. To be considered *scholarship,* service activities must be tied directly to one's special field of knowledge and relate to, and flow directly out of, this professional activity. Such service is serious, demanding work, requiring the rigor—and the accountability—traditionally associated with research activities.

The *scholarship of application,* as we define it here, is not a one-way street. Indeed, the term itself may be misleading if it suggests that knowledge is first "discovered" and then "applied." The process we have in mind is far more dynamic. New intellectual understandings can arise out of the very act of application—whether in medical diagnosis, serving clients in psychotherapy, shaping public policy, creating an architectural design, or working with the public schools. In activities such as these, theory and practice vitally interact, and one renews the other.

Such a view of scholarly service—one that both applies and contributes to human knowledge—is particularly needed in a world in which huge, almost intractable problems call for the skills and insights only the academy can provide. As Oscar Handlin observed, our troubled planet "can no longer afford the luxury of pursuits confined to an ivory tower. . . . [S]cholarship has to prove its worth not on its own terms but by service to the nation and the world."[13]

The Scholarship of Teaching

Finally, we come to the *scholarship of teaching.* The work of the professor becomes consequential only as it is understood by others. Yet, today, teaching is often viewed as a routine function, tacked on, something almost anyone can do. When defined as *scholarship,* however, teaching both educates and entices future scholars. Indeed, as Aristotle said, "Teaching is the highest form of understanding."

As a *scholarly* enterprise, teaching begins with what the teacher knows. Those who teach must, above all, be well informed, and steeped in the knowledge of their fields. Teaching can be well regarded only as professors are widely read and intellectually engaged. One reason legislators, trustees, and the general public often fail to understand why ten or twelve hours in the classroom each week can be a heavy load is their lack of awareness of the hard work and the serious study that undergirds good teaching.

Teaching is also a dynamic endeavor involving all the analogies, metaphors, and images that build bridges between the teacher's understanding and the student's learning. Pedagogical procedures must be carefully planned, continuously examined, and relate directly to the subject taught. Educator Parker Palmer strikes precisely the right note when he says knowing and learning are communal acts.[14] With this vision, great teachers create a common ground of intellectual commitment. They stimulate active, not passive, learning and encourage students to be critical, creative thinkers, with the capacity to go on learning after their college days are over.

Further, good teaching means that faculty, as scholars, are also learners. All too often, teachers transmit information that students are expected to memorize and then, perhaps, recall. While well-prepared lectures surely have a place, teaching, at its best, means not only transmitting knowledge, but *transforming* and *extending* it as well. Through reading, through classroom discussion, and surely through comments and questions posed by students, professors themselves will be pushed in creative new directions.

In the end, inspired teaching keeps the flame of scholarship alive. Almost all successful academics give credit to creative teachers—those mentors who defined their work so compellingly that it became, for them, a lifetime challenge. Without the teaching function, the continuity of knowledge will be broken and the store of human knowledge dangerously diminished.

Physicist Robert Oppenheimer, in a lecture at the 200th anniversary of Columbia University in 1954, spoke elegantly of the teacher as mentor and placed teaching at the very heart of the scholarly endeavor: "The specialization of science is an inevitable accompaniment of progress; yet it is full of dangers, and it is cruelly wasteful, since so much that is beautiful and enlightening is cut off from most of the world. Thus it is proper to the role of the scientist that he not merely find the truth and communicate it to his fellows, but that he teach, that he try to bring the most honest and most intelligible account of new knowledge to all who will try to learn."[15]

Here, then, is our conclusion. What we urgently need today is a more inclusive view of what it means to be a scholar—a recognition that knowledge is acquired through research, through synthesis, through practice, and through teaching.[16] We acknowledge that these four categories—the scholarship of discovery, of integration, of application, and of teaching—divide intellectual functions that are tied inseparably to each other. Still, there is value, we believe, in analyzing the various kinds of academic work, while also acknowledging that they dynamically interact, forming an interdependent whole. Such a vision of scholarship, one that recognizes the great diversity of talent within the professoriate, also may prove especially useful to faculty as they reflect on the meaning and direction of their professional lives.

Notes

1. Charles Wegener, *Liberal Education and the Modern University* (Chicago: The University of Chicago Press, 1978), 9–12; citing Daniel, C. Gilman, *The Launching of a University and Other Papers* (New York: Dodd Mead & Co., 1906), 238–39 and 242–43.

2. Richard I. Miller, Hongyu Chen, Jerome B. Hart, and Clyde B. Killian, "New Approaches to Faculty Evaluation—A Survey, Initial Report" (Athens, Ohio; submitted to The Carnegie Foundation for the Advancement of Teaching by Richard I. Miller, Professor of Higher Education, Ohio University, 4 September 1990.)

3. William G. Bowen, *Ever the Teacher: William G. Bowen's Writings as President of Princeton* (Princeton, N.J.: Princeton University Press, 1987), 269.

4. Harriet Zuckerman, *Scientific Elite: Nobel Laureates in the United States* (New York: The Free Press, A Division of Macmillan, 1977), 282–88; citing *The World Book Encyclopedia*, vol. 14, 1975.

5. National Research Council, *Physics Through the 1990s* (Washington, D.C.: National Academy Press, 1968), 8.

6. Lewis Thomas, "Biomedical Science and Human Health: The Long-Range Prospect," *Daedalus* (Spring 1977), 164–69; in Bowen, *Ever the Teacher*, 241–42.

7. Mark Van Doren, *Liberal Education* (Boston: Beacon Press, 1959), 115.

8. Michael Polanyi, *The Tacit Dimension* (Garden City, N.Y.: Doubleday, 1967), 72; in Ernest L. Boyer, *College: The Undergraduate Experience in America* (New York: Harper & Row, 1987), 91.

9. Clifford Geertz, "Blurred Genres: The Refiguration of Social Thought," *The American Scholar* (Spring 1980), 165–66.

10. Ibid.

11. Lyman Abbott, "William Rainey Harper," *Outlook,* no. 82 (20 January 1906), 110–111; in Frederick Rudolph, *The American College and University: A History* (New York: Alfred A. Knopf, 1962), 356.

12. Christopher Jencks and David Riesman, *The Academic Revolution* (Garden City, N.Y.: Doubleday, 1968), 252.

13. Oscar Handlin, "Epilogue—Continuities," in Bernard Bailyn, Donald Fleming, Oscar Handlin, and Stephan Thernstrom, *Glimpses of the Harvard Past* (Cambridge, Mass.: Harvard University Press, 1986), 131; in Derek Bok, *Universities and the Future of America* (Durham, N.C., and London: Duke University Press, 1990), 103.

14. Parker J. Palmer, *To Know As We Are Known* (New York: Harper & Row, 1983).

15. *The New York Times,* 27 December 1954, D27.

16. Parker J. Palmer to Russell Edgerton, president of the American Association for Higher Education, 2 April 1990.

Selected Bibliography

The following works are cited in Part One or are of interest relative to some of the topics covered in this book.

Books and Reports

Boyer, Ernest. *Scholarship Reconsidered: Priorities of the Professoriate.* Carnegie Foundation for the Advancement of Teaching. Princeton: Princeton University Press, 1990.

Cahn, Steven M. *Scholars Who Teach.* Chicago: Nelson-Hall, 1978.

———. *Saints and Scamps: Ethics in Academia.* Totowa, N.J.: Rowman and Littlefield, 1986.

———. *Morality, Responsibility and the University: Studies in Academic Ethics.* Philadelphia: Temple University Press, 1990.

D'Souza, Dinesh. *Illiberal Education: The Politics of Race and Sex on Campus.* New York: Macmillan/Free Press, 1991.

Dziech, Billie Wright, and Linda Weiner. *The Lecherous Professor: Sexual Harassment on Campus,* 2nd edition. Urbana: University of Illinois Press, 1990.

Eble, Kenneth. *The Aims of College Teaching.* San Francisco: Jossey-Bass, 1983.

Hall, Roberta M., and Bernice R. Sandler. *The Classroom Climate: A Chilly One for Women?* Project on the Status and Education of Women. Washington, D.C.: Association of American Colleges, 1982.

Hook, Sidney. *Education for Modern Man.* New York: Alfred A. Knopf, 1963.

Kimball, Richard. *Tenured Radicals: How Politics Has Corrupted Our Higher Education.* New York: Harper and Row, 1990.

Mill, John Stuart. *On Liberty.* New York: Bobbs-Merrill, 1956.

Rich, John Martin. *Professional Ethics in Education.* Springfield, Ill.: Charles Thomas, 1984.

Robinson, George M., and Janice Moulton. *Ethical Problems in Higher Education.* Englewood Cliffs, N.J.: Prentice-Hall, 1985.

Shils, Edward. *The Academic Ethic.* Chicago: University of Chicago Press, 1983.

"Statement on Professional Ethics." *Policy Documents and Reports of the American Association of University Professors,* December 1969, p. 40.

Strike, Kenneth. *Liberty and Learning.* New York: St. Martin's Press, 1982.

Sykes, Charles. *The Hollow Men: Politics and Corruption in Higher Education.* Washington, D.C.: Regnery Gateway, 1990.

———. *Profscam.* New York: St. Martin's Press, 1990.

Wolff, Robert Paul. *Ideal of the University.* Boston: Beacon Press, 1969.

Articles

Arons, Arnold. "Teaching Science." *Scholars Who Teach,* ed. Steven M. Cahn. Chicago: Nelson-Hall, 1978, pp. 101–30.

Audi, Robert. "The Ethics of Graduate Teaching." *Morality, Responsibility and the University: Studies in Academic Ethics,* ed. Steven M. Cahn. Philadelphia: Temple University Press, 1990, pp. 119–33.

Baumgarten, Elias. "Ethics in the Academic Profession: A Socratic View." *Journal of Higher Education* 53:3 (1982), pp. 283–95.

Benditt, Theodore M. "The Research Demands of Teaching in Modern Higher Education." *Morality, Responsibility and the University: Studies in Academic Ethics,* ed. Steven M. Cahn. Philadelphia: Temple University Press, 1990. pp. 93–108.

Blanshard, Brand. "Current Issues in Education." *Monist* 52 (January 1968).

Callahan, Joan C. "Academic Paternalism." *International Journal of Applied Philosophy* 3:1 (1986), pp. 21–31.

Cahn, Steven M. "The Uses and Abuses of Grades and Examinations." *Scholars Who Teach,* ed. Steven M. Cahn. Chicago: Nelson-Hall, 1978, pp. 217–41.

Churchill, Larry R. "Ethics and Moral Values in Teaching." *Journal of Higher Education* 53:3 (1982), pp. 296–306.

Cooley, Rita W. "Teaching Social Science." *Scholars Who Teach,* ed. Steven M. Cahn. Chicago: Nelson-Hall, 1978, pp. 131–61.

Dill, David. "Introduction." *Journal of Higher Education* 53:3 (1982), pp. 244–53.

Gewirth, Alan. "Human Rights and Academic Freedom." *Morality, Responsibility and the University,* ed. Steven M. Cahn. Philadelphia: Temple University Press, 1990.

Gurland, Robert H. "Teaching Mathematics." *Scholars Who Teach,* ed. Steven M. Cahn. Chicago: Nelson-Hall, 1978, pp. 75–100.

Searle, John. "Storm over the University." *New York Review of Books,* December 6, 1990.

———. "Reply to Gerald Graff," *New York Review of Books,* May 16, 1991.

Schurr, George M. "Toward a Code of Ethics for Academics." *Journal of Higher Education* 53:3 (1982), pp. 319–33.

Wilder, Hugh T. "The Philosopher as Teacher: Tolerance and Teaching Philosophy." *Metaphilosophy,* vol. 9, Nos. 3 and 4 (July–October 1978), pp. 311–23.

Wilson, Everett. "Power, Pretense and Piggybacking: Some Ethical Issues in Teaching." *Journal of Higher Education* 53:3 (1982), pp. 268–81.

Index

243

Peter J. Markie teaches Philosophy at the University of Missouri-Columbia, where he holds the rank of professor and has served as chair of the department. He has taught widely (from logic to the history of philosophy to ethics to the philosophy of psychology) and at all levels (from introductory undergraduate courses to graduate seminars). His previous publications have been in the history of philosophy (most notably *Descartes's Gambit*, Cornell University Press, 1986), ethics, and the philosophy of psychology. He received his degrees from the New York University (BA) and the University of Massachusetts-Amherst (MA, Ph.d.)